FIRST
PERSON

FIRST PERSON

Tales of Management Courage and Tenacity

Edited with an Introduction by

THOMAS TEAL

A HARVARD BUSINESS REVIEW BOOK

The *Harvard Business Review* articles in this collection are available as individual reprints. Discounts apply to quantity purchases. For information and ordering contact Customer Service, Harvard Business School Publishing, Boston, MA 02163. Telephone: (617) 495-6192, 9 a.m. to 5 p.m. Eastern Time, Monday through Friday. Fax: (617) 495-6985, 24 hours as day.

The paper used in this publication meets the requirements of the American National Standard for Permanence of Paper for Printed Library Materials Z39.48-1984

Library of Congress Cataloging-in-Publication Data

First person : tales of management courage and tenacity / edited with
  an introduction by Thomas Teal.
       p.   cm. — (The Harvard business review book series)
   ISBN 0-87584-674-2 (alk. paper)
   1. Management—Case studies.   I. Teal, Thomas.
II. Series.
HD31.F527   1996
658—dc20   95-46818
                                      CIP

CONTENTS

In 1984, Robert Frey bought a small manufacturing company with marginal profits, high labor costs, and poor union relations. Today the company has superior profits, lower labor costs, and excellent union relations. Frey describes how he forced empowerment and profit sharing on his employees—and now the workers are pushing him to give them still more responsibility.

This account is Ralph Stayer's description of the successful transformation of Johnsonville Sausage, which began with Mr. Stayer changing himself. In 1980, the company was growing and profitable—but the workers weren't committed and motivation was poor. Changing the company meant letting go of his authority and giving his workers a chance to lead.

Recently, Timothy W. Firnstahl, owner of five successful restaurants in Seattle, came close to losing them all. In this account he tells how he turned the recession to his advantage. He looked to Mikhail Gorbachev and cut off central command—that is, corporate headquarters. Because Firnstahl's line managers now manage themselves, he's done away with bureaucracy and found a gold mine.

What is the best company in Brazil to work for? Ricardo Semler's Semco, where top management lets workers make corporate decisions, come to work whenever they want, and study the company books at will—and where the company enjoys a 40% growth rate! The three key principles that hold this heretical management model together: work force democracy, profit sharing, and free access to information.

Accepted thinking about economic development has long considered it ridiculous to supply Third World villages with state-of-the-
art telecommunications technology. But Sam Pitroda, who brought
digital communications to India, argues that successful development depends on such technology. What's more, telecommunications is a powerful democratizing tool.

When Kye Anderson was 13, her father suffered a fatal heart
attack. For her, the result was a single-minded career in medical
technology. She launched her own company and fueled its growth.
Then, lacking the management skill to take the company into its
next phase, she stepped aside. Here Anderson tells how she came
back to the company with a fresh understanding of what management is really all about.

INTRODUCTION

THOMAS TEAL

LOOK CLOSELY AT ANY COMPANY in trouble and you'll probably find that the problem is management. Ask employees about their jobs and they'll complain about management. Study large corporations and you'll discover that the biggest barrier to change, innovation, and new ideas is very often management. Make an inventory of the things that have stifled your own creativity and held back your own career; summarize the critical factors that have stood in the way of your organization's runaway success; name the individuals chiefly responsible for the missed opportunities you yourself have witnessed. Managers will top every list.

There is so much inferior management in the world that some people believe we would be better off in flat organizations with no managers at all. *Most* of us spend the better part of our working lives convinced that we could do the boss's job better than the boss. Something about management looks so easy that we watch one anemic performance after another and never doubt that we could succeed where others repeatedly fail. Of course, a few of us would be great managers. But just as clearly, most of us would not. We know this is true because so many of us eventually get the chance to try.

As for the argument that management is unnecessary, think for a moment about what the world was like before scientific management rationalized production, democratized wealth and leisure, commercialized science, and effectively doubled life expectancy. Good management works miracles.

ix

And still the troublesome fact is that mediocre management is the norm. This is not because some people are born without the management gene, or because the wrong people get promoted, or because the system can be manipulated, though of course all these things happen. The overwhelmingly most prevalent explanation is much simpler. It's because capable management is so extraordinarily difficult that few people look good no matter how hard they try. The fact is, most of those lackluster managers we all complain about are doing their *best* to manage well.

what is asked of managers

In one form or another, managing has become one of the world's most common jobs, and yet we, the managed, make demands on managers that are nearly impossible to meet. For starters, we ask them to acquire a long list of traditional management skills—finance, cost control, resource allocation, product development, marketing, technology, that sort of thing. In addition, we demand that they master the management arts—writing, speaking, strategy, negotiation, judgment, high ethics, clairvoyance—and that they assume full responsibility for organizational success, play the role of friend and mentor, and, of course, make a great deal of money and share it generously. Finally, we require them to demonstrate the qualities that define leadership and integrity—things like vision, fortitude, sensitivity, commitment, insight, intelligence, and the ability to inspire others. Practicing this common profession *adequately*, in other words, requires people to display on an everyday basis the combined virtues of George Washington and Mahatma Gandhi. No wonder most managers seem to underperform.

First Person is a book of stories about what it takes to achieve the exceptional A+ management performance that most of us are willing to accept as a passing grade. These are stories about the hazards and frustrations of management and about those occasional exhilarating moments of breakthrough. All of them deal with the

routinely impossible problems that managers confront
every day in the ongoing effort to create better products,
happier customers, bigger profits, greater rewards, and a
healthier, more fulfilling work environment. But all of
the stories deal as well—deal primarily, in fact—with the
human or superhuman dimensions of good management
just mentioned. For among the preposterous demands
we make, we actually care more about character than
technical finesse. More than anything else, management
is a problem in human relations. As the list of requirements in the previous paragraph glides upward from
acquirable skills to primal virtues, each item on the list
grows less and less dispensable.

So this is a book of stories about how difficult management really is. All 13 articles first appeared in the
Harvard Business Review between 1989 and 1994—most
of them in a department called "First Person." I had the
good fortune to edit all of them and to get to know the
12 remarkable people and exceptionally thoughtful managers who wrote them.

Not all these stories are success stories in the usual
sense. Not all of them end happily. But they all include
struggle and error leading to insight, and all of them say
something vital about the nature of good management—
even when good management is not enough.

The articles are grouped into three sections dealing
with three kinds of management challenges. The first
part, "The Hard Work of Being a Soft Manager," is about
the often unwelcome responsibilities that go along with
treating subordinates fairly and humanely. Doing the
right thing may seem like a straightforward matter of
morality, conscience, organizational policy, and the
law. These three stories offer another perspective. Doing
the right thing can mean stifling the instinct for self-
preservation. It can mean engaging in a struggle that you
know you cannot win. It can mean confronting loss,
pain, even death, armed only with the cold comfort that

you are doing, if not the best there is, at least the best you can. These are sobering articles. Two of them lack the upbeat, optimistic outcome we've come to expect in articles about the human side of business. Their great virtue is only that they're true, that they teach useful lessons, and that one of these lessons is that managers who face impossible situations are not alone. Gary Banas's article won an award the year it was published from the New England Corporate Consortium for AIDS Education. After the awards presentation a young woman came up and thanked us for publishing it. "I thought I was the only person who'd been through this," she said. "I thought I had failed everyone, myself included. You have no idea what it meant to me to have someone point out that there never was any way to win."

In the third article, Bill Sells tells a story of managing at Manville at a time when the company was failing— and many of its employees dying—from two deadly afflictions: asbestos-related disease and two or three generations of managers who had neglected to grasp or at least to act on the deeper meaning of responsibility.

To the extent that Sells' story is a human tragedy, it belongs with the stories by William H. Peace and Banas. To the extent that it combines its life-and-death drama with a struggle for organizational change, it makes a good bridge to the second section, "Empowerment or Else," which deals with the arduous task of moving organizations in unfamiliar directions, sometimes to places they don't want to go. The section begins with Bob Frey's remarkably candid story—reprinted in the *Washington Post* and elsewhere—of how he coaxed, cajoled, and flatly coerced his labor force into sharing profits, decision making, and responsibility. Two more studies in change management follow. Ralph Stayer used profit-sharing and smart psychology to make his workers care enough and worry enough to seize the power that he offered them—and that he simultaneously withheld. His story is direct but full of subtlety, a pragmatic look at how difficult it can be for a manager to recognize and overcome his own ambivalence toward change. Tim Firnstahl, on the other hand, had empowered his employees years before (and written about it in two *Harvard Business Review* articles). In 1990, chased by an economic crisis that was killing restaurants left and right (and inspired by the example of Mikhail Gorbachev), he made an all-or-nothing bet that would either save his business or do it in. He eliminated his entire corporate staff and transferred virtually all management power to his local restaurant operators.

This middle section of the book ends with two articles by Ricardo Semler, the Brazilian industrialist who practices common sense as if it were one of the martial arts and pursues organizational logic with an inventiveness that can leave the reader breathless. "Managing without Managers" is a testament to sanity, self-discipline, and the value of radical delegation (all of which Semler himself calls treating adults like adults). "Why My Former Employees Still Work for Me" is a study in chaos management. Semler appears to have built a system so shapeless and ad hoc that it would give an anarchist sleepless nights. What he's actually done is to identify the areas in which management *must* maintain control, then delegate or eliminate everything else. His company doesn't even know how many employees it has, which Semler regards as useless information, but the company has been making money and maintaining performance during some of the worst economic times in Brazilian history.

Ricardo Semler's experiments in organizational structure amount very nearly to a life's work, which is the focus of the book's third section, "The Purpose at the Heart of Management." Four of these five articles are brief autobiographies, focused on business but including a good deal of personal history. The one partial exception, Ken Veit's "Reluctant Entrepreneur," is an autobiography in the making. We see only one part of an ongoing career, but the part we see deserves a niche in business mythology. Veit's story is a disaster epic—an entrepreneurial *Andrea Doria* rammed not by one ship in the night but by half a dozen. It's also the story of a business survivor, a man who spends a year in the small-business version of an open boat in stormy seas but who never stops calculating, planning, learning lessons, and actually finding hope and opportunities.

Each of the articles in this section of the book tells a story about the invention or the reinvention of an enterprise. Hal Rosenbluth took a family company that had been invented twice already—the first time by his great grandfather in the 1890s—and by seeing opportunity where others saw only a threat, revolutionized the business once again. John Thorbeck rebuilt several companies, in part by giving close attention to their history and trying to recapture their former values and competencies without turning back the clock. His particular interests are the marriage of values and realities and the conflicts among business constituencies that can rise up and tear companies apart. Sam Pitroda, who grew up poor in one of the poorest states of India, conceived and set in motion the implementation of a massively ambitious strategy for introducing telecommunications to India's 600,000 villages, using equipment ingeniously designed for Third World use and manufactured in India itself. Finally, Kye Anderson traces her business and the relentless passion behind it to the sudden death of her father when she was 13. All the stories in this book shed light on the qualities of really first-rate managers—optimism, energy, persistence, decency, the inability to accept defeat, the inability to stop trying. Kye Anderson's story adds a new dimension (which Sam Pitroda also hints at): the sense of purpose, almost a sense of destiny, that drives many managers—especially entrepreneurial ones—to innovate, build, proselytize, and take all opposition by storm.

Easy as it is to point out mediocre managers—and we've established that you could hardly swing a cat in the average workplace without hitting several—it is very difficult to describe the attributes of the excellent managers in these articles. The effort tends to produce long lists of admirable qualities without capturing the essence. Let me make two suggestions, one modest and one probably outrageous.

The modest suggestion is that the 12 people who wrote these articles are outstanding examples of what managers should be, even though they don't all enjoy unbridled success in the conventional meaning of the word and even though they don't all possess every attribute of managerial greatness. Clearly all have passed muster with their subordinates, who are probably as zealous and overpunctilious as any, and that matters. Clearly all have learned valuable lessons about managing and are able to pass those lessons on, which also matters. Clearly, too, they are people who understand the difficulty of management and stand in constant critical judgment of themselves, which may matter most of all. Management is a process as much as an outcome. The measure of business success is whether or not the company makes money and survives its crises, but the success of individual managers is a question of how they manage day by day. Doing that job well not only contributes to success, it *is* a kind of success, whether or not the company succeeds. All in all, stories like these are almost certainly a better guide to the essence of what makes a good manager than any definition or list of skills and traits that anyone is likely to come up with.

The second suggestion is that what distinguishes a really great manager is more than intelligence, intuition, leadership, luck, or a deep understanding of human behavior. I mentioned earlier that most of us demand something in a manager that is larger than life. In really great managers, we get it. The words "courage" and "tenacity" in the subtitle of this collection sum up a quality that separates the sheep from the goats in a crisis; it is in many ways the quality of heroism. People whose concept of the heroic is inextricably tied to burning buildings and reckless self-sacrifice may find this suggestion offensive. Heroism certainly isn't a word we're comfortable using in the same breath with the word self-interest, and there's no escaping the fact that managers do what they do at least partially to serve themselves, even to make money, even to make a lot of money. Still and all, creating value where none existed; saving and creating jobs; doing what's right, productive, and beneficial; standing alone, often without support, often against formidable opposition; doing the hard intellectual work of conceiving a vision and the hard moral work of staying true to it—aren't these the kinds of acts we associate with heroism? Even if there *are* rewards? Even if the eventual rewards are great? For that matter, quite a few of our traditional storybook heroes—and our modern media heroes as well—reap lavish benefits.

One of the most striking things about the CEOs of small companies is their sometimes conspicuous, if awkward, resemblance to the heroes of the Romantic Age—their isolation, their single-mindedness, the fact that they are perpetually swimming against the current, against the wishes of one or more of their supporters, against convention, against heavy odds. Consider a few of the challenges that arise again and again in these 13 stories:

- *Management as an exercise in imagination.* If a company's vision and strategy are to differentiate its offerings and create competitive advantage, then they must be original. Conceiving and implementing a distinct vision takes not only wit and intelligence but determination as well. Original has to mean unconventional and it often means counterintuitive. It takes a good deal of backbone to flout convention and intuition successfully. (Rosenbluth, Anderson, and Semler learn this lesson by experience. Firnstahl discovers that it applies to organizational structure as well as to vision.)

- *Management as an exercise in persuasion.* Getting people to do what is best—for customers, for the business, even for themselves—is often a struggle because it means getting people to *understand* and *want* to do what's best. (Frey and Stayer face this problem in exaggerated form.)

- *Management as an exercise in tension.* Putting yourself in the hot seat of responsibility is stressful, partly because you have to serve at least two masters—one organizational, one moral—and partly because you'll get no sympathy for doing it, not even if you do it well. (Banas and Sells experience this in a tragic form; Veit is a good example on an almost—but not quite—comic level.)

- *Management as an exercise in diplomacy.* Watching out for the interests of conflicting constituencies is an intricate political task, often doomed to failure but still indispensable. Sometimes it's hard even to identify the constituencies. (Pitroda, Thorbeck, Banas, and Sells all wrestle with the politics of their situations.)

- *Management as an exercise in sensitivity.* Learning to understand the needs of subordinates—and developing a thick-enough skin to respond to their wishes and needs, sometimes with a resounding "No"—takes insight and nerve. (Frey and Banas confront this problem repeatedly.)

- *Management as an exercise in leadership.* Even a move toward widespread empowerment and leaderlessness takes leadership if it's not to become an exercise in abandonment instead. What's more, pushing people toward shared responsibility and authority—and repressing your own instinct to control—is like pulling teeth, often like pulling your own teeth. The truth is, people often fail to embrace the opportunities they claim to want. (Frey, Semler, and Stayer cope with all these problems in elaborate forms.)

The list could go on but is long enough to make the point. Management can be as complex and selfish as any other human activity, but it can also be as idealistic and as noble. Management at its finest has a heroic dimension, because it deals with eternal human challenges and offers no excuse for failure and no escape from responsibility. The evidence is on the next 260 pages.

Yet for those who simply refuse to entertain the suggestion that a manager's day-to-day work might involve some trace of heroism—and among them we can probably include the articles' authors, who don't appear to see themselves as heroes—let me advance a more modest claim.

All the managers in these stories are competent in the sense that they are dauntless. They do what has to be done. Nothing stops them; not much even slows them down. And in the course of doing what has to be done, the managers in this book and thousands of others like them put on displays of uncommon behavior—determination, integrity, daring, even gallantry. I doubt anyone can read the first selection in this book, William Peace's short story of managerial conscience, without a sense that Peace's mentor, and Peace himself, graze the shell of something authentically noble and courageous, however industrial and self-interested, however quotidian the scale. All the stories that follow underscore the message. Management is terrifically difficult. It takes exceptional people to do it well. But even doing it well *enough* is a much more arduous and honorable task than we ordinarily suppose.

The Hard Work of
Being a Soft Manager

1

The Hard Work of Being a Soft Manager

WILLIAM H. PEACE

I AM A SOFT MANAGER. Unlike the classic leaders of business legend with their towering self-confidence, their unflinching tenacity, their hard, lonely lives at the top, I try to be vulnerable to criticism, I do my best to be tentative, and I cherish my own fair share of human frailty. But like them, I too have worked hard to master my management style, and, on the whole, I think it compares favorably with theirs.

In my vocabulary, soft management does not mean weak management. A tentative approach to a critical decision in an unfamiliar environment is not a sign of indecision but of common sense. Criticism from your subordinates is not necessarily a sign of disrespect; they may be offering the wisdom and experience of a different perspective.

Conversely, tough management does not necessarily mean effective management. Self-confidence can be a cover for arrogance or fear, resolute can be a code word for autocratic, and hard-nosed can mean thick-skinned.

I believe that openness is a productive management

technique and that intentional vulnerability is an effective management style. The "soft" management I believe in and do my best to practice is a matter of making hard choices and of accepting personal responsibility for decisions. I have a couple of stories that illustrate what I mean.

In the early 1980s, I was general manager of the Synthetic Fuels Division of Westinghouse. Unfortunately, the decline in oil prices that followed the second oil shock in 1979 had led Westinghouse top management to decide to get out of the synthetic fuels business, so my staff and I had to find a buyer and consummate a sale within a few months or face the prospect of seeing our division dismantled and liquidated.

In an effort to make ourselves attractive, we had already trimmed the work force from 240 to about 130, most of them engaged in the design, testing, and marketing of a coal gasification process that we were confident would one day produce electric power from coal efficiently, cleanly, and economically. While we believed in the technology, we realized that, in the midst of a recession, there weren't many buyers for energy businesses that could offer only future profits.

For the employees in the division, closure would mean more than unemployment. It would mean shattering the dream of building a great new business, a dream many of us had been working toward for more than five years. Unfortunately, even with the reduced work force we had a dilemma. The continuing financial drain we represented tended to shorten the corporation's patience, but if we cut employment too much, we would have nothing left to sell. Moreover, as winter approached, my staff and I became concerned that Westinghouse was about to set an absolute deadline for selling the division.

My senior managers and I approached this dilemma as gingerly as we could, with much discussion and no foregone conclusions. We decided that a further reduction in force of 15 people was both necessary to sustain the corporation's goodwill and tolerable, perhaps even desirable, from the point of view of selling the business. We then examined various alternatives for selecting the people to lay off. We agreed that our criteria would not include performance as such. Instead, we decided to choose jobs with the lowest probable value in the eyes of a potential buyer, provided only that they were not essential to the task of selling the business. For example, we decided we could get along with two technicians in the chemistry lab instead of three.

After about an hour of give-and-take, some of it heated, we agreed to a list of 15 names, and as the meeting drew to a close, one department head said to the others, "Well, let's go tell them." It had been our practice in past layoffs to choose an hour when all managers with people on the reduction list would call them in and give them the bad news.

"No," I said, "I'm going to tell them myself."

"But that's not necessary," someone said.

"I think it is necessary," I said.

I was concerned that a further reduction in force might lead the remaining employees to conclude that management had given up on selling the business and that it was only a matter of time before we laid off everyone else as well and closed the business down. If they were to draw that conclusion, many of our most valuable people would leave. During months of uncertainty about the future of the division, our best engineering and marketing people had located opportunities with other companies, and they were now sitting on those offers waiting to see what would happen to Synthetic Fuels. They needed to hear the real reasons for the layoffs from me—personally.

I asked my senior managers to send all employees on the reduction-in-force list to a conference room early the following morning. I wanted to explain as truthfully as I could what it was we were doing and why.

Walking into the conference room the next morning was like walking into a funeral home. The 15 employees sat around the table in mourning. Most of the women were crying. Most of the men, stunned and dejected, were staring at the tabletop. Their managers sat in chairs against the wall, clearly wishing they were somewhere else. I had not expected my staff to announce the purpose of the meeting, but, obviously, people knew.

I summoned my courage and took the chair at the head of the table. I told the employees we were going to lay them off and that all of us, I in particular, felt very bad about it. I went through our reasoning on the reduction in force, putting particular emphasis on our belief that this RIF would improve our chances of selling the division—as opposed to closing it. I told them we were, in effect, sacrificing a few for the benefit of many. I explained the criteria we had used and observed that while we felt our thinking was sound and believed we had matched people to the criteria in good faith, we understood that they might well disagree. I said we were doing the best we could—imperfect as that might be—to save the business. I asked them not to blame their managers. I ordered them not to blame themselves—our decision was in no way a value judgment on them as individuals, I said. If they wanted someone to blame, I urged them to blame me.

These remarks took about 15 minutes, and then I asked for questions. The initial responses were all attempts to discredit the selection process. "But why *aren't* you taking performance into account?" one woman asked. "My supervisor has told me my performance is excellent. What's the point of doing a good job if you only get laid off?"

"I've been here for 11 years," said a male technician. "Why shouldn't I get more consideration than someone who was hired only a couple of years ago?"

I responded by repeating that under the circumstances,

we believed only two criteria were relevant: first, that the position be nonessential to the selling process and, second, that it be one that prospective buyers would see as having relatively little value to them in the short term.

The questions kept coming, and for a time the tearful, funereal mood persisted, but eventually other questions began to surface. Did we really think the division could be sold? Did we think there really was a future for synthetic fuels? Why couldn't Westinghouse wait a little longer? The question period went on for a good 45 minutes and was without doubt one of the most painful I've ever attended. And yet, as it ended, I felt a certain new closeness to those 15 people. I shook hands with each of them and wished them good luck. I thought I sensed that most of them understood and even respected what we were trying to do, however much they might object to our final choice of sacrificial lambs.

For weeks the meeting stayed fresh in my mind. We'd hear, for example, that now Nancy's husband had been laid off from his job, and I would remember Nancy sitting at the conference table with tears streaming down her face, and the memory would be so bleak that I'd think, "Why did I insist on meeting with all of them myself? Why didn't I just let their bosses break the news?"

At the same time, however, I was beginning to notice a change I hadn't expected: the remaining employees seemed to have a renewed determination to hold the business together. For example, tests on the pilot plant continued with a new optimism; whenever I was in the test structure, the technicians seemed cheerful, positive, and entirely focused on the task at hand. And at a meeting to discuss the status of another project we wanted to hold onto, not only was the lead engineer still with us—pockets undoubtedly filled with attractive offers from oil companies—but he was explaining his ideas for reducing the project's capital costs.

A couple of months later, we did finally sell the

business, and what happened next was even more grati-
fying. The new owner gave us funds for some additional
work, and we suddenly had the chance to rehire about
half of the 15 people we'd laid off. *Without exception,*
they accepted our offers to return. One or two even gave
up other jobs they'd found in the meantime. One secretary gave up a good position with a very stable and rep-
utable local company to rejoin her friends at our still
somewhat risky operation with all its grand dreams.

It gradually became apparent to me that my very painful meeting with those 15 employees had been a kind of
turning point for Synthetic Fuels. Clearly, this was due in
part to the two messages I sent in that meeting on behalf
of senior management—first, that we would do everything in our power to keep the business alive and salable
and, second, that we saw layoffs as an extremely regret-
table last resort. But as time goes by, I am more and more
convinced that the "success" of that meeting was also
due in part to the fact that it made me vulnerable to the
criticism, disapproval, and anger of the people we were
laying off. If that sounds cryptic, let me explain by telling another story, a story I remembered only later when I
began to analyze what had happened at Synthetic Fuels.

In the early 1970s, I worked for the vice president of
the Westinghouse Steam Turbine Division, which was
located just south of the Philadelphia airport in a sprawling complex of factories that had employed more than
10,000 people during World War II and was still a union
stronghold. My boss, Gene Cattabiani, then in his forties,
had a reputation as a good engineer and a "people person." In fact, his success in previous assignments had
had much to do with his ability to get along with the
people above and below him.

One of the most difficult issues facing Gene at Steam
Turbine was an extremely hostile labor-relations environment. In the 1950s, the Union of Electrical Workers
represented the entire hourly work force. It was a tough,

unfriendly union, so much so that the McCarthy hearings had labeled it communist.

I had seen two faces of this union. On the one hand, its leaders were as stubborn as mules at the negotiating table, and its strikes were daunting. Several men once threatened to throw a small boulder through my windshield when I tried to cross a picket line to get to work. In 1956, the violent, confrontational mood of one nine-month strike led to a shooting death outside the plant.

On the other hand, I had also seen thoughtfulness and warmth. One year when I was chairman of the United Way campaign, we asked the union leaders to serve with me on the organizing committee. It was a very successful campaign, partly because they worked so hard to get the hourly work force to contribute, though few had ever given in the past.

By and large, however, attitudes were polarized. Most managers viewed shop floor workers as lazy and greedy, a distinct business liability. On their side, most union members viewed management as incompetent, overpaid, and more or less unnecessary.

When Gene took over, the Steam Turbine Division was not particularly profitable. There was a compelling need to cut costs and improve productivity, and it was clear that much of the opportunity for improvement was on the shop floor. Yet the historic animosities between labor and management made it seem unlikely that any fruitful negotiation could take place.

Gene decided it was up to him to break this impasse and begin to change attitudes on both sides by treating union leaders and the work force with respect, honesty, and openness. To me this made a great deal of sense. If managers began treating union members as human beings, with dignity and worth, they might just respond by treating us the same way.

But it was not just a matter of style. The business was in trouble, and unless the union understood the extent of the problem, it would have little incentive to cooperate. Historically, union leaders had assumed that the business was very profitable. They believed their people deserved a thick slice of what was in their view a large pie. By the time Gene arrived, however, the pie had become pretty skimpy and was threatening to vanish altogether. Gene decided it was essential to inform the union of the real state of the business.

In the past when there was any informing to be done, the labor-relations vice president would call a meeting with the union leadership and tell them what he wanted them to know. Not surprisingly, since they saw everything management said as entirely self-serving, union leaders had always viewed these meetings with disdain. This time, however, Gene decided he would do it differently. He would give a presentation on the state of the business to the entire hourly work force, a thing that had never been done in the long history of the division.

Many of us wondered if this was really necessary. We knew the rank and file saw the vice president and general manager—Gene—as the ultimate enemy. Wouldn't it be easier, we wondered, and maybe more effective, to have someone else make the presentation? Maybe they would listen to the financial manager. But Gene clung—stubbornly, I thought—to his decision.

To reach the entire work force, Gene would have to repeat the presentation several times to groups of hundreds of workers. The format was a slide presentation, simple but complete and clear, followed by questions from the floor.

The initial presentation was a nightmare. Gene wanted the work force to see that the business was in trouble, real trouble, and that their jobs depended on a different kind of relationship with management. But the workers assumed that management was up to its usual self-serving tricks, and there on stage, for the first time, they had the enemy in person. They heckled him merci-lessly all through the slide show. Then, during the ques-tion-and-answer period, they shouted abuse and threats. As far as I could tell, they weren't hearing Gene's mes-sage—or even listening. I felt sure he had made a mis-take in deciding to give the presentation himself.

But Gene persisted. With obvious dread but with grim determination, he made the full series of presenta-tions. While I could see no evidence that people even understood his state-of-the-business message, much less believed it, I did begin to see an important change. When Gene went out on the factory floor for a look around (which his predecessors never did unless they were giving customers a tour), people began to offer a nod of recognition—a radical change from the way they used to spit on the floor as he walked by.

Even more remarkable was his interaction with heck-lers. Whenever he spotted one, he would walk over and say something like, "You really gave me a hard time last week," to which the response was usually something like, "Well, you deserved it, trying to pass off all that bull!" Such exchanges invariably led to brief but very open dialogues, and I noticed that the lathe operators or blading mechanics he talked to would listen to what Gene said—really listen.

Suddenly, Gene was credible. He had ceased to be an ordinary useless manager and had become a creature of flesh and blood, someone whose opinions had some value. Gene was my boss, and I liked him for his warmth, honesty, and sense of humor. But I knew it had to be more than personality that won him respect in the eyes of that hard-bitten, cynical work force.

Now, years later, as I thought about those presenta-tions to the hourly workers and about Gene's daily inter-actions with subordinates and peers as well, I realized that he often set up encounters in such a way that the people he met felt free to complain or argue, even to attack. Gene made himself vulnerable to people, and it was this deliberate vulnerability that seemed to draw people to him. Because he avoided defensiveness and opened himself to criticism, people were much more inclined to believe that the strength and force of his position was not merely contrived and rhetorical but real.

But there was more to it than that. By making the presentations himself, Gene took the heat for his own point of view. Had he let someone else deliver the message, he would have avoided some of the most unpleasant consequences of his position—not the business consequences, which he would have suffered in any case, but the personal consequences, the face-to-face consequences of conveying bad news. People want to confront the source of their difficulties. Gene gave them the chance, and they respected him for it.

From those presentations on, union-management relations took a sharp turn for the better, and Gene rapidly built credibility with the work force. He made important changes in Steam Turbine's work rules and gave individual employees broader, more flexible assignments. He also imposed layoffs, and he raised standards with respect to both throughput and error-free performance. With each change, Gene continued to open himself to arguments, complaints, and anger—all of which gradually diminished as results continued to improve and as Gene's vulnerability and courage continued to disarm opponents.

Combined with many other changes that reached well beyond the factory floor, the division's increased productivity powered Steam Turbine to greatly improved financial performance, and before long, Gene became an executive vice president. More important from my point of view, Gene became a role model for me—more of a role model than I realized at the time. He taught me how important it is to be a flesh-and-blood human being as well as a manager. He taught me that "soft" qualities like openness, sensitivity, and thoughtful intelligence are at least as critical to management success as "harder" qualities like charisma, aggressiveness, and always being right. Most important of all in the light of what happened at Synthetic Fuels, he taught me the value of vulnerability and the benefits of taking the heat for your own acts and policies.

What I had done in my meeting with the 15 employees at Synthetic Fuels was to repeat, in a smaller format, Gene's experience at Steam Turbine. As a result, it was a turning point not only for the division but for me as well. I went well beyond anything I had done previously in opening myself to others. On the surface, I was motivated by what I saw as a business need and didn't give much thought to how vulnerable the meeting would make me. Deep down, I think I was also motivated by Gene's example, by an internalized picture of the soft manager succeeding in the face of hard challenges.

Being a soft manager is no job for the fainthearted. On the contrary, it takes a certain courage to be open-minded, well-informed, and responsible, to walk straight into adversity rather than seek to avoid it. Staying open to different possibilities can, of course, lead to vacillation, but it can also lead to tougher, better decisions from among a wider range of choices. The object of soft management is certainly not to be lax or indecisive.

By the same token, whenever I'm tempted to insulate myself from the painful emotional consequences of some business decision, Gene's experience reminds me that it's more productive to listen to objections and complaints, to understand what subordinates are thinking and feeling, to open up to their arguments and their displeasure. It was this kind of vulnerability that made Gene credible to the people whose help he most needed in order to succeed.

Unfortunately, openness and vulnerability are anathema to some people. I have worked with at least two men who found my management style upsetting. Both were supremely self-confident, bright, and articulate, the kind of men who take complete charge of situations and of other human beings. I'm sure it's very uncomfortable (at an unconscious level, perhaps even frightening) for people who like to feel they are in absolute control of their surroundings to see someone like me stand so close to what they must experience as a precipice of indignity and lost authority.

In any case, they didn't like me, and I didn't like them. I believe they saw my vulnerability as exactly what they wanted to be rid of in themselves. I know I saw their exaggerated self-assurance as arrogance and insensitivity, which I wanted no part of in myself.

My position on soft management comes down to this: proponents of all management styles will probably agree that to manage other people effectively, a person needs a battery of qualities that are not easily acquired, and that these include intelligence, energy, confidence, and responsibility. Where I differ from a lot of my colleagues is in believing that candor, sensitivity, and a certain willingness to suffer the painful consequences of unpopular decisions belong on the list of necessary characteristics. Being vulnerable to the give-and-take of ordinary emotional crossfire and intellectual disagreement makes us more human, more credible, and more open to change.

William H. Peace, *formerly an executive with Westinghouse and the Carrier division of United Technologies, moved to England in 1987.*

He now lives in Buckinghamshire, England, where he operates his own international consulting practice, specializing in process reengineering and team building. "The Hard Work of Being a Soft Manager" is now used as a case at several business schools.

2

Nothing Prepared Me to Manage AIDS

GARY E. BANAS

THE TROUBLE WITH almost everything I read about AIDS or AIDS in the workplace is that it's too cut and dried. Popular advice to managers is strikingly unhelpful because it always seems to involve choices that are neat and easy. Confidentiality, equity, and accommodation are among the prescribed managerial practices, but these words describe a world very distant from the world of real people doing real work in real organizations.

I know, because in the course of less than four years, two of my subordinates developed AIDS. One after the other, I saw two men and the people they supervised suffer through AIDS and its inevitable consequences: debility, denial, impaired performance, and death for the men themselves, deteriorating productivity and morale for their subordinates. Nothing I thought I'd learned from pamphlets and seminars prepared me for either ordeal. For that matter, the first ordeal did not prepare me for the second.

My whole reason for writing this article, including the parts that don't reflect particularly well on myself, is to make this one point: Don't let anyone kid you, when you confront AIDS in the workplace, you will face untenable choices that seem to pit your obligation to humanity against your obligation to your organization. Contrary to popular opinion, you will almost certainly fall short in both areas.

Most of my early education in the proper managerial approach to AIDS occurred while I was personnel officer for the southwestern district of the Comptroller of the Currency. I attended and even organized AIDS awareness seminars, and I stayed conscientiously abreast of AIDS literature. By the mid-1980s, I reckoned myself one of the nation's leading personnel directors in the effort to recognize and respond to AIDS as an emerging work-place issue. In early 1987, I moved to our New York office as director for administration, and it was here that I came face to face with the disease for the first time.

In the spring of that year, one of my mid-level super-visors, a capable manager whom I'll call Frank—and whose job I won't identify too closely—began showing signs of serious illness. He was losing a great deal of weight. He was also beginning to miss work, and his absences grew longer and more frequent. At first, he'd call in the morning to say he was sick, or he'd leave early in the afternoon for a doctor's appointment or because he felt ill. Within a few weeks, he was out sick for days at a time. In addition, he became short-tempered with his staff and began avoiding me altogether. More important, the quality and timeliness of his work rapidly declined. His required reports were often late or incomplete, and he was often unavailable or unprepared for essential meetings.

Before he became ill, Frank was candid about his homosexuality. He would jokingly volunteer to others, for example, that he belonged to a high-risk group for AIDS. Yet now he was very guarded about his medical condition. Since I had known him only a few months before his illness came on, I could understand his reluctance to confide in me. But all of us could see that he was sick.

After more than a month—and several attempts to get him to tell me what was wrong—Frank went to the hospital for the first time. When I visited him, he told me he was suffering from a rare form of tuberculosis. He also said he was responding to medication and assured me he would soon recover his full health.

Two weeks later, he did come back to work but told me his diagnosis had changed. He was now taking medication for intestinal parasites. After asking for a pledge of strict confidence, Frank also told me he had been tested for the AIDS virus and was HIV-positive.

I can't say I was surprised. Because of the attention AIDS has received in the media, Americans probably know more about it than they know about the common cold. Where I would have a tough time discussing colds without some reference to chicken soup, I can speak knowledgeably about opportunistic infections, Kaposi's sarcoma, the side effects of AZT, and the immune system in general.

What Frank didn't realize when he asked for and got my pledge of secrecy was that the rumor mill had already conducted an amazingly accurate medical evaluation of his symptoms. There were a number of reasons for the widespread interest in his illness. First, he was highly visible in the organization. Second, everyone knew he was gay. Add the fact that he was the first suspected AIDS case in the office—at a time when the disease was getting extraordinary media coverage—and it's easy to see how idle speculation translated quickly into common knowledge.

Frank's case points up the difficulty any manager faces in maintaining employee confidentiality and in balancing human and organizational needs. I cannot begin to count the phone calls and visits I received from Frank's colleagues and subordinates seeking confirmation of their suspicions. Early on, I could respond to their often subtle questioning with a forthright, "I don't know." Once Frank told me he was HIV-positive, I resorted to dodging their questions.

As necessary as I thought they were, my evasions fooled no one. What they did do was weaken organizational credibility, increase everyone's discomfort and insecurity—except perhaps Frank's—and damage morale, more even than I realized at the time. Openness and honesty are vital; employee confidentiality is critical. In this typical AIDS-related trade-off, both suffered.

Telling Frank's staff was not the only problem. There was also the question of telling my supervisor. As Frank's absences from the office lengthened, productivity in his unit deteriorated. I took on much of the essential work myself, including Frank's budget planning, but I didn't have the time to supervise his unit's daily routine operations. As a new director, I was concerned about how top management viewed my own performance, so I very much wanted to discuss Frank's illness with my executive-level superior.

Without going into detail, I asked Frank for permission to tell my supervisor, and he gave it. Greatly relieved, I went to my boss and felt a tremendous burden lift from my shoulders. For the first time, I was able to talk openly about my own feelings and the work-related questions that Frank's illness raised. My supervisor was also concerned about declining unit performance, and he promised his support for whatever approach I thought best. I came away from the meeting reassured that he was aware of my difficulties and felt I was doing an effective job.

In late August, after another long hospitalization, Frank called on a Friday to tell me he would be back at work the following Monday. I'd seen him in the hospital only a few days before and was astonished to hear he felt well enough to come back to the office. Of course, I hoped his condition would take another turn for the better—many AIDS patients have periods of relative improvement in their long downhill struggle—but now I began to suspect that Frank didn't realize how sick he really was. He told me he would begin with a half-day schedule and that within a few weeks he hoped to return to work full-time. I told his staff to expect him on Monday.

Before Friday was over, his subordinates asked to see me, and I met with them late that afternoon. Several said how pleased they were to hear his condition had improved, but all confessed that they were worried about his return. One of them, apparently a designated spokes-person, said they all believed Frank had AIDS. They didn't ask me to confirm this, but they did want my assurance that they couldn't catch it in the office. One of them asked if it was safe to use the bathroom after Frank. Another even wondered about the water fountain. After all of the formal and informal AIDS education I knew they'd had, both in and out of the office, these two questions surprised me. I reminded them that AIDS could not be transmitted through casual contact, even assuming they were right about Frank's illness.

At the end of the meeting, I thanked them for their extra efforts during Frank's absence and said I hoped things would soon return to normal. I doubt I eased any of their fears, but I think just getting their anxieties into the open helped. To their credit, every one of them appeared for work on Monday.

As it turned out, Frank had to leave after only two hours on the job, and that was the last time he ever came to the office. He spent most of the next three months either alone in his apartment or in the hospital.

Frank still admitted only to being HIV-positive, but his two hours in the office convinced me he had an advanced case of AIDS and would never again be fully able to do his job. The visit also forced me into a decision I had been avoiding: whether to keep Frank on despite his illness or to take the steps necessary to replace him.

Since I'm lucky enough to work for an organization that puts a premium on employee health and well-being, this was not a question of termination. The Comptroller of the Currency has long had an official policy covering employees with life-threatening illnesses, and we fully support accommodations such as working at home, flexible hours, leave-sharing, and moving people to less stressful jobs. We also do our best to keep employees in paid positions for as long as they wish to work.

Although Frank's extended absences and loss of productivity gave us ample grounds for enforced retirement or some other removal action, I knew his sense of self-worth was almost completely tied up in his career. He had little contact with his family and, as far as I could tell, few close friends. His job was the most important thing in his life, and I had no desire to strip a dying man of what mattered to him most. I was convinced that any effort to take away his job would undermine his optimism and further shorten his life.

For the short term, I gave one of his subordinates a temporary promotion in order to have someone directing traffic. In addition, everyone rolled up their sleeves and pitched in to get the work done. But these were makeshift arrangements. In September, I finally decided to ask Frank to consider reassignment to a nonsupervisory position. Because of his seniority, he would have to make a formal request for a reduction in rank, and if he balked, I'd have to initiate a lengthy and potentially hostile removal process. I broached the subject on one of my hospital visits. I told him it wouldn't mean a cut in pay. I said I hoped it would relieve him of any concern he might have about his inability to manage his unit.

To my surprise, Frank immediately agreed to request

the reassignment. It was sad to watch him relinquish his whole career without a murmur of protest, but I was enormously relieved.

From that day until his death in November, I visited Frank as often as I could. I helped him fill out his health-insurance claim forms, and I passed along the latest office gossip. He was failing rapidly, and he had the hospital put my name on the emergency contact list. At Frank's request, I called his younger brother, explained that Frank was near death, and asked him to come to New York to be with him.

Frank died two days after his brother's arrival. A group of us from the office made arrangements for a memorial service, and I wrote and delivered a eulogy. Except for Frank's brother, the only people who attended were from the agency.

I was saddened by Frank's death, but, at the same time, my superiors and colleagues praised my sensitive response to a difficult management crisis, and I have to admit that their approval pleased me. I felt I had set a standard for other managers to follow. No inner voice warned me that my approach to Frank's case might be of little value when I confronted AIDS a second time.

Immediately after Frank stepped aside in September, I began recruiting for his replacement. Jim, who had worked for me in Dallas, was one of my principal candidates. I had known him about four years, considered him a friend as well as a capable colleague, and was delighted when he agreed to transfer to New York. He arrived in January 1988.

Because he was familiar with our organizational priorities and my own management style—and because he was just plain good at his job—Jim quickly restored former production levels, improved morale, and generally made my life a lot easier. I was now able to focus on areas I had neglected over the previous six months and, being still relatively new as director for administration in a large and diverse operation, to go on discovering what I was director of. The next 18 months were comparatively easy ones for Jim and for me.

Then one morning in the spring of 1989, Jim walked into my office for a quarterly status reports meeting, sat down stiffly in his chair, and told me quite calmly that he had just learned he was HIV-positive.

I had a hard time taking it in, and when I did, I was more than surprised. I was devastated. Deep inside, I'm sorry to say, a selfish voice was saying, "Why me?" and "Not again!" Aloud I said, "I'm terribly sorry to hear that, Jim. Please let me know if there's anything I can do to help."

My response was superficial and inadequate, but it was the best I could do at that moment. Having been through this once before, my compassion was mingled with dread. I didn't want to watch Jim suffer, and I didn't want to grapple again with the problems that his suffering might cause for his staff and for me. Although he still looked the picture of health, I began mentally calculating the time remaining before he would have to leave his job.

Jim explained that he was beginning AZT treatments and that his doctor was optimistic about his ability to live a long life. Having seen Frank's health deteriorate rapidly over the course of five months, I had my doubts. I resolved to deal with the situation quickly and effectively.

I told Jim there were others in the organization who needed to know and that I would discuss his condition with my supervisor. He agreed to this limited release of information but was adamant that I tell no one else. He insisted he was not like Frank in any way and said he didn't want people in the office talking about him the way they had talked about Frank.

Despite my long professional association with Jim, I knew very little about his personal life. While we saw each other socially from time to time, it was usually at parties or office functions. Though I considered him a friend, to this day I have no idea how he became infected with the AIDS virus. His sense of privacy was exceptionally strong.

Several months passed without any noticeable decline in Jim's condition. I started hoping that he might enjoy many years of good health before his virus developed into AIDS. By late June, however, he was beginning to show the familiar signs of weight loss. When I asked him about it, he said he felt great. He said his doctor was adjusting his medication to improve his appetite.

I took him at his word. I now think Jim was in denial, but even I was cautiously optimistic. He seemed able to carry a full work load and was only occasionally absent from the office for doctor's appointments. Because I was focusing so intently on his physical health, I was slow to notice the decline in his performance and slow to remember Frank's initial denial of any performance problem.

By now, Jim's unit had begun to miss occasional deadlines, and I was hearing periodic complaints about unit response time. Given Jim's history of superior performance, I wrote these off to the increasing work load. Yet the complaints persisted, and new problems cropped up—simple errors uncorrected, critical organizational objectives ignored, major projects never completed and never assigned to subordinates. My supervisor started pressuring me about several projects that were stalled.

I mentioned these concerns to Jim without suggesting any link between his illness and unit performance. I believed at the time, and I still believe, that Jim had developed an active case of AIDS by June of 1989, but not because he told me so. In fact, Jim never acknowledged that his HIV had developed into full-blown AIDS. Absent that acknowledgment, I raised his performance problems the same way I would have raised them with any other manager. I had received complaints, I said, and I expected him to analyze and correct them.

Nevertheless, I was sufficiently worried about Jim's state of mind that I met with several members of his staff a few days later to get their views on whether or not Jim was losing his ability to function as a manager. One employee, whom I'll call Liz, was so candid that she forced me to recognize the truth: AIDS was affecting not only Jim's performance but also the performance of every one of his subordinates.

Liz was the senior staffperson in Jim's unit and had been extremely loyal to Jim personally. She and others had covered for him as best they could for several months, but now she'd had enough. Liz was also getting complaints—from the unit's internal customers as well as from our Washington headquarters for a number of late and inaccurate reports. But the final straw had come from Jim himself. According to Liz, Jim had recently told her that I was dissatisfied with unit performance and that he blamed her and the rest of the staff. He'd gone on to say that he would take corrective action unless there was immediate improvement.

Liz was in tears as she told this story. She and others had worked extra hours and run interference for Jim, and he'd laid the blame for the entire problem at their door. When I asked her why she hadn't told me earlier, Liz said she'd felt sorry for Jim, hadn't wanted to make more trouble for him, and, in any case, found it awkward to go over his head. She also told me that she and others had come to the conclusion that Jim had AIDS.

I tried to assure Liz that I didn't blame her or anyone else in the unit for declining performance, but I'm afraid the damage had already been done. Several days later, I found Liz ill in one of the office corridors—she was hyperventilating—and sent her home for the day. Several months later, she told me she had a job offer from another organization, and I encouraged her to accept it for the sake of her own health.

Because AIDS takes the lives of its primary victims, we naturally lose sight of the fact that it injures others as well. Unlike Frank and Jim, Liz didn't come close to dying, but she paid a price for their illness in stress and overwork. Others did too. During the four-year period from the onset of Frank's illness to the end of Jim's, we saw a 200% turnover in unit personnel. Today only one person remains who worked for both men.

One of the most difficult dilemmas a manager faces in this situation is how to weigh the obvious, painful needs of the dying person against the less dramatic but clearly compelling needs of the organization. I have no ready answers. I only know that managers will be plunged into moral and professional choices at the most mundane, specific level, that there will be little precedent for many of these choices, and that almost all will cause injury to someone. Fatal disease permits no win-win solutions, only lose-lose ones. A manager's task is to minimize the losses—to people and to organizations.

After talking to Liz, I was more troubled than ever about Jim's competence, his apparent paranoia, unit morale—and my own performance as his supervisor. Once again, confidentiality had lost its meaning as a protector of privacy and become a source of uncertainty and fear. Once again, subordinates were paying the price for Jim's denial. I had allowed the situation to go on too long. I decided it was time to replace him.

As in Frank's case, I never had to consider outright termination. I hoped Jim would accept reassignment to a less critical position the way Frank had. Alternatively, Jim had enough years of service to qualify for disability retirement. All things considered, I was naively confident that Jim would step aside graciously—if not for himself, then for the good of the organization. I was about to see a new face of denial.

I began my meeting with Jim by discussing his

declining performance and suggesting a link with his health. But before I had a chance to offer him a different job, Jim vehemently rejected my appraisal of his work. If there were unit deficiencies, he said, they depended on the substandard performance of his staff and a work load too large for his unit to handle. As for the alleged complaints about his performance, people were simply blaming their own inadequacies on him. And since there was nothing wrong with his performance, AIDS was clearly not a contributing factor. He accused me of treating him unfairly because I was bitter about having to deal with two HIV-infected employees in a row.

I was stung. My spontaneous, angry reaction was to tell him he should consider himself lucky to be working for someone with experience in dealing with this situation. Then, cooling off quickly, I responded more professionally. I was determined to say what had to be said, even if it sounded cold and clinical.

In any case, Jim was not receptive to a change of title and position. I made the offer, and he turned it down. He reminded me that I would have to take formal action to remove him from his post. I said I was aware of the organizational requirements. I said I was prepared to take that course unless his performance immediately improved. It was now June; I gave him until September to demonstrate such improvement.

Several days after this stormy encounter, Jim put in a request for a month's vacation. I was surprised and angry all over again. If Jim was determined to resist my efforts to help him, I thought he should be spending more hours at work, not going on vacation. Fortunately, I was not so angry that I lost all perspective. I knew this might be the last vacation Jim would ever have, so despite my real convictions about organizational priorities, I approved his request.

As it happened, Jim became extremely ill on the plane and had to spend the first two weeks of his vacation in the hospital. He called to explain that he'd been diagnosed with meningitis, which he claimed was completely unrelated to his AIDS.

When he returned to the office, Jim looked awful. He had lost a great deal of weight, he was losing his hair, and he confessed to difficulty keeping down any food at all. Nevertheless, Jim seemed genuinely optimistic about the new medication he was taking for what he still insisted was meningitis and nothing more.

For that matter, his health actually seemed to improve for a time. But despite extraordinary efforts and long hours, Jim was unable to improve his performance. As we approached my September deadline, a flood of complaints rolled in from other managers about the unit and about Jim specifically. He simply wasn't getting the job done. Once again, I rolled up my sleeves, personally managed several program areas, and got our Washington headquarters to provide temporary staff assistance. But my efforts weren't enough. Jim's unit was central to the organization, and now its reputation was gone, its staff thoroughly demoralized, and its manager too ill to function. Worst of all, it was clearly my job to fix it. I had no alternative but to proceed with a formal performance action against him.

As a manager, it was the most agonizing task I ever faced. On the one hand, I knew that removing Jim was necessary to meet my responsibilities as a manager. On the other hand, I believed that taking action against him meant failing my responsibilities as a human being. Although I was well practiced in the art of terminating unproductive employees, I had never had to force the removal—or, in this case, the reassignment—of an employee who was facing death.

At the end of September, I handed Jim a formal notice of proposed performance action. It informed him that unless his performance improved significantly by year's end, he would be rated "unacceptable" and terminated, demoted, or reassigned. In early January, after the holidays, I presented Jim with an unacceptable rating. As expected, he disputed its accuracy.

Over the next several days, Jim and I carried on an intense and painful negotiation. My goal never was to fire him. The unacceptable rating was simply a way of getting him to ask for reassignment. I told Jim that if I had to force him out of his job, I would set out my reasons in plain English. But if he gave up his supervisory position of his own free will, he could name any reason he wished. I told him I would reconsider his unacceptable rating when I received his voluntary request for reassignment.

We talked several times a day, clarifying our respective positions, each of us trying to get the other to relent. In the end, "for reasons of health," Jim "volunteered" for reassignment to a nonmanagerial position. In return, I raised his performance rating to "acceptable." I felt manipulative, but I also felt I had done my job.

I would like to say that this solved the work-related problem. I was able to replace Jim with another proven manager, and the change improved staff morale and restored much of the unit's responsiveness and credibility. But Jim continued to dispute his performance rating even after I raised it to acceptable. He went so far as to file a grievance in order to get a rating high enough to carry a salary increase. The grievance procedure sustained my action, but it was a shallow victory. Jim avoided me; we rarely spoke unless I called for a formal meeting. Sadly, his performance continued to deteriorate even with reduced responsibility, so we had a series of stiff, formal meetings right through 1990. I was doing my job, but I had lost a friend and, I was afraid, a piece of my better self.

Things proceeded to get worse for both of us. Jim's absences grew longer and more frequent, and he was hospitalized several times. I'd minimized his diminishing effectiveness by limiting his responsibility, but Jim still couldn't do his job. At the end of the year, nevertheless, I gave him another acceptable rating so he could keep his new position. Although I considered it a gift—in fact, Jim's work was far from acceptable—he filed another grievance. At the very same time, however, he also submitted an application for disability retirement and went on sick leave pending its approval. When I asked him why he was contesting his rating when he meant to retire anyway, Jim explained angrily that he needed a better rating to find a new job. My supervisor was the grievance officer in his case, and, with my concurrence, he increased Jim's final rating to "fully successful."

Unlike Frank, Jim had solid support from his family and was able to return to his hometown and live with his mother for the last year of his life. He died in January 1992.

Every manager knows that people differ in their ability to accept constructive criticism and acknowledge performance deficiencies. Looking back, it amazes me that I expected the same reaction from Jim that I got from Frank. I suppose I was misled by their obvious similarities. Both were terribly sick, both lost their effectiveness, both fell into a clear physical category—AIDS victim—for which I felt trained and ready. But the dying are as different as the healthy. AIDS is not an "issue" but a disease, and the people who get it are human beings first and victims second. Some of what I learned in dealing with Frank applied equally to Jim. Much did not. The differences as well as the similarities have taught me some valuable lessons.

To begin with, there is a critical distinction to be made between employees who are HIV-positive and those who have developed active AIDS. Distressingly enough, my experience indicates that it is managers who must make this distinction, since the people affected may not volunteer or even admit to themselves how far their illness has progressed.

Employees who are HIV-positive are fully capable of

providing normal, productive work. Supervisors should base every decision regarding their recruitment, evaluation, and promotion on merit alone and not on some imprecise notion of life expectancy or anticipated future decline in performance.

This much is basic. The real challenge for managers is dealing with employees in the advanced stages of AIDS, when performance is declining, attendance and dependability are haphazard, confidentiality has been jeopardized or swept aside by the rumor mill, and unit productivity and morale have begun to suffer serious damage. By extension, a manager's own performance will now be in question as well.

The broader issue is how to achieve a balance between organizational needs and the fair and compassionate treatment of a formerly successful employee. The narrower issues, unfortunately, tend to focus not so much on equity, counseling, and organizational success as on compromise, candor, and damage control.

Perhaps the most difficult aspect of AIDS for a manager is the inability or reluctance of AIDS victims to recognize how far their health has actually deteriorated. Both Frank and Jim tried hard to maintain their optimism. Both insisted that the variety of ailments they fell victim to were unrelated to AIDS. Both assured me repeatedly that new medications or new dosages would improve their condition. From time to time, I even shared their false hopes of recovery, and that was perhaps my greatest failing. The conflict between compassion and organizational efficiency is bleak enough without adding wishful thinking to the mix.

In Jim's case, clearly it would have been better for the organization if I had reassigned him earlier. Yet doing so would have required me to ignore or at least challenge his optimism about a partial or complete recovery, and I cannot believe I have the right to challenge that kind of hope. In the end, I had no choice but to proceed along the grueling and decidedly unsympathetic route of performance documentation.

Jim's case was further complicated by its duration. Only four months elapsed from the observed onset of Frank's disease until he agreed to step aside. Jim continued to work for some two years, his effectiveness diminishing more and more swiftly as time went on, before I forced him to accept reassignment. As medical breakthroughs improve the quality of life and prolong the careers of AIDS patients, the problem of decreasing job performance will probably grow more acute—and more distressing.

The next time I confront AIDS, especially in a supervisor, I will know that the disease affects everyone around it, not just the person who is ill. As performance flags, colleagues and subordinates will find themselves absorbing additional duties, redoing unsatisfactory work, and piecing together uncompleted projects. When the AIDS patient is a supervisor, a considerable amount of work may remain unassigned and simply fall through the cracks.

On top of the extra work load, productivity will suffer in other ways as well. People will discuss a coworker's deteriorating health, and if the nature of the illness is confidential, then they will spend additional time speculating about diagnosis, life-style, and the danger of infection. In the future, I will encourage employees with AIDS to consider seriously the advantages of confiding in their coworkers.

The next time I recognize performance impairment as a result of AIDS, I will also start focusing attention on the needs and concerns of the other workers in the unit. Had I paid closer attention to Jim's staff, I think I would have realized much sooner that they were covering for him.

The last lesson I learned was the importance of keeping my own supervisor informed of my difficulties.

While I was quick to alert him to the existence of an AIDS case among my subordinates, I was slow to ask for help. There were two reasons for this lapse. The first was my training in the lean-and-mean school of management technique. The second was my miscalculation of the effect of AIDS on the unit as a whole. When I finally did seek support from my supervisor, my request for additional staff was approved without hesitation. I only wish I had asked sooner.

I am glad to say that once we stopped being subordinate and supervisor, Jim and I were able to recover some semblance of our past friendship. I am grateful to him for that. For me, one of the most numbing side effects of Jim's illness was my own anguish at having to put the interests of the organization ahead of Jim's need to take pride in his work and status.

I wished Jim well. I made mistakes, but short of neglecting my responsibility to the organization, I think I did all I could to ease his work life and eventual withdrawal. Yet in the end, I needed to know he forgave me for doing my job.

AIDS is a challenge to our humanity as well as to our reason because it robs us of a little bit of both.

*Since 1987, **Gary E. Banas** has been Director for Administration at the Comptroller of the Currency of the U.S. Department of the Treasury, Northeastern District, in New York City. In 1992, the New England Corporate Consortium for AIDS Education gave "Nothing Prepared Me for AIDS" its annual award for distinguished media con-*

tribution in the fight against AIDS. Over the past three years, sponsored by the National Leadership Coalition for AIDS, Gary Banas has spoken at seminars across the United States on the subject of managing AIDS. He is currently on sabbatical, doing course work at the Woodrow Wilson School of Public Administration at Princeton University.

3

What Asbestos Taught Me about Managing Risk

BILL SELLS

AS A MANAGER WITH Johns-Manville and its successor, the Manville Corporation, for more than 30 years, I witnessed one of the most colossal corporate blunders of the twentieth century. This blunder was not the manufacture and sale of a dangerous product. Hundreds of companies make products more dangerous than asbestos —deadly chemicals, explosives, poisons—and the companies and their employees thrive. Manville's blunder was not even its frequently cited failure to warn workers and customers of what it knew to be the dangers of asbestos during the 1940s, when so much of the damage to workers' health was done. Given the exigencies of war and the widespread indifference to environmental dangers at that time, it would have taken more than warnings to prevent the tragedy.

In my opinion, the blunder that cost thousands of lives and destroyed an industry was a management blunder, and the blunder was denial. Asbestosis—a nonmalignant lung disease brought on by breathing asbestos fibers—had been known since the early 1900s, and the first indications of a connection between asbestos and lung cancer appeared in the 1930s. But Manville managers at every level were unwilling or unable to believe in the long-term consequences of these known hazards. They denied, or at least failed to acknowledge, the depth and persistence of management accountability.

Had the company responded to the dangers of asbestosis and lung cancer with extensive medical research, assiduous communication, insistent warnings, and a rigorous dust-reduction program, it could have saved lives and would probably have saved the stockholders, the industry, and, for that matter, the product. (Asbestos still has applications for which no other material is equally suited, and, correctly used, it could be virtually risk free.) But Manville and the rest of the asbestos industry did almost nothing of significance— some medical studies but no follow-through, safety bulletins and dust-abatement policies but no enforcement, acknowledgment of hazards but no direct warnings to downstream customers—and their collective inaction was ruinous.

The fundamental lesson I've learned in my 30 years in the asbestos and fiberglass industries is that, to be more than an empty gesture, responsibility must be overt, proactive, and farsighted. At Manville, denial became endemic to the corporate culture, so much so that even after top executives had recognized health and safety as a critical issue, many middle- and lower-level managers continued to hide behind rationalizations and the letter of what they took to be the law.

I am not going to write about what and when Manville managers knew or didn't know about the dangers of asbestos. In one sense, it hardly matters because the standard for product liability that I see applied today—partly as a result of the asbestos litigation—seems to build on the principle that companies are responsible for product hazards whether or not they knew about product dangers. This is a retroactive standard, of course, but it is the same standard we apply to every other management activity. We expect executives to anticipate and pre-evaluate market trends, capital requirements, staffing needs, research, new product developments, competitive pressures, and much, much more. We also expect them constantly to question their companies' practices and procedures. When executives fail to foresee the future at least enough to prevent business setbacks, they pay a penalty in compensation, promotion, or job security. Now juries and the courts demand no less in the area of product liability. For the New Jersey Supreme Court, not even "unknowability"—the absence of any scientific evidence that a product may be harmful—is an adequate defense.[1]

To protect employees, customers, stockholders, society, and the business itself from product and production hazards, managers must go well beyond appearances, union demands, and the letter of the law. They must anticipate and lead the drive to head off environmental hazards and risks. They must study, analyze, assess, communicate, and prevent the damage their methods and products might cause.

I am not speaking on some abstract moral plane. I learned these lessons the hard way, as a participating eyewitness to some of the worst outcomes a corporation can experience. Employees and customers suffered disabilities and died, and Manville was eventually required to help fund a personal-injury-settlement trust fund with $150 million in cash, $1.6 billion in bonds, 80% of the company's common stock, and, beginning in 1992 and continuing for as long as there are claims to settle, 20% of company profits.

Remarkably, however, my experiences as the manager of an asbestos plant and later as the head of Manville's fiberglass group also taught me that what is now called product stewardship—the active acceptance of product and production responsibility—yields short-term as well as long-term benefits, among them profit, survival, and even competitive advantage.

I WENT TO WORK for Manville in June 1960, fresh from college and four years in the Marine Corps. When I joined it, Manville was the largest producer of asbestos products in the United States and the largest producer of asbestos fiber in the Western world, with 500 product lines and 33 plants and mines across the United States and Canada. To me, Manville seemed an ideal employer —an old-guard, blue-chip industrial giant, a member of the Fortune 500 and the Dow-Jones industrial average. "The bluest of the blue," *Forbes* once called it.

Since its founding in 1858, Manville had specialized in asbestos, a "miracle" substance with unique properties— fireproof, lightweight, durable, strong, an excellent insulator—that made it indispensable for hundreds of industrial and commercial applications. During World War II, the government declared asbestos a strategic material, and its use mushroomed. So did its misuse. In wartime shipyards, workers installed asbestos below decks in conditions of intense heat and dust described by one eyewitness as a glimpse of hell. Even outside the shipyards, asbestos plants and fabricating shops tolerated dust standards that were later shown to be far too high.

Later, often decades later, the people who worked in those plants, shops, and shipyards began to develop asbestos-related diseases, including several forms of cancer. Tens of thousands were disabled or died. Claims that they and their survivors brought against the company came to hundreds of millions of dollars. In 1982, Manville filed for Chapter 11 protection and was on its way to the top of *Fortune's* list of least admired corporations. The company was reorganized in 1988, and its stockholders—many of them Manville workers or retired workers—lost as much as 98% of their equity.

In 1960, I was ignorant of company history; I knew very little about the dangers of the product, which few employees understood well and still fewer discussed; and of course I had no inkling of the future. I started in sales, moved to marketing, and then, in 1968, I switched to production as a manager in training. After some brief hands-on experience as a supervisor at the Manville, New Jersey, plant, I packed up my family and headed for Waukegan, Illinois, to see if I could turn around a plant that made asbestos-cement pipe and ranked at the bottom of the heap in both productivity and profit.

The plant lay at the back of a sprawling complex built in the 1920s, its view of Lake Michigan obscured by a landfill several stories high. The road wound through this mountain of asbestos-laden scrap, and as I drove it for the first time, I stopped to watch a bulldozer crush a 36-inch sewer pipe. A cloud of dust swirled around my car.

Corrugated asbestos-cement panels covered the out-side of the nearly windowless building. Inside, a forklift picked up a pallet of finished couplings and moved off in the dingy light, leaving a trail of dust. People told me things had improved. At one time, they said, you couldn't see from one end of the building to the other. But I saw asbestos dust on every ledge and purlin, and I wondered what I had gotten myself into.

Waukegan was a grueling experience right from the start. In sales, when you stop work, the selling function stops. In a continuous manufacturing operation, the machines keep running and endless problems devour every moment, night and day. Whenever the phone rang at home, I would hold my breath until I knew it wasn't someone calling from the plant. No one ever called with good news.

The task I'd been set was to increase productivity, but over the next two years, I discovered that low productiv-ity had its roots in more basic problems. For example,

conventional wisdom had it that the plant's poor performance was due to poor labor relations and a recalcitrant
union that blocked productivity improvements. The
truth, I learned, was a good deal more complex. For
one thing, the plant's profit squeeze had caused previous
managers to defer proper maintenance, which greatly
increased downtime. For another, the lack of proper
maintenance in the area of dust control was seriously
affecting employee behavior. For a third, Manville's management culture had developed an unhealthy streak of
cynicism. Too many engineers and middle managers
had come to the conclusion—incorrectly, as events were
to show—that workers were necessarily a part of the
problem and not of the solution, that money could not
be found for adequate upkeep, and that change was
impossible.

Sometimes just by chance, sometimes by self-educa-
tion and determination, sometimes in sheer desperation,
I managed to turn most of this conventional wisdom on
its head. But my learning curve was a series of painful
shocks and confrontations.

To begin with, I lost my innocence about asbestos-
related diseases. I encountered several new words:
dusted, *red case*, and *mesothelioma*. *Dusted* was a shop-
floor term for a person incapacitated by asbestosis.
Severe lung changes, identified by X ray during physical
examinations, were called *red cases*. When the doctor
found changes like these, he would direct me to assign
the worker in question to a "nondusty" area, which was
a good deal easier said than done.

People at the plant seldom talked about asbestos diseases. Everyone knew who had high past exposures, and
there was dismay but no surprise when a dusted worker
got lung cancer. In the early 1960s, however, a new disease called mesothelioma struck several people who were
not red cases. It was hard enough for people to get used
to the progressive nature of asbestos-related diseases and

learn to live with the possibility of permanent disability or death. Mesothelioma, a cancer of the lung or stomach lining, was a new and even more insidious threat. It came without warning; it sometimes occurred in people whose asbestos exposure had been minimal; and it was swift, untreatable, excruciating, and invariably fatal.

Deaths had already begun to occur in the work force by the time I arrived in Waukegan, and I came to be a regular visitor at Victory Memorial Hospital. A young man just 25 years old, with a wife and children, died of mesothelioma. Others developed lung cancer. I got to know the doctor who treated most of these cases, and I started borrowing his medical journals and read dozens of articles on the subject. I began paying more and more attention to dust collection and abatement, hoping to bring Waukegan up to the standard of more modern plants. I pushed dust-reduction programs, and I organized a cleanup of inaccessible ledges and hard-to-reach beams and sills to reduce the levels of background dust. I even started wearing my own respirator in high-exposure areas, though, like everyone else, I was not nearly skeptical enough about the levels then considered "safe."

One memory still haunts me. Early one morning, I stopped at the hospital to see one of our lathe operators with mesothelioma only to be told that he had died a few hours before. The family was upstairs, and my heart was pounding as I walked into the room, acutely aware of my role as representative of the management system responsible for this premature death. The man's wife had known for months that this day was coming, but the finality of death and the uncertainty of the future were written all over her face. Her young son stared solemnly at her and then at me. I managed a few words of thin comfort, but I still remember the woman's face and my own feeling of helplessness.

A few days later, I learned that another plant in the Waukegan complex was going to close for good, and that set me up for another stark realization: our workers lived with two quite different kinds of fear.

The announcement was set for 11:30 A.M., and I arrived early. Clearly, the word was out. Groups of employees stood around talking, and I headed for the conference room as quickly as I could. Turning to go up the stairs, I found a man old enough to be my father sitting by himself with tears streaming down his cheeks. His face too came to haunt me over the years. People might dread the possibility of lung cancer or mesothelioma, but they also dreaded the possibility of losing the very jobs that put them at risk. And it was my responsibility to protect them from either outcome.

AS THIS REALIZATION sank in, however, I began to see that these two responsibilities did not have to be at odds with each other. On the contrary, they were closely related, just like my two business goals.

My primary business mission in Waukegan was to improve plant profitability; my secondary objective was to gain union cooperation and support. Since people rarely do their best work for an employer who neglects their welfare, an improvement of environmental conditions was clearly essential to achieving either end. This seems like common sense today, but it was not accepted wisdom in the late 1960s.

Labor relations, productivity, dust abatement, profitability, health and safety—it struck me that at some level these were all the same issue. If there was anything at all I really wanted to know about the plant, the answer was always somewhere on the shop floor—perhaps not in one place or with one individual or in sophisticated technical terms, but there nonetheless. By getting to know more of the workers and more about their work, I realized that key operating indicators like downtime, material usage, quality, and productivity were as much a function of attitudes as they were of mechanics. I remembered what I'd been told about recalcitrant unions, and I suddenly saw that we had the labor relations we deserved.

Another piece of conventional thinking that plagued the Waukegan pipe plant was the whole question of maintenance.

Despite its early neglect of the problem, Manville had become a pioneer in industrial dust collection by the late 1940s. It had developed what were in effect gigantic vacuum cleaners with hundreds of dust filters and dozens of dust lines reaching out to dust hoods on every machine in virtually every corner of the plant. When profits got tight, unfortunately, Waukegan managers began to defer maintenance, and, in the early days, I took the same dead-end approach. Instead of replacing a damaged dust line, we mended it with duct tape. Instead of replacing or rebuilding a dust collector, we sent mechanics to shovel their way in every weekend and jerry-rig repairs. Soon we were spending most of our time retaping the tape and repairing the repairs, which put the maintenance curve out in front of us to stay. I watched us repeat the same repairs over and over again when the only real problem was the lack of proper repairs to begin with.

For more than a year, I was captive to the conventional notion that equipment that doesn't make a product makes no contribution to profit, but slowly I changed my mind. First, I saw that a cleaner plant would function more smoothly and help to reduce downtime. Then, as the morale and productivity benefits of a better plant environment became more and more apparent, I became a convert to the idea of cleanliness for its own sake. Finally, early one Sunday morning toward the end of my second year, the plant engineer and the production superintendent called me in to examine a massive breakdown. It was clear to all three of us that we couldn't go on the way we had, and pretty soon we were walking through the plant with a pad of paper, making a long list of everything that needed fixing. The list included a massive general cleanup.

We had already taken steps to reduce airborne fiber levels and clear away the accumulated dust of decades, but there was much still to do. The plan called for large investments in maintenance and dust-collecting capacity as well as dozens of practical improvements. We described in detail all the environmental improvements we required and presented our analysis to the division staff in Manville, New Jersey. They offered practical suggestions, private advice that I not try to do everything at once, and the cynical prediction that if I were foolish enough to present the plan to top management, I'd get tossed out on my ear.

In fact, top management knew more than middle management about the importance of environmental quality. At my next semi-annual meeting with chairman and CEO Clinton Burnett and members of his staff, I conducted a tour of the plant and then laid out my plan, complete with charts and drawings. Or at least I started to. Before I had finished, Burnett interrupted to ask how much the whole thing was going to cost. With only the tiniest catch in my voice, I told him half a million dollars. "Fine," he said, turning to his staff. "Does anyone have a problem with that?"

With our capital expenditures approved, we proceeded to rebuild, replace, clean, or otherwise refurbish nearly everything in the building. We made big improvements and thousands of small ones. We installed experimental cardboard dust hoods to test for effective configurations before fabricating permanent hoods of metal. We repaired our dust collectors thoroughly and properly, and we installed air locks and built stairs in place of ladders.

As dust counts fell, so did our costs. We had probably made not a single change that someone hadn't thought of years earlier; the difference was that now we were actually making them. As a result, people began to identify other problems and fix them. The plant's productivity rose. People seemed to *care* more than they had before.

But even as we turned the corner on productivity and began to win our own small battle to save Waukegan from closing, the war as a whole was already lost. Negative public perception of asbestos was growing, and the market was beginning to crumble. By the late 1970s, asbestos plants were closing down right and left. In 1982, Manville filed for Chapter 11 reorganization, which was finally granted in 1988.

Our ultimate acknowledgment of the asbestos problem in the 1980s, which even then was grudging and half-hearted in some parts of the company, had come 50 years too late. During the 1970s and 1980s, I had to say good-bye to every member of my Waukegan administrative staff. They had become my friends, and now, one by one, they contracted mesothelioma and died.

IN RETROSPECT, IT SEEMS self-evident that clean air and a clean environment should have top priority in asbestos plants, especially in plants where some workers have already fallen ill and even died from asbestos-related diseases. But all through the decades of the 1940s, 1950s, and 1960s, managers skirted many of the real issues and gave surprisingly short shrift to others. Denial is itself an insidious disease. Once given a toe-hold, it finds its way into management acts and decisions at every level.

For example, it was common practice in Waukegan to test for dust under the best possible circumstances to make the plant look good on paper. It took a lecture by a medical expert at a plant managers' meeting to make me see that the only way to monitor dust emissions mean-ingfully was to test our *dirtiest* products and equipment

under the *worst* conditions, which is exactly what we
began to do in about 1970, when we implemented our
grand environmental plan.

Another thing I often saw people do was hide behind
procedures and standards when common sense would
have served them better as a guide. I remember writing a
request for funds to repair a dust hood on a coupling
lathe and having one of my engineers attach a report
stating that he had tested the area and found dust levels
within company guidelines. There was nothing *wrong*
with his report. Procedurally it was quite correct. But
just to make sure my request would be approved, I took
his pen and wrote on the report that I could see dust in
the area.

If an organization's culture encourages denial, problems get buried. Corporate cultures are built by successful people, good men and women who are often
pillars of their communities as well as business leaders.
The executives at Manville were good people too, and
nevertheless they fostered a culture of self-deception
and denial. Consider all the various forms this took:

First was the conviction that asbestos was inherently
useful, necessary, and therefore "good." I remember hearing colleagues argue that the world could never get along
without it; substitutes were not economically viable and
never would be. Today 18 asbestos companies have filed
for bankruptcy, asbestos is effectively eliminated from
commerce, and asbestos-free substitutes exist for every
former use.

Another powerful form of denial was the conviction
that we were already doing everything possible to reduce
risk. Manville acknowledged that the product was potentially harmful but insisted that employees, unions, customers, regulators, scientists, and insurance companies
all knew of the dangers. Furthermore, we had modern
dust-collection equipment and a standard for airborne
fibers that bettered the national standard at the time by

half. We also issued regular bulletins about acceptable procedures and exposure levels. What more could we possibly do?

I have already shown how that attitude led to a pernicious form of self-deception in some older facilities like Waukegan, where cost consciousness or an individual manager's failure to think ahead led to ineffective dust abatement. But even at the new plants, where state-of-the-art equipment really did keep dust to a minimum, we might have asked whether our airborne-fiber standards were really adequate. True, in the late 1960s, the allowable limit set by the American Conference of Governmental Industrial Hygienists was 12 fibers per cubic centimeter and Manville's was 6. But did we know that number was low enough? Were we funding research to find out? The answer is no. By 1972, OSHA had set its standard at 5 fibers per cc and then lowered it to 2 in 1976. By 1986, even 2 had been reduced 90% to an allowable level of 0.2 fibers per cc.

Worse yet, while environmental standards in most Manville plants were perhaps low enough to protect our own workers, there was a big additional health problem farther downstream in fabricating shops and among people installing asbestos products like brake shoes.

A third form of denial was the tendency to believe that the fault lay elsewhere. During World War II, for example, the U.S. government controlled the use and applications of asbestos as a strategic and critical war material. Surely the government should bear some responsibility for the ensuing problems. The government eventually escaped responsibility by claiming "sovereign immunity," but that claim might have failed if Manville had assumed more responsibility at the time—during the war—and tried to persuade the shipyards to improve working conditions. Protests might not have solved the problem—with ships burning and sinking almost daily, those in charge clearly put production ahead of potential long-term health hazards—but a paper trail of responsible warnings could have saved the company by involving the government in subsequent product liability claims.

Another potential scapegoat was tobacco. In 1979, a study revealed that asbestos workers who smoked suffered 50 times more asbestos-related lung cancer than those who did not. Surely the tobacco industry too should share responsibility. Ironically, the cigarette manufacturers found refuge in the government-mandated warning labels that have served them as a defense against product liability claims.

A fourth form of denial derives from the very nature of corporations. Companies exist to go on existing, and corporate existence is a matter of monthly and quarterly goals. Manville managers never knowingly took any action that placed their customers or stockholders at risk over the short term. The long-term consequences of their actions were another matter.

Finally, there is a form of denial called "Don't tell me what I don't want to hear." Early in my career, my boss chided me because I strongly disagreed with him on some issue. "Bill, you're not loyal," he said. And I said, rightly, I think, "No, no, you've got it wrong. I'm the one who *is* loyal."

Every CEO needs to remember that what he or she knows is only a small part of the legal equation. Today's legal standard also convicts people for what they *should have known*. Manville did not violate the written law, but juries found that the company did violate the public trust. *Caveat vendor* has replaced *caveat emptor* in the courts.

IN 1972, I LEFT Waukegan for Manville's Denver headquarters to manage all Manville pipe production; in 1974, I became general manager of the industrial products division; and in 1978, I was appointed vice president for production and engineering. Then, in 1981, I took charge of the Fiber Glass Manufacturing Division. Predictably, I encountered dozens of large and small production headaches, but after years of dealing with health issues in the asbestos business, it was a joy to tackle normal business problems again.

Fiberglass was by then the leading profit producer in the company. Although widely seen as an alternative to asbestos, fiberglass is, in fact, only a partial substitute. Like asbestos, fiberglass will not burn, but it will melt at high enough temperatures. Like asbestos, fiberglass is an excellent insulator, but it will not stand up to the intense wear and other demanding applications that gave asbestos such industrial value.

Fiberglass differed from asbestos in another critical respect as well. Despite more than 40 years of scientific studies, there was little evidence connecting fiberglass to anything more serious than irritation from prolonged exposure. Most recently, in the early 1980s, a government laboratory in Los Alamos, New Mexico, had carried out an inhalation study using laboratory animals, which gave fiberglass a completely clean bill of health. Even lung irritation from the high experimental dosages appeared to be completely reversible once the animal was removed from the exposure. After more than 20 years with asbestos, I was now dealing with a truly benign substance.

Of course, we were taking no chances. The environmental controls in our fiberglass plants were well maintained and extremely effective, and workplace monitoring was routine. The product also carried a warning label about the potential for irritation.

During the early 1980s, Manville consolidated fiberglass marketing and manufacturing into a single Fiber Glass Group, and I became group president. Encouraged by Dr. Bob Anderson, who was Manville's corporate medical director, I became a strong proponent of aggressive scientific research.

In October 1986, Bob was in Copenhagen attending a symposium on man-made mineral fibers chaired by Sir Richard Doll, a world-renowned epidemiologist. The conference was uneventful until its last few moments. In his concluding remarks, Doll summarized the most important presentations and then ended with this comment: "If I now abandon the firm basis of scientific judgment . . . I do so because I know that, in the absence of such a conclusion, many people may think that the whole symposium has been a waste of time. Let me therefore add . . . accepting that [fiberglass and other man-made mineral fibers] are not more carcinogenic than asbestos fibers, we can conclude that exposure to fiber levels of the order of 0.2 respirable fibers per [cubic centimeter] is unlikely to produce a measurable risk even after another 20 years have passed."

Confirming the fact that low exposure to man-made mineral fibers would not produce measurable risk was not news, and exposures, especially in fiberglass, were extremely low. But 0.2 was the *asbestos* standard. What Doll had done was to establish a link between a known carcinogen and fiberglass!

Bob called me immediately, and the first words out of his mouth were, "Bill, our lives may have just changed forever." We both knew from experience that once a public perception is created, changing it can be extremely difficult. I hung up the phone and thought, I don't deserve two of these in one lifetime.

The best scientific and health information available indicated to us that fiberglass posed little if any risk to workers or users. But wasn't it possible that Manville executives reached the same conclusion about asbestos in the 1930s? I leaned back in my chair, ran through all the perceived failings of the asbestos industry in my head, and compared them to the situation we were now facing with fiberglass.

Had we done enough scientific research? Were our

environmental controls and conditions the best in the world? Had workplace monitoring given us an accurate assessment of risk for factory workers as well as fabricators and installers? Had our audits found all the environmental and safety problems? And were we fixing these problems as soon as we found them?

I kicked myself mentally on realizing that our score wasn't an A+ but, unfortunately, more like a B. If anyone should have known better, it was I. But at least there was no question about what we had to do now. First and foremost, we were going to communicate.

Manville's new president, Tom Stephens, was well schooled in the roots of the asbestos tragedy. Like me, he had learned more than a little about corporate denial and more than a lot about corporate responsibility. Within hours, we had posted Doll's remarks on all plant bulletin boards and begun the process of communicating with all our customers, first by phone and then in person. This was the first move in a communications campaign that continued for years, to the mystification of many. From the start, for example, our fiberglass competitors criticized us for not thinking through what they called the "probable impact of our actions." But we did think them through. Our competitors did not understand the history of asbestos.

Doll's remarks were only the first of many challenges. In June 1987, the International Agency for Research on Cancer (IARC) met in France, debated human and animal scientific studies separately, and concluded that the human evidence was not sufficient to consider fiberglass a possible cause of lung cancer. But on the basis of animal implantation work—glass fibers that were surgically implanted directly into the body cavities of laboratory rats—and over the protests of scientists who felt that inhalation tests were more accurate predictors of a potential hazard, the IARC classified fiberglass wool as "possibly carcinogenic to humans."

The IARC cautions that its findings are not to be considered assessments of risk, but the difference between hazard and risk is often confusing. Hazard defines the potential to produce harm; risk reflects the probability that this hazard will be realized. For example, radiation is hazardous, but when your dentist covers you with a lead shield and takes low-dosage X rays, there is little if any risk. The IARC is chartered to assess hazard only. By U.S. law, however, IARC findings automatically trigger a lot of state and federal product-safety regulations, and the trigger goes off without any risk assessment. Moreover, the regulations require companies to communicate the hazard, not the risk. Outside of scientific circles, these rules create a great deal of confusion.

In October 1987, the International Program on Chemical Safety (IPCS) of the World Health Organization declared that animal-inhalation studies were the most relevant way of assessing potential hazards to human beings. That finding agreed with our own convictions on the subject, but it would take several years to complete new studies and several more for the IARC to consider the new evidence.

We included the IARC finding in our product literature and added a "possible cause of cancer" warning label on all fiberglass-wool products.

"I will tell you the truth," I told all our customers, "and if I don't know, I will tell you I don't know, along with what I am doing to find out." Put very simply, our communications policy was, "You'll know when we know." We gave regular briefings on fiberglass safety and health to customers, employees, union officials, community leaders, and regulatory agencies by phone, letter, brochure, videotape, live television, and group meetings.

If there wasn't one crisis, there were three. We finally realized that truth, like beauty, was in the eye of the beholder. Regulatory agencies, the media, nonfiberglass competitors, and the fiberglass industry—all interpreted the truth to serve themselves. At the time, I didn't understand this aspect of the problem, and it led to conflict and frustration. Take the regulatory agencies.

The IPCS conclusion that inhalation was the preferred method for assessing a potential hazard led the fiberglass industry to fund a new inhalation study. We assembled a panel of independent scientists in Denver, and for two days they hammered out a protocol to achieve the highest possible scientific standard for the study. Then we signed a contract with a laboratory in Geneva, the only one in the world that met the panel's quality standards.

We sent the protocols to the appropriate regulatory bodies in advance of the study and routinely briefed them on its progress. After two years, the tests concluded with entirely negative results—*no* evidence that respirated fiberglass fibers affected the rate of lung cancer in laboratory rats. We were elated.

But the regulatory agencies did not find the results as conclusive as we did. Scientific conclusions are based on assumptions—change the assumptions, and you get a different conclusion—and the protocols and assumptions of this study were industry's, not OSHA's or the EPA's. The scientists who consulted for us had designed an extensive chronic-inhalation study using state-of-the-art inhalation technology. We knew that a positive finding would establish fiberglass as a hazardous substance, and while we didn't expect that outcome, we were prepared for the possibility. We were not prepared for the regulators' response to a negative finding, which seemed merely to arouse their automatic skepticism about industry intentions. They seemed to feel that a study that found no hazard in the product could not, by definition, be "most protective" of society.

It taught us that we should have involved the regulators in the formulation of assumptions and protocols. A negative finding that was based on their own assumptions would have been more difficult for them to pick apart.

The media presented another challenge. When the inhalation study came in with negative results, we declared victory in our internal publications and wanted the media to do the same. We continuously presented our view of truth to the press by explaining the IARC's hazard-assessment process, the difference between hazard and risk, the physical differences between asbestos and fiberglass, and our conviction that fiberglass posed little if any risk to workers. But reporters are even more suspicious than regulators. By adding our own side of the story to every disclosure, we managed to convince them they were getting less than the whole truth. As a result, they grasped at any source of negative information or simply reminded their readers of the IARC's original classification. We got headlines like, "Evidence Grows on Possible Link of Fiberglass and Lung Illness" or "Could Fiberglass Become the Asbestos of the 1990s?" The lesson that taught me was never to give in to pressure to try to make ourselves look good in risk communications. Let public relations do that work for itself. In risk communications, stick to the facts.

Nonfiberglass competitors were yet another problem. Our candid communication policy delighted many of them. The more we disclosed, the more information they had to twist and distort with customers. The issue also gave them an umbrella to put some new competitive products on the market (none of which, by the way, were subjected to hazard or risk assessment). We had to use legal means to stop the most blatant distortions, and most attempts to sensationalize the issue backfired. Our best weapon was our communication policy itself, because most customers understood that we were telling them everything we knew.

We learned that truth is relative, but we also learned that a consistent, conscientious commitment to the truth is a weapon powerful enough to overcome relativity, cynicism, and a great deal of fear. Driven by business as well as liability concerns, our customers wanted us to keep them up-to-date, and that was a perfect fit with our you'll-know-when-we-know policy. As customers began to depend on us for the latest news on fiberglass and health, relationships steadily improved, and I started receiving letters from customers supporting our actions. Our policy was so effective that its critics changed their tune from "You are going to destroy the industry" to "You must be doing this to gain competitive advantage."

Through all the turmoil and adverse publicity, fiberglass has remained the preferred material for residential insulation and has retained or improved its market position in the industrial, commercial, filtration, and aerospace segments. In fact, 1993 was one of the best sales years in the history of the fiberglass-wool industry.

IN ITS PRODUCT liability defense, the asbestos industry argued that it did not violate the law. The law required no warnings; a supplier's liability was limited to simple negligence. Moreover, the medical data were not conclusive until the 1960s. While technically correct, this defense was tied to the legalities of the past, and in the mid-1970s, with the benefit of hindsight, juries began to make judgments on the basis of what companies should have done, should have known, and should have disclosed. Increasingly, they judged the asbestos industry guilty of not meeting this new, higher, retroactive standard and required it to pay punitive damages for its failure to do so.

When I learned to fly an airplane on instruments, I was taught that my senses were always wrong and that the instruments were always right. As managers, our senses are finely tuned to deal with short-term changes and seldom help us with the blind landings that are still years away. When the pressure to cut short-term costs is high, it simply goes against the grain to increase spending for environmental controls with an uncertain long-term payback. What I learned as a businessman in the asbestos and fiberglass industries was that the instruments of long-term guidance are called principles. More specifically, they're called responsibility and product stewardship.

Product stewardship—defined as product responsibility extending through the entire stream of commerce, from raw material extraction to the ultimate disposal of a used-up or worn-out product—can cost a lot of money. But so can the alternative. Moreover, product stewardship probably represents the legal standard of tomorrow. Environmental regulations grow steadily tougher, and the imputed knowledge from these regulations will almost certainly carry over into the area of product liability.

I cannot possibly say how many companies are putting themselves and their employees and customers at this kind of risk today. I think I do know that voluntary product stewardship adds up to competitive advantage over the short term and a greatly improved chance of survival and profit into the future.

NOTE

1. *Beshada v. Johns-Manville Products Corp.*, 90 N.J. 191, 447 A. 2d 539 (1982).

Bill Sells *runs his own consulting firm, Sells & Associates, in Evergreen, Colorado, specializing in environmental compliance as a byproduct of corporate cost reduction and productivity-improvement programs. He continues to promote the kind of product stewardship this article espouses. He takes every opportunity to enlighten industries that see proactive environmental responsibility as costly but not cost effective, and to educate managers who think they're helping their companies by focusing narrowly on short-term, limited goals.*

The Personal Injury Trust that Manville was required to help fund with $1.6 million in bonds, $150 million in cash, 80% of its stock, and 20% of its profits is still very much in operation, granting liquid damages on top of workmen's compensation to people, or the families of people, who suffered injury or death as a direct result of their contact with asbestos. Claims averaging $40,000 to $50,000 each roll in at the rate of about 45,000 per year. In the beginning, the legal questions were so tangled—and the rate of spurious claims so high—that for several years the courts put a hold on all settlements. Today, claims are again being settled—most of them for about 10% of the damages requested—at a rate of 5,000 or 6,000 per year. The backlog is cur-

rently about 200,000 cases and growing. Sadly, a big share of the money already paid out has gone to lawyers and questionable claims, while many people whose lives were devastated by asbestos have received very little from the fund set up to help them. The real tragedies of asbestos mismanagement seem likely to continue for years to come.

Empowerment or Else

1

Empowerment or Else

ROBERT FREY

ALMOST TEN YEARS AGO, a partner and I bought a small, troubled company in Cincinnati that made mailing tubes and composite cans—sturdy paper containers with metal ends. The product line had not changed in 20 years. Profits were marginal. Labor costs were out of control, job definitions were rigid, and union relations were poor.

Today we make a new mix of highly differentiated, specially protected, environmentally responsible composite cans; our work force is flexible and deeply involved in our success; strict job descriptions are a thing of the past; we have not raised the contract wage for eight years; and our relations with the union are excellent. What's more, the company is doing well in a demanding market and making a lot of money.

How did we achieve this startling turnaround? Employee empowerment is one part of the answer. Profit sharing is another.

But the kind of change we experienced doesn't come simply from treating people well. People hate change.

Change of *any* kind is a struggle with fear, anger, and uncertainty, a war against old habits, hidebound thinking, and entrenched interests. No company can change any faster than it can change the hearts and minds of its people, and the people who change fastest and best are the people who have no choice.

I had no choice because the company was close to failure, and I was overwhelmed and exhausted. At my wit's end, I decided to share my problems and profits with my employees.

And why did they have no choice? Because I gave them none. I forced empowerment and profit sharing on them pretty much against their will.

Cin-Made was founded in 1902. Before we acquired it, the company was owned and run by a woman I'll call Lucille, who had lived and breathed it for 25 years and knew it inside out. She turned down my first offer for the company almost a year before we finally closed the deal.

Lucille micromanaged every detail of the business from billing to maintenance. No one made any decision, however small, without her consent. She'd do all the negotiating, production planning, and costing, for example, then go out to the line and give people their marching orders. Controlling every action in the company took time. Lucille worked 75- and 80-hour weeks, every evening, and most weekends.

But if Lucille was an autocrat, she was a benevolent, maternal autocrat. She saw her employees as family. She threw costume parties for them. She loved listening to their personal problems, she kept track of their kids, and she showed them a good deal of loyalty. Among other things, she kept people on the payroll when she should have let them go. When she did fire people, she'd have second thoughts and hire them back again. She knew what was best for her people, and she made sure they got what they needed.

Or at least that's how Lucille saw the situation. She

believed her employees loved her dearly. But they certainly didn't love her when it came to contract time.

Cin-Made was in a highly competitive market for many of its products, and prices were holding steady or actually declining while costs went up, especially labor costs. In 1981, Lucille signed a union contract providing for three consecutive years of across-the-board 9% raises. So her labor costs rose 27% while orders and income declined. As a result, the company had gone from profits of 1% to 2% on sales to no profits at all. She kept the company out of the red by drawing virtually no salary herself and by gradually letting her managers go. By taking on all that work herself, she held the company near the break-even point.

In the second year of the contract, she went to the union and told them she was going broke. While the company had made small profits in the past, she said, Cin-Made was making nothing now.

"Believe me," she told them, "I can't afford this contract." But if the union would trust her and roll back the increases to 4% or 5% per year, the company might survive.

The union had three responses: we don't trust you; we don't believe you; we aren't giving anything up.

Lucille took her case to the employees as a whole and lost by an overwhelming margin. No more than two or three members of her "family" took her side. It was a crushing experience.

When my partner and I approached her with a second offer at the end of 1983, she was looking ahead to a new round of contract negotiations in September 1984 and honestly didn't feel that she had the strength. It must have seemed hopeless. If she didn't cut labor costs, the company would go under. But if she did cut labor costs, the union would go out on strike, and the company would go under nevertheless.

To Lucille, my partner and I must have looked like

white knights. I had operational experience in the paper industry, and my partner was good with people and an excellent salesman. Lucille figured that the two of us could rescue her company, save her family (however ungrateful), and keep her employed at the job she loved.

We bought the company in April 1984. In the beginning, as agreed, Lucille was still in charge. Everybody on the floor asked Lucille what to do, and I followed her around trying to understand the products, trying to figure out how to cost them, trying to soak up Lucille's knowledge of the business, all of which was in her head.

I think she found me a slow learner and, in that, typically masculine. Lucille was a female chauvinist and proud of it. She believed in women. Her work force was 90% female, and all her managers had been women until she was forced to let them go. No male manager had ever succeeded at Cin-Made.

Heaven knows, I felt slow much of the time. But I struggled very hard during those first couple of months, and I began to penetrate company costs. I put together financials we could understand and some proper inventory and tracking systems. I discovered that the equipment was in much worse condition than I had believed. Mostly, however, I made mistakes.

The company's sole maintenance man for all its old, failing equipment told me he'd received a much better offer elsewhere. I guessed he was bluffing; we did nothing, and a few days later, he was gone.

A second key man tried to hold me up for a $2-an-hour raise, and I agreed to give him half that much in the form of what we called a merit raise, which didn't have to go through the union. "But you can't tell anyone," I said. "This has to be our secret."

Within minutes, he was out on the factory floor telling everyone I'd given him an extra $1 an hour and bragging that he had me over a barrel.

I went on making mistakes. An engineer by training,

I'd stand around with a stopwatch timing people's every move. One day as I watched people at one of our anti-quated, sluggish machines, I remarked to someone that it looked to me like work that a moron could do. By noon, the whole work force had heard that I thought they were mentally retarded.

When I brought in some modern automated equip-ment to meet a large new order, employees hated it. For one thing, we had to create a new job description, some-thing Cin-Made hadn't seen in 20 years. For another, the new equipment ran much faster than the old, and people were afraid they might get hurt. In the old days, about the worst accident anyone ever had was cutting a finger on a sharp metal edge. Now people figured they could lose a hand, and lots of safety training didn't seem to make them any happier.

All in all, I did not make myself popular. Employees saw me as a brash, young, arrogant know-it-all with poor people skills making lots of changes and amazing blun-ders. By and large, they were right. These were the peo-ple whose help I needed to turn the company around, and I was busily turning them into enemies. It was also at about this time that we lost our biggest customer.

Cin-Made was relatively cash rich when we bought it, but what with paying our debts (the purchase was essen-tially a leveraged buyout), losing orders, and dribbling away the last drops of employee goodwill, we were run-ning out of cash in a big hurry despite taking no salaries ourselves. By midsummer, we were losing $30,000 a month.

Over the short haul, there were only two things we could do in that situation—raise prices or cut expenses —and we decided to do both.

Cin-Made's product line was too big, and too many of our products were marginally profitable. My partner and I were already leaning toward a more specialized market niche—composite cans with special linings for chemical products—so we raised prices as much as 25% on many other items. Many of our least profitable customers left; we even helped them find other suppliers. Better yet, we now made money on those who chose to stay.

Next we turned to expenses. There were no managerial salaries to eliminate, because as yet there were no managers. We weren't paying ourselves anything, and we had to pay Lucille for a couple of years to teach us. That left employee wages and benefits. As Lucille had realized, the company couldn't survive with the wage-and-benefits package it had. Most of our competitors were nonunion and paid their workers much less than we did. Moreover, our work force was getting 5 to 6 weeks of vacation, 13 holidays, and a comprehensive health plan completely paid for by the company.

Since Lucille's three-year union contract expired in September that year, we went to the union and told them we were going to have to cut wages and benefits by 25%.

The union was apoplectic. They had seen two guys with lots of money buy this company, and they weren't about to take a cut in pay. On the contrary, they wanted yet another raise and a long list of new benefits. We said, sure, we have some personal money, but this business has to survive on its *own* merits. We got nowhere. In September 1984, six months after we bought the company, the union went out on strike.

Lucille, my partner, and I worked the factory, along with the office staff and a couple of workers who crossed the picket line. I discovered how decrepit and difficult the equipment really was. The job wasn't so easy after all, and, even more surprising, I did it badly. They had a lot of fun with that on the picket line. Now there really *was* a moron running the machines.

We negotiated day and night, and federal mediators flew in to help, but we remained miles apart. My partner and I agreed to a smaller wage cut—25% was only our opening shot—but the union still adamantly demanded an increase. Then, as time passed, the strike began to weaken. The numbers we brought to the table gradually convinced the strike leaders that the company really was in trouble, and slowly they began to accept the fact that there was no reason for us to put any more of our money into Cin-Made unless the business could stand on its own two feet. More important still, the workers began to waver. This was not a rich work force. Lucille had paid them well, but they had little savings and no strike fund to speak of. Three or four more came back to work. A lot of the other workers began to worry that the company really would go under and they'd lose their jobs forever.

Finally, the union gave in. They offered to continue the existing contract for another year.

We said no. We sent them a carefully worded letter stating that unless they immediately accepted our last offer—a 12.5% cut in wages and benefits, reduced vacation, fewer holidays—we would take the legal remedies available to us, including permanent replacement of the work force. We dressed it all up in flowery language, but the letter was very threatening. The state of the business made it vital that our employees accept lower wages and benefits, so vital that we were willing to use threats to get what we wanted. The company's survival depended on it. For that matter, so did their jobs.

The letter worked. The union committee met again and decided we meant what we were saying. They didn't like us, but they'd seen enough to believe we'd make good on our threat. Moreover, our present employees were not going to find new jobs easily. They had little education, they were getting older, and they had very specific skills for which there was no other market. We were the only composite-can factory in Cincinnati.

In the end, the committee told the members roughly this: "As much as you hate these two men, as much as you hate this situation, as much as you hate a pay cut, these guys are playing for keeps. It's going to be very tough to find new jobs. So swallow your pride, go back to work, and then spend your free time looking for new jobs with people you don't hate."

It was good advice, and they took it. We signed a new two-year contract, and our work force went back to their jobs with lower wages, fewer holidays, reduced benefits, and a maximum three weeks of vacation instead of six. As part of the bargain, we promised to restore 9% of the 12.5% wage cut by the end of the second year.

It was a critical victory. The financial hemorrhage slowed, stopped, and eventually became a profit stream. I was able to hire some managers to run accounting and marketing and to help me operate the plant. We were able to proceed with the development of new products and gain essential market share in the new niches we had targeted.

Still, the year that followed was miserable. By all the rules of the old labor-management game, we had won. But the biggest part of our victory prize was a factory full of angry, defeated employees determined to oppose innovation and grieve every tiny infraction of the letter of the contract. We had costs under control, and we had the worst imaginable labor climate—a financial victory and a human relations disaster. I had deliberately exploited their lack of economic choice to make them do a thing they didn't want to do, and that was a very bitter pill for them to swallow. I saw it as necessary trauma. The workers saw it as unnecessary greed.

Grievances increased to about one a week, a few of them perfectly legitimate, most of them petty and pedantic. The workers stuck to their job descriptions like glue and opposed every suggestion that they be flexible. We often made mistakes about who was entitled to put in overtime, and they filed a grievance every time, demanding that we pay the people who should have worked but didn't. I consistently apologized and did my best to learn the rules, but I just as consistently refused to pay for work not done.

I engaged in petty behavior of my own. Lucille had always bought supper for people working overtime, but as the new contract didn't *specify* dinner money, I cut off my nose to spite my face and denied the first request, roughly $4 each for four or five people. If I was going down, they were going down with me. Pretty soon we couldn't get people to work overtime at all.

The atmosphere was deeply adversarial. They played their game, I played my game, and none of us seemed smart enough to stop the game playing and get on with running the company.

As that year passed, I realized with increasing clarity that our victory was not making me a happy man or a successful business owner. In fact, the strike had taught me several valuable lessons, though I was slow to grasp them. For one thing, the workers' jobs weren't as easy as I'd thought. For another, the company really couldn't get along without its employees and their special knowledge of the equipment, the products, and the customers. I began to understand that the contempt I'd felt for my workers was a piece of extremely poor judgment.

Despite their bitterness, the employees could also see that we'd reached an impossible dead end. Although they suspected my motives and disliked my style, we both realized that to save the company, we had to work together. Like it or not, we had a marriage, and there was no good way to get a divorce.

What the company needed was an atmosphere of teamwork and participation, whereas the atmosphere we had was adversarial and acrimonious. Acrimonious because we all had short tempers and big egos. Adversarial because management and labor have always been adversaries. Unions were *created* to be adversarial.

Adversarial was what my training and experience as a manager had prepared me for.

And yet life was too short. The strain on everyone, especially on me, was too great. I knew that the company would never succeed, perhaps not even survive, unless we all gave it the same total commitment. But the workers didn't see Cin-Made as their company; they saw it as the owners' company. That had to change. I didn't want to be their worthy adversary; I wanted to be their worthy partner. As we ended the first year of the new contract and headed into the second, I began putting together a plan for change.

I wanted to share this company with my employees. In the beginning, it was the pain I wanted to share as much as the profit. I wanted the workers to worry. Did any one of them ever spend a moment on a weekend wondering how the company was doing, asking herself if she'd made the right decisions the week before? Maybe I was unrealistic, but I wanted that level of involvement. After a bad start, I had begun to see that they knew more about the company and its operations than I or the new managers I'd hired. They were better qualified to plan production for the next day, the coming week, the month ahead. They had more immediate knowledge of materials, workload, and production problems. They were ideally placed to control costs and cut waste. But how could I give them some reason to care?

I began holding monthly informational meetings called state-of-the-business talks to let them know how the company was doing. The only trouble was that the workers had no stake in the company. If they wanted more money or less work or another holiday, it didn't come out of their pockets; it came out of mine. That led me to the idea of profit sharing. If they got part of the profits, then extra costs and expenses would come out of their pockets too.

I bought some books and sent away for materials and

studied corporate profit-sharing plans. I couldn't find anything I liked. In the first place, all the plans I read about sounded manipulative. The rules were subject to change without notice. The profits shared were whatever management declared them to be. The plans were handouts, a form of charity. Not surprisingly, they completely failed to convey any sense of the cause-and-effect relationship between productivity and profits, between work and success.

Another problem was the complexity of the rules. There were threshold limits; there were profits behind, above, and beyond the normal expected rate of return; and there were minimums and maximums and categories and schedules and language that struck me as pure bafflegab.

Worst of all, the plans never paid out much money. And my idea was to pay out *lots* of money, enough to create a tangible connection between the way people worked and the profits they shared, enough to get everyone passionately involved in the effort to cut costs, increase sales, and make money.

I wanted to do something radical. I wanted to divide employee income into fixed and variable components. I wanted to make profit sharing—the variable component—so big that it would serve as an incentive to keep wages—the fixed component—frozen. Over the years, the variable component would become a larger and larger percentage of income and work more and more effectively as an incentive. Over the years, consequently, we would lower the risk of doing business while at the same time offering bigger and bigger rewards to our employees.

I did a bunch of calculations and decided it would work. I even believed it would be attractive, at least to the work force. As for my partner, my creditors, and my family, they would probably think I was crazy to offer so much. But what the hell, I thought. If this works, we'll all be better off. If nothing else, I'll sleep better at night from not feeling so damned lonely. My employees will share my profits, but they will also share my anxieties.

I asked myself what was the most money I could share with my employees and still have enough for taxes, new equipment, R&D, and something for me and my partner.

The answer was 30%. Hourly workers would get equal shares of 15% of before-tax profits, apportioned by hours worked (except overtime). Managers and office staff would divide another 15% on the basis of performance appraisals. (The total has now risen to 35%—18% for workers, 17% for managers—to accommodate a new 401(k) pension plan and some other refinements.).

As we moved toward the middle of the contract's second year, I decided to anticipate the union's predictably unreasonable demands and negotiating strategies. I refused to go back to the old labor-management game of bribes, blackmail, strikes, and wage hikes. I was not going to give them a raise. Yet I was perfectly prepared to give them more *money,* provided that it be in shared profits. Wages were still 3% below the prestrike level, and, given the adversarial atmosphere, I needed to take the bull by the horns.

So in the late spring of 1986, before they'd had time to formulate their bargaining position, I called them together and announced that I wanted to extend the contract for a third year. We needed labor peace, I said, to continue work on our new products and strategies.

There would be no raise. On the other hand, I would restore the final 3% of the earlier wage cut by the end of the extended year. On top of that, I would give them something they hadn't asked for: a share of the company's profits. I would take 15% of current-year profits and distribute them the following year, the year of the contract extension. Because of my monthly state-of-the-business talks, they already knew that the company was now earning a decent profit. I showed them exactly

where we stood and made some projections they understood to be reasonable for the remaining three months of
the fiscal year.

To my surprise, they agreed. I think there were three
reasons, and the profit sharing—untested and unfamiliar—was probably the least of them. More important was
the restoration of that final 3%, which they hadn't
expected to get without a fight. More important still was
the bad economy. By 1985, my employees knew they
didn't have much choice. People at other companies were
not getting raises either. And jobs were very scarce.

Once again, severe economic conditions were serving
the cause of change. But this has never troubled me.
Within reason, I'm willing to use whatever will help me
introduce systems that are fair and just and highly beneficial to the business, which means highly beneficial to
employees, customers, and me. In this case, I wanted to
get my employees involved. I wanted to establish a pattern of cause and effect by establishing a pattern of big
wage increases, bigger than anything they'd ever seen,
but only *after* the money had been earned. Profit sharing
was only partly a matter of fairness. For me, an even
more critical goal was to open my employees' eyes to
where wages came from, to the trade-offs they would
have to make between benefits and profits.

Having won this first round, I took the opportunity to
move the agenda ahead by making two constructive pronouncements that I'd been thinking about for months:

I DO NOT choose to own a company that has an adversarial relationship with its employees.

EMPLOYEE participation will play an essential role in
management.

To my surprise, the very act of making these two
statements seemed to increase the level of adversarial
behavior.

First of all, my three managers felt they were *paid* to

be worthy adversaries of the unions. It's what they'd been trained for. It's what made them good managers. Moreover, they were not used to participation in any form, certainly not in decision making. One of them devised at least a dozen ways of delaying and obstructing the flow of necessary numbers to the employees. As for profit sharing, another of my managers declared it to be a form of communism. They all saw both of my statements as clear threats to their positions.

The workers were not much better. My managers believed that managers should manage and that hourly workers should do what they were told. The trouble was, most of the workers were perfectly happy with that arrangement. They wanted generous wages and benefits, of course, but they did not want to take responsibility for anything more than doing their own jobs the way they had always done them. Now I was stirring up the pot by telling everyone they had to change.

It was bad enough forcing them to use new equipment, but I was also forcing them to change job descriptions, to change work habits, to think differently about themselves and the company. What my employees were telling me, in deeds and words, was, "We don't want to change, and we're much too old to change. Anyway, we don't come to work to *think*."

I wouldn't take no for an answer. Once I had made my two grand pronouncements, I was determined to press ahead and make them come true. It may seem contradictory to use confrontational, even coercive, methods to reduce adversarial relations and empower employees, but I believe it was what I had to do. My reasoning was simple. We would continue to be adversaries as long as we had opposing interests. We would continue to have opposing interests until we shared a common interest in the company's success. We would share that common interest only when we shared both the profits and the responsibilities that go along with success.

But which of us is ever eager to take on new responsibilities? Certainly not Lucille's work force, not after years of security and obedience. They never dreamed how much responsibility I wanted to lay on their shoulders, but they disliked what little they had seen so far.

Yet behavioral change begets attitudinal change, not the other way around. If you force people's behavior to change, their attitude will change as well. And that new attitude will eventually drive even better and more spectacular results. A manager has to force change. My role was to make sure that people changed at a faster pace than they would ever have chosen for themselves. My role was to push the process of change and never be satisfied with results for more than a moment at a time. I pushed the process hard.

I made people meet with me, then instead of *telling* them what to do, I *asked* them. They resisted.

"How can we cut the waste on this run?" I'd say, or, "How are we going to allocate the overtime on this order?"

"That's not my job," they'd say.

"Why not?" I'd say.

"Well, it just isn't," they'd say.

"But I need your input," I'd say. "How in the world can we have participative management if you won't participate?"

"I don't know," they'd say. "Because that's not my job either. That's your job."

And I'd lose my temper.

In the beginning, I really did lose my temper every time I heard the words, "It's not my job." Later on, when I discovered my outbursts were having some effect, I started faking them a bit. Whenever anyone said, "It's not my job," I'd go berserk. Sometimes I didn't know myself if I was really mad or simply playacting, but people had to understand that those were words they weren't allowed to utter.

Gradually, I induced my managers to share more information with employees. I also got them to learn how to share power or to quit and let me replace them with managers who would. When I introduced profit sharing, I expanded my regular state-of-the-business meetings. I still showed them month-to-date sales, year-to-date sales, and monthly and year-to-date profits. Now I also began using those meetings to make profit projections and examine other numbers, such as scrap rates and materials prices and operation efficiencies. The information shared with employees grew more and more complex—and more and more "confidential." I made it a practice to answer any and all questions about the company's results. I told them the company's books were open and that the union could come in and audit them any time it chose. I don't see how a company can hope to make profit sharing credible if its workers cannot *know* what the profits are.

Gradually, union relations improved. We realized early that we could not leave the union behind, so I sat down with the officers and told them I wanted to work with them for the benefit of everyone: workers, owners, customers, and most of all the company, which was all of us together. I promised them we were not out to get the union. They were skeptical but said they were willing to judge me by my actions.

Gradually, I began giving my best people new responsibilities. For example, I expanded the duties of the union steward, a woman named Ocelia Williams, from sheet-metal cutting to inventory planning to materials ordering to head of the metals department, though it took some arm-twisting to get the man who thought he ran that shop to accept her authority. We also gave her a special training course in leadership and a lot of coaching in the art of negotiating with suppliers. (For her version of Cin-Made's turnaround, see "Ocelia Williams.")

Gradually, hourly workers in general began to take on

some of the work of problem solving and cost control. I pushed and prodded and *required* people to help solve problems related to their own jobs. Sometimes I felt like a fool, albeit a very pleased fool, when they came up with simple solutions to problems that had persistently stumped me and my managers. Always I pushed too hard, making progress but still making enemies.

Gradually, my worst managers left, especially after I started assessing performance and doling out raises on the basis of their ability to coach and work with hourly employees. I could be an abrasive boss at times. I *had* to have managers with a human touch.

My key move was to hire a plant manager who had both technical genius and a willingness to become what I was not, an attentive and dedicated listener to the people who worked for him. Over time, he became the recognized leader of the movement toward empowerment on the factory floor.

We began working on quality. One customer had returned a shipment of 40,000 cans because the metal ends were coming off. My new plant manager and eight hourly workers took a ten-week night school course in statistical process control (SPC) at the University of Cincinnati. They gathered data on the pressure it took to blow the ends off those cans, and, with some engineering help, the group worked out a solution to the problem.

The plant manager began teaching SPC techniques to the rest of the work force, including many who needed help with basic math and found the whole notion threatening. I encouraged him to pressure them, to make them learn, like dragging someone along on a roller coaster because you know he'll like it once he tries it. He took a slightly more humane approach. He coaxed them into volunteering to learn the math and the SPC techniques. He also told them they could stop any time they felt overwhelmed. But because he held their hands, and

OCELIA WILLIAMS

When I first came to Cin-Made, the place was like a circus. There was a ten-minute break every hour, and people walked off the line any-time at all to go to the ladies room or get a candy bar. It was pathetic. The trouble was, most of these people had never worked anyplace but Cin-Made. I came here from Georgia-Pacific. I'd seen a real factory with real work discipline, but most of the others never had.

A lot of that was Lucille's fault. She was a good woman, but she let her workers take advantage of her.

Then Bob Frey and his partner bought the company and wanted to cut our pay by 25%. I couldn't believe he could *want* that big a cut when he knew what we were making. The low wage here was $6.48 in those days, a little over $13,000 a year. And he wanted us to give up a quarter of it. I was horrified.

Worse yet, he made us do it. He sent us a letter telling us to come back to work or lose our jobs. What choice did we have? The following year was tough. We worked because we needed the jobs, not because we liked them, and certainly not because we liked who we were working for.

Then when he introduced profit sharing, I was apprehensive. So were the others. None of us thought we could trust him. But, again, what choice did we have? By then I was the union shop steward, and Bob

and I were fighting like cats and dogs. I kept trying to get him to see that the employees were human beings, that they'd given up a lot, that they thought he was giving them the shaft by cutting vacations and holidays and making them pay a big piece of their own insurance.

In my opinion, that was when he started to change. The strike had shown him there was a lot he didn't know—how hard people worked, for example—but now he seemed to be learning. We told him what a bad listener he was, and he took a class on listening. It even helped, a little.

That was also when he started giving us more information about the company in his state-of-the-business talks. I always asked a lot of questions, and I started to believe he was telling us the truth, not only the good news but also the bad.

And that was when I started to change my mind as well, about Bob and about the company. I started to respect him, even to like him. In the second year of the profit sharing when there *were* no profits, for example, we knew it ahead of time. We knew it month by month from those meetings. That made a big difference, at least to me.

Some of the others were still suspicious. The union president kept saying, "Profit sharing sucks!" and "Team building sucks!" She thought it was nonunion, our taking so much responsibility. That bothered me. I kept asking myself if I was truly union. But I couldn't see how we were going to protect ourselves and keep our jobs if the company went under. And I couldn't see how the company could work unless we all took our share of the responsibility. A lot of people thought those ideas were off the wall.

Then, finally, the profit sharing started to give us quite a lot of money. And the union president took some classes and discovered that other companies have cut-off points in their plans. But we get 18% from dollar one, and it goes on for as much money as the company makes. Even she came around. Now she's a Frey supporter.

So in the end, I like my job more than I ever used to. I do better work. I make more money. Yes, I suppose Bob Frey is getting rich on those same profits, but that's life. He has more invested in this company than I do. And that's fine.

---

because they really cared about quality, within a year he had every one of them entering process statistics into the computer data bank and doing their own scrap and efficiency tracking.

Gradually, the conflict and chaos I had spread around me began to lessen, especially as new managers took over and employees learned to take responsibility. No managers at all is hopelessly utopian. No human system is that perfect, but good systems don't need much. We were taking big strides toward my goal of a few managers spending a little time doing a little coaching and giving a little advice.

Gradually, the union committee took on much of what I would call labor force management: allocating overtime, scheduling layoffs, deciding when to take on temporary workers and when to let them go. Moreover, the company and the union now jointly administer a program of merit raises, with which we've rewarded about 75% of employees for acquiring competencies above and beyond their basic skills. In addition, workers now interview all job candidates, including new managers. We hire no one without the approval of their future colleagues and subordinates.

Gradually, too, we developed an employee committee to schedule operations. Cin-Made's specialized product strategy makes it tremendously difficult to do centralized short- and long-term planning of labor, materials, equipment, production runs, packing, and delivery. With the help of one or two staff people from the front office, hourly workers now do all this planning. Often, but not always, a manager sits in to provide input, but the workers make all the decisions. I'm sure they rarely make exactly the right decisions, because in a business like ours it is not possible to anticipate every problem and change, but I'm equally sure that they make better decisions than I would make. For example, one area that we track and chart religiously is customer deliveries. At the moment, we have a 98% on-time record.

But when the committee does make bad decisions—and from time to time it must—I don't necessarily know. That is the ultimate point of everything I've tried to do. Now a bad decision comes out of their pockets as well as mine.

Progress in all these areas was painful and painfully slow. Some employees have never entirely accepted the idea that they should share the company's risks as well as its profits. But, of course, it is precisely the profit sharing that has turned the tide at Cin-Made in favor of shared responsibility.

Three times each year, on September 30, December 20, and March 30, every hourly worker gets a check for his or her equal share of the pretax profits from the previous fiscal year, which ends on June 30. For the first four years, employee shares were modest, and we made limited headway. Averaged over a full work year, that first year's individual share came to $0.58 for each standard hour worked. We had no profits at all the second year because we acquired and closed a small competitor and also bought and moved into a new building. In the third and fourth years, while we were still struggling with quality problems, a slow market, and a lack of strategic direction, employee shares came to $0.41 and $0.11 an hour, respectively.

In 1989, we finally generated a comprehensive strategic focus for product development, marketing, and cost control, and in fiscal 1990, it began to pay off in earnest. Profit sharing that year came to $2.82 an hour on top of fixed wages. Over the last four years, the average profit-sharing bonus has been $2.62 an hour—a 36% increment to income.

The effect has been electrifying. Full-time employees now routinely monitor the work of temps to reduce waste and increase efficiency. Strict adherence to job descriptions is a thing of the past. Absenteeism has fallen to nearly nil. Productivity is up 30%. Grievances are down to one or two a year. Except for merit raises, there has been no increase in fixed wages since 1984, yet our work force makes more money than comparable industrial workers.

In 1990, during our last contract negotiations, we ran into two hurdles that tested our progress. First, a group of hourly employees had decided that they wanted an across-the-board pay raise on top of profit sharing. The impulse was understandable. Their weekly pay checks hadn't grown in six years, whereas day-to-day living expenses obviously had. At the same time, of course, they wanted to keep those three big checks each year.

I was disappointed, but I walked them through the reasoning once more. To begin with, I said, you can't have raises *and* profit sharing. Wages don't come from shareholders or from an owner's deep pockets. They come from the profits the company generates and from no other place. But profit is attached to risk. If you'll take the same kind of risk I'm taking, if we're all in this game together, then you can go on sharing 18% of every pretax dollar we make. True, not every year will be as profitable as every other, but lately we've been doing pretty well.

On the other hand, I said, for the first time, I'm willing to give you a raise if you really want it. But it's got to be a choice: you can have a raise or you can have profit sharing. You can't have both. If you choose the raise, I'll match the best percentage increase your union can negotiate anywhere in the country with any employer. But I'll keep the 18%, or what's left of it, because all the risk will be mine again.

It was a calculated gamble. I didn't want them to give up profit sharing, and I guessed they wouldn't choose security over income. But if they did, so be it. I couldn't push them forever. And higher wages for them would mean a lot more money for me.

They decided to speak to the membership. After comparing the wages of union members in other companies with their own combined incomes, fixed and variable, the workers changed their minds. Some of them concluded that my easy acquiescence meant that I wanted to take away their profit sharing. They voted nearly unanimously to drop the request for a raise and insist on the continuation of the profit-sharing program.

The second hurdle was vacation. They'd been stuck at three weeks since the strike in 1984, and now they wanted another week.

Fine, I said. I don't care if you want more vacation or more holidays or a dental plan. But there's only one pot of money, and that's profits. You can use your share any way you like. You can have them in cash or in vacations.

You see, there's nothing here to negotiate, I said. There are no concessions you can squeeze from me. Or, to put it the other way around, there are no concessions

I won't make. It's your money. You can distribute it any way you please.

They decided they would rather have the money, but I honestly didn't care which way they voted. If they have finally grasped the concept, the details hardly matter.

The process of change is an endless series of small battles. Someone must always force the action, yet empowerment is only possible when workers and managers are capable of taking the power offered them and using it aggressively and well. I have forced the action persistently and hard, but the people at Cin-Made have exceeded my expectations, and probably their own, in learning to take collective action, in setting and achieving hugely ambitious goals, in seizing empowerment with both hands and making themselves almost totally responsible for the company's success. Today I discover to my surprise that whereas once I pushed them forward, now they are pushing me. The skirmishes ahead of us revolve around two issues.

First, I am concerned about eventual ownership succession. To protect Cin-Made's future and the employees' jobs, I want to create an employee stock ownership plan that will allow them to buy the company. They're not quite ready for this idea. In the long run, it will increase their income and security, but for the next few years, it could cost them a good deal of their profits.

The second issue involves my more immediate future. My employees want me to reduce my role as president relatively quickly and turn over even more power to the people responsible for day-to-day operations. In this case, I'm the one who's not quite ready. I still like my job.

On the first issue, I push and they hold back. On the second, they press and I resist. Forcing change has begun to cut both ways.

Robert Frey *is the owner and president of The Cin-Made Corporation in Cincinnati, Ohio, and, recently, of two new packaging companies as well, all three operating from the same plant. Since this article was published, his story has been included in several books; and articles about him have appeared in a number of magazines including* Fortune *and* Inc. *In 1994, he was named to the board of directors of the National Labor-Management Association, and in 1995 he was made a member of the Radcliffe Public Policy Institute to study the new economic equation: family, workplace, economy, and the way they relate.*

Perhaps more important than these honors, his businesses are doing well. Revenues per employee are up 20% over the last two years. Overall sales have grown from $3.6 million last year to a projected $5.9 million in 1995–1996. Because of the new companies, there were no profits to share in fiscal 1994–1995. Cin-Made itself did well, but the two startups, predictably, lost all the profits Cin-Made earned.

Nevertheless, Frey's work force is now seeking a five-year contract to enshrine the present profit-sharing arrangement and to perpetuate their present level of self-administration, which now has them not just doing all their own production planning but also ordering raw materials, setting their own pay rates, and hiring their fellow employees. In fiscal 1995–1996, Frey and his employees expect profit-sharing to set records.

Ocelia Williams *is still with the company.*

2

How I Learned to Let
My Workers Lead

RALPH STAYER

IN 1980, I WAS the head of a successful family business—Johnsonville Sausage—that was in great shape and
required radical change.

Our profits were above the average for our industry,
and our financial statements showed every sign of
health. We were growing at a rate of about 20% annually,
with sales that were strong in our home state of
Wisconsin and steadily rising in Minnesota, Michigan,
and Indiana. Our quality was high. We were respected in
the community. I was making a lot of money.

And I had a knot in my stomach that wouldn't go
away. For one thing, I was worried about competition.
We were a small, regional producer with national competitors who could outpromote, outadvertise, and under-
price us any time they chose.

In addition to our big national competitors, we had a
host of local and regional producers small enough to
provide superior service to customers who were virtually

*Author's note: I wish to acknowledge the contribution of my partner, James A.
Belasco, to this article.*

their neighbors. We were too big to have the small-town advantage and too small to have advantages of national scale. Our business was more vulnerable than it looked.

What worried me more than the competition, however, was the gap between potential and performance. Our people didn't seem to care. Every day I came to work and saw people so bored by their jobs that they made thoughtless, dumb mistakes. They mislabeled products or added the wrong seasonings or failed to mix them into the sausage properly. Someone drove the prongs of a forklift right through a newly built wall. Someone else ruined a big batch of fresh sausage by spraying it with water while cleaning the work area. These were accidents. No one was deliberately wasting money, time, and materials; it was just that people took no responsibility for their work. They showed up in the morning, did halfheartedly what they were told to do, and then went home.

Now, I didn't expect them to be as deeply committed to the company as I was. I owned it, and they didn't. But how could we survive a serious competitive challenge with this low level of attentiveness and involvement?

GETTING TO POINTS B AND A

In 1980, I began looking for a recipe for change. I started by searching for a book that would tell me how to get people to care about their jobs and their company. Not surprisingly, the search was fruitless. No one could tell me how to wake up my own work force; I would have to figure it out for myself.

And yet, I told myself, why not? I had made the company, so I could fix it. This was an insight filled with pitfalls but it *was* an insight: the fault was not someone else's, the fault was mine.

Of course, I hadn't really built the company all alone, but I had created the management style that kept people from assuming responsibility. Of course, it was counterproductive for me to own all the company's problems by myself, but in 1980 every problem did, in fact, rest squarely on my shoulders, weighing me down and—though I didn't appreciate it at the time—crippling my subordinates and strangling the company. If I was going to fix what I had made, I would have to start by fixing myself. In many ways that was my good luck, or, to put the same thought another way, thank God I was the problem so I could be the solution.

As I thought about what I should do, I first asked myself what I needed to do to achieve the company's goals. But what were the company's goals? What did I really want Johnsonville to be? I didn't know.

This realization led me to a second insight: nothing matters more than a goal. The most important question any manager can ask is, "In the best of all possible worlds, what would I really want to happen?"

I tried to picture what Johnsonville would have to be to sell the most expensive sausage in the industry and still have the biggest market share. What I saw in my mind's eye was definitely not an organization where I made all the decisions and owned all the problems. What I saw was an organization where people took responsibility for their own work, for the product, for the company as a whole. If that happened, our product and service quality would improve, our margins would rise, and we could reduce costs and successfully enter new markets. Johnsonville would be much less vulnerable to competition.

The image that best captured the organizational end state I had in mind for Johnsonville was a flock of geese on the wing. I didn't want an organizational chart with traditional lines and boxes, but a "V" of individuals who knew the common goal, took turns leading, and adjusted their structure to the task at hand. Geese fly in a wedge, for instance, but land in waves. Most important, each individual bird is responsible for its own performance.

With that end state in mind as Point B, the goal, I turned to the question of our starting point, Point A. Johnsonville was financially successful, but I was dissatisfied with employee attitudes. So I conducted an attitude survey to find out what people thought about their jobs and the company and to get an idea of how they perceived the company's attitude toward them. I knew there was less commitment than I wanted, but I was startled all the same to find that Johnsonville attitudes were only average—no better than employee attitudes at big, impersonal companies like General Motors.

At first I didn't want to believe the survey, and I looked for all kinds of excuses. The methodology was faulty. The questions were poorly worded. I didn't want to admit that we had an employee motivation problem because I didn't know how to deal with that. But however strong the temptation, the mistakes and poor performance were too glaring to ignore.

The survey told me that people saw nothing for themselves at Johnsonville. It was a job, a means to some end that lay outside the company. I wanted them to commit themselves to a company goal, but they saw little to commit to. And at that stage, I still couldn't see that the biggest obstacle to changing their point of view was me. Everything I had learned and experienced to that point had convinced me that anything I didn't do myself would not be done right. As I saw it, my job was to create the agenda and then motivate "them" to carry it out.

In fact, I expected my people to follow me the way buffalo follow their leader—blindly. Unfortunately, that kind of leadership model almost led to the buffalo's extinction. Buffalo hunters used to slaughter the herd by finding and killing the leader. Once the leader was dead, the rest of the herd stood around waiting for instructions that never came, and the hunters could (and did) exterminate them one by one.

I realized that I had been focused entirely on the financial side of the business—margins, market share, return on assets—and had seen people as dutiful tools to make the business grow. The business *had* grown—nicely—and that very success was my biggest obstacle to change. I had made all the decisions about purchasing, scheduling, quality, pricing, marketing, sales, hiring, and all the rest of it. Now the very things that had brought me success— my centralized control, my aggressive behavior, my authoritarian business practices—were creating the environment that made me so unhappy. I had been Johnsonville Sausage, assisted by some hired hands who, to my annoyance, lacked commitment. But why should they make a commitment to Johnsonville? They had no stake in the company and no power to make decisions or control their own work. If I wanted to improve results, I had to increase their involvement in the business.

This was an insight that I immediately misused. Acting on instinct, I ordered a change. "From now on," I announced to my management team, "you're all responsible for making your own decisions." I went from authoritarian control to authoritarian abdication. No one had asked for more responsibility; I forced it down their throats. They were good soldiers, and they did their best, but I had trained them to expect me to solve their problems. I had nurtured their inability by expecting them to be incapable; now they met my expectations with an inability to make decisions unless they knew which decisions I wanted them to make.

After more than two years of working with them, I finally had to replace all three top managers. Worst of all, I now see that in a way they were right. I didn't really *want* them to make independent decisions. I wanted them to make the decisions I would have made. Deep down, I was still in love with my own control; I was just making people guess what I wanted instead of telling them. And yet I had to replace those three managers. I needed people who didn't guess so well, people who couldn't read my mind, people strong enough to call my bluff and seize ownership of Johnsonville's problems whether I "really" wanted to give it up or not.

I spent those two years pursuing another mirage as well—detailed strategic and tactical plans that would realize my goal of Johnsonville as the world's greatest sausage maker. We tried to plan organizational structure two to three years before it would be needed—who would be responsible for what and who would report to whom, all carefully diagrammed in boxes and lines on charts. Later I realized that these structural changes had to grow from day-to-day working realities; no one could dictate them from above, and certainly not in advance. But at the time, my business training told me this was the way to proceed. The discussions went on at an abstract level for months, the details overwhelmed us, and we got nowhere.

In short, the early 1980s were a disaster. After two years of stewing, it began to dawn on me that my first reactions to most situations were usually dead wrong. After all, my organizational instincts had brought us to Point A to begin with. Pursuing those instincts now would only bring us *back* to Point A. I needed to start thinking before I acted, and the thought I needed to think was, "Will this action help us achieve our new Point B?"

Point B also needed some revision. The early 1980s taught me that I couldn't give responsibility. People had to expect it, want it, even demand it. So my end state needed redefining. The goal was not so much a state of shared responsibility as an environment where people insist on being responsible.

To bring people to that new Point B, I had to learn to be a better coach. It took me additional years to learn the art of coaching, by which, in a nutshell, I mean communicating a vision and then getting people to see their own behavior, harness their own frustrations, and own their own problems.

Early in the change process, for example, I was told that workers in one plant disliked working weekends, which they often had to do to meet deliveries. Suspecting that the weekends weren't really necessary, I pressed plant managers to use the problem as an opportunity. I asked them if they had measured production efficiency, for instance, and if they had tried to get their workers to take responsibility for the overtime problem. The first thing everyone discovered was that machine downtime hovered between 30% and 40%. Then they started coming to terms with the fact that all that downtime had its causes—lateness, absences, sloppy maintenance, slow shift startups. Once the workers began to see that they themselves were the problem, they realized that they could do away with weekend work. In three weeks, they cut downtime to less than 10% and had Saturdays and Sundays off.

Managing the Context

The debacle of ordering change and watching it fail to occur showed me my limitations. I had come to realize that I didn't directly control the performance of the people at Johnsonville, that as a manager I didn't really manage people. They managed themselves. But I did manage the context. I provided and allocated the resources. I designed and implemented the systems. I drew up and executed the organizational structure. The power of any contextual factor lies in its ability to shape the way people think and what they expect. So I worked on two contextual areas: systems and structures.

Systems

I first attacked our quality control system. Quality was central to our business success, one of our key competitive advantages. But even though our quality was better than average, it wasn't yet good enough to be great.

We had the traditional quality control department with the traditional quality control responsibilities—catching errors before they got to the customer. Senior management was a part of the system. Several times a week we evaluated the product—that is to say, we *checked* it—for taste, flavor, color, and texture.

One day it struck me that by checking the product, top management had assumed responsibility for its quality. We were not encouraging people to be responsible for their own performance. We were not helping people commit themselves to making Johnsonville a great company.

This line of reasoning led me to another insight: the first strategic decision I needed to make was who should make decisions. On the theory that those who implement a decision and live with its consequences are the best people to make it, we changed our quality control system. Top management stopped tasting sausage, and the people who made sausage started. We informed line workers that from now on it would be their responsibility to make certain that only top-quality product left the plant. In the future, they would manage quality control.

It surprised me how readily people accepted this ownership. They formed teams of workers to resolve quality problems. For example, one team attacked the problem of leakers—vacuum-packed plastic packages of sausage that leaked air and shortened shelf life. The team gathered data, identified problems, worked with suppliers and with other line workers to develop and implement solutions, even visited retail stores to find out how retailers handled the product so we could make changes that would prevent their problems from occurring. The team took complete responsibility for measuring quality and then used those measurements to improve production processes. They owned and expected to own all the problems of producing top-quality sausage, and they wanted to do the best possible job. The results were amazing. Rejects fell from 5% to less than 0.5%.

Clearly this new quality control system was helping to create the end state we were after. Its success triggered changes in several other systems as well.

Teams of workers in other areas began to taste the product every morning and discuss possible improvements. They asked for information about costs and customer reactions, and we redesigned the information system to give it to them.

We began to forward customer letters directly to line workers. They responded to customer complaints and sent coupons for free Johnsonville sausage when they felt it was warranted. They came to own and expect responsibility for correcting the problems that customers raised in their letters.

People in each section on the shop floor began to collect data about labor costs, efficiency, and yield. They posted the data and discussed it at the daily tasting meeting. Increasingly, people asked for more responsibility, and the information system encouraged them to take it. We were progressing toward our end state, and as we made progress we uncovered deeper and more complex problems.

One of these arose when people on the shop floor began to complain about fellow workers whose performance was still slipshod or indifferent. In fact, they came to senior management and said, "You don't take your own advice. If you did, you wouldn't let these poor performers work here. It's your job to either fix them or fire them."

Our first reaction was to jump in and do something, but by now we had learned to think before acting. We asked ourselves if accepting responsibility for this problem would help us reach Point B. The answer was clearly no. More important, we asked ourselves who was in the

best position to own the problem and came to the obvious conclusion that the people on the shop floor knew
more about shop-floor performance than we did, so they
were the best ones to make these decisions.

We offered to help them set performance standards
and to coach them in confronting poor performers, but
we insisted that since they were the production-perfor-
mance experts, it was up to them to deal with the situation. I bit my tongue time and time again, but they took
on the responsibility for dealing with performance problems and actually fired individuals who wouldn't perform
up to the standards of their teams.

This led to a dramatic change in Johnsonville's human
resource system. Convinced that inadequate selection
and training of new workers caused performance problems, line workers asked to do the selection and training
themselves. Managers helped them set up selection and
training procedures, but production workers made them
work. Eventually, line workers assumed most of the traditional personnel functions.

The compensation system was another early target for
change. We had traditionally given across-the board
annual raises like most other businesses. What mattered
was longevity, not performance. That system was also a
stumbling block on our way to Point B, so we made two
changes.

First, we eliminated the annual across-the-board raise
and substituted a pay-for-responsibility system. As people took on new duties —budgeting, for instance, or
training—they earned additional base income. Where the
old system rewarded people for hanging around, regardless of what they contributed, the new one encouraged
people to seek responsibility.

Second, we instituted what we called a "company
performance share," a fixed percentage of pretax profits
to be divided every six months among our employees.
We based individual shares on a performance-appraisal

system designed and administered by a volunteer team of line production workers from various departments. The system is explained in "How Johnsonville Shares Profits on the Basis of Performance."

These system changes taught me two more valuable lessons. First, just start. Don't wait until you have all the answers. When I set out to make these changes, I had no clear picture of how these new systems would interact with one another or with other company systems and procedures, but if I had waited until I had all the answers, I'd still be waiting. A grand plan was impossible; there were too many variables. I wasn't certain which systems to change; I just knew I had to change something in order to alter expectations and begin moving toward my goal.

Second, start by changing the most visible system you directly control. You want your first effort to succeed. I knew I could control who tasted the product because I was doing the tasting. I also knew it was a highly visible action. Everyone waited to hear my taste-test results. By announcing that I wasn't going to taste the product anymore and that the people who made it were, everyone knew immediately that I was serious about spreading responsibility.

Structures

Along with the system changes, I introduced a number of changes in company structure. Teams gradually took over a number of the functions previously performed by individual managers in the chain of command, with the result that the number of hierarchical layers went from six to three.

Teams had already taken on responsibility for selecting, training, evaluating, and, when necessary, terminating fellow employees. Now they began to make all decisions about schedules, performance standards, assignments, budgets, quality measures, and capital

How Johnsonville Shares Profits on the Basis of Performance

Every six months, we evaluate the performance of everyone at Johnsonville to help us compute shares in our profit-sharing program. Except "we" is the wrong word. In practice, performance evaluations are done by the employees themselves. For example, 300 wage earners—salaried employees have a separate profit-sharing pool and a different evaluation system—fill out forms in which they rate themselves on a scale of 1 to 9 in 17 specific areas grouped into three categories: performance, teamwork, and personal development.

Scores of 3, 4, or 5—the average range—are simply entered on the proper line. Low scores of 1 or 2 and high scores of 6 to 9 require a sentence or two of explanation.

Each member's coach fills out an identical form, and later both people sit down together and discuss all 17 areas. In cases of disagreement, the rule is only that their overall point totals must agree within nine points, whereupon the two totals are averaged to reach a final score. If they cannot narrow the gap to nine points, an arbitration group is ready to step in and help, but so far mediation has never been needed.

All final scores, names deleted, are then passed to a profit-sharing team that carves out five categories of performance: a small group of superior performers (about 5% of the total), a larger group of better-than-average workers (roughly 20%), an average group amounting to about 50% of the total work force, a below-average group of 20%, and a small group of poor performers who are often in some danger of losing their jobs.

The total pool of profits to be shared is then divided by the number of workers to find an average share—for the purpose of illustration, let's say $1,000. Members of the top group get a check for 125% of that amount or $1,250. Members of the next group get 110% ($1,100), of the large middle group, 100% or $1,000, and so on down to $900 and $750.

Yes, people do complain from time to time, especially if they think they've missed a higher share by only a point or two. The usual way of dealing with such situations is to help the individual improve his or her performance in enough areas to ensure a higher score the next time. But overall satisfaction with the system is very high, partly because fellow workers invented it, administer it, and constantly revise it in an effort to make it more equitable. The person currently in charge of the Johnsonville profit-sharing team is an hourly worker from the shipping department.

improvements as well. In operations, teams assumed the supervisors' functions, and those jobs disappeared. Those former supervisors who needed authority in order to function left the company, but most went into other jobs at Johnsonville, some of them into technical positions.

The function of the quality control department was redefined. It stopped checking quality—now done by line workers—and began providing technical support to the production people in a cooperative effort to *improve* quality. The department developed systems for continuous on-line monitoring of fat, moisture, and protein content, for example, and it launched a program of outside taste testing among customers.

The traditional personnel department disappeared and was replaced by a learning and personal development team to help individual employees develop their own Points B and A—their destinations and starting points—and figure out how to use Johnsonville to reach their goals. We set up an educational allowance for each person, to be used however the individual saw fit. In the beginning, some took cooking or sewing classes; a few took flying lessons. Over time, however, more and more of the employees focused on job-related learning. Today more than 65% of all the people at Johnsonville are involved in some type of formal education.

The end state we all now envision for Johnsonville is a company that never stops learning. One part of learning is the acquisition of facts and knowledge—about accounting, machine maintenance, marketing, even about sky diving and Italian cooking. But the most important kind of learning teaches us to question our own actions and behavior in order to better understand the ways we perform, work, and live.

Helping human beings fulfill their potential is of course a moral responsibility, but it's also good business. Life is aspiration. Learning, striving people are happy people and good workers. They have initiative and imagination, and the companies they work for are rarely caught napping.

Learning is change, and I keep learning and relearning that change is and needs to be continuous. For example, our system and structural changes were reciprocal. The first led to the second, which then in turn led to new versions of the first.

Initially, I had hoped the journey would be as neat and orderly as it now appears on paper. Fortunately—since original mistakes are an important part of learning—it wasn't. There were lots of obstacles and challenges, much backsliding, and myriad false starts and wrong decisions.

For example, team leaders chosen by their team members were supposed to function as communication links, leaving the traditional management functions of planning and scheduling to the group itself. No sooner had the team leaders been appointed, however, than they began to function as supervisors. In other words, they immediately fell into the familiar roles they had always seen. We had neglected to give them and the plant managers adequate training in the new team model. The structure changed, but mind-sets didn't. It was harder to alter people's expectations than I had realized.

Influencing Expectations

I discovered that change occurs in fits and starts, and that while I could plan individual changes and events, I couldn't plan the whole process. I also learned that expectations have a way of becoming reality, so I tried to use every available means —semantic, symbolic, and behavioral—to send messages that would shape expectations to Johnsonville's advantage.

For example, we wanted to break down the traditional pictures in people's minds of what managers do and how subordinates and employees behave, so we changed the words we used. We dropped the words employee and subordinate. Instead we called everyone a "member" of the organization, and managers became "coordinators" or "coaches."

Our promotion system had always sent a powerful message: to move up the ladder you need to become a manager and solve problems for your people. But this was now the wrong message. I wanted coordinators who could build problem-solving capacities in others rather than solve their problems for them. I recast the job requirements for the people whose work I directly coordinated (formerly known as "my management team"), and they, in turn, did the same for the people whose work they coordinated. I took every opportunity to stress the need for coaching skills, and I continually de-emphasized technical experience. Whenever someone became a coordinator, I made sure word got around that the promotion was for demonstrated abilities as a teacher, coach, and facilitator.

This new promotion standard sent a new message: to get ahead at Johnsonville, you need a talent for cultivating and encouraging problem solvers and responsibility takers.

I discovered that people watched my every action to see if it supported or undermined our vision. They wanted to see if I practiced what I preached. From the outset I did simple things to demonstrate my sincerity. I made a sign for my desk that said THE QUESTION IS THE ANSWER, and when people came to me with questions, I asked myself if they were questions I should answer. Invariably, they weren't. Invariably, people were asking me to make decisions for them. Instead of giving answers, I turned the tables and asked the questions myself, trying to make them repossess their own problems. Owning problems was an important part of the end state I'd envisioned. I wasn't about to let people give theirs to me.

I also discovered that in meetings people waited to hear my opinion before offering their own. In the beginning, I insisted they say what they thought, unaware that I showed my own preferences in subtle ways—my tone of voice, the questions I asked—which, nevertheless, anyone could read and interpret expertly. When I realized what was happening, I began to stay silent to avoid giving any clue to where I stood. The result was that people flatly refused to commit themselves to any decision at all. Some of those meetings would have gone on for days if I hadn't forced people to speak out before they'd read my mind.

In the end, I began scheduling myself out of many meetings, forcing others to make their decisions without me. I also stopped collecting data about production problems. I learned that if I had information about daily shortages and yields, I began to ask questions that put me firmly back in possession of the problems.

Eventually, I came to understand that everything I did and said had a symbolic as well as a literal meaning. I had to anticipate the potential impact of every word and act, ask myself again and again if what I was about to do or say would reinforce the vision or undermine it, bring us closer to Point B or circle us back to Point A, encourage people to own their own problems or palm them off on me. My job, as I had come to see it, was to put myself out of a job.

WATERSHED

By mid-1985, we had all come a long way. Johnsonville members had started wanting and expecting responsibility for their own performance, and they usually did a good job. Return on assets was up significantly, as were margins and quality. But on the whole, the process of change had been a journey without any major mileposts or station stops. Then Palmer Sausage (not its real name) came along and gave us our watershed—a golden opportunity and a significant threat to our existence.

Palmer is a much larger sausage company that had contracted with us for private-label products during a strike in the early 1980s. Our quality was so high that they kept us on as a supplier after the strike ended. Now Palmer had decided to consolidate several facilities and offered to let us take over part of the production of a plant they were closing. It represented a huge increase in their order, and the additional business was very tempting: it could be very profitable, and it would justify the cost of a new and more efficient plant of our own. The upside was extremely attractive—if we could handle it.

That was what worried me. To handle an expanded Palmer contract, we'd have to hire and train a large group of people quickly and teach our present people new skills, keep quality high on both the Palmer products and our own, work six and seven days a week for more than a year until our new plant was ready, and run the risk if Palmer cancelled—which it could do on 30-days notice—of saddling ourselves with big layoffs and new capacity we no longer had a market for. Maybe it wasn't a bet-the-company decision, but it was as close as I'd like to come.

Before 1982, I would have met for days with my senior team to discuss all these issues, and we would probably have turned down the opportunity in the face of such an overwhelming downside. But by 1985, it was clear to me that the executive group was the wrong group to make this decision. The executives would not be responsible for successfully implementing such a move. The only way we could do Palmer successfully was if everyone at Johnsonville was committed to making it work, so everyone had to decide.

Until that moment, my senior team had always made the strategic decisions. We took advice from people in the operating departments, but the senior staff and I had dealt with the ultimate problems and responsibilities. We needed to move to a new level. This was a problem all of our people had to own.

My senior managers and I called a meeting of the entire plant, presented the problem, and posed three questions. What will it take to make it work? Is it possible to reduce the downside? Do we want to do it?

We asked the teams in each area to discuss these questions among themselves and develop a list of pros and cons. Since the group as a whole was too large to work together effectively, each team chose one member to report its findings to a plantwide representative body to develop a plantwide answer.

The small groups met almost immediately, and within days their representatives met. The discussion moved back and forth several times between the representative body and the smaller groups.

To make it work, the members decided we'd have to operate seven days a week, hire and train people to take new shifts, and increase efficiency to get more from current capacity. They also thought about the downside risk. The biggest danger was that we'd lose the added business after making all the investments and sacrifices needed to handle it. They figured the only way to reduce that downside potential was to achieve quality standards so high that we would actually improve the already first-rate Palmer product and, at the same time, maintain standards on our own products to make sure Johnson-ville brands didn't fall by the wayside.

Two weeks later, the company decided almost unanimously to take the business. It was one of the proudest moments of my life. Left to our traditional executive decision making, we would have turned Palmer down. The Johnsonville people, believing in themselves, rose to the challenge. They really did want to be great. (See "Ralph Stayer's Guide to Improving Performance").

The results surpassed our best projections. Learning took place faster than anticipated. Quality rose in our

Ralph Stayer's Guide to Improving Performance

Getting better performance from any group or individual, yourself included, means a permanent change in the way you think and run your business. Change of this kind is not a single transaction but a journey, and the journey has a specific starting point and a clear destination.

The journey is based on six observations about human behavior that I didn't fully grasp when I started, though I'd have made faster progress and fewer mistakes if I had.

1. People want to be great. If they aren't, it's because management won't let them be.

2. Performance begins with each individual's expectations. Influence what people expect and you influence how people perform.

3. Expectations are driven partly by goals, vision, symbols, semantics, and partly by the context in which people work, that is, by such things as compensation systems, production practices, and decision-making structures.

4. The actions of managers shape expectations.

5. Learning is a process, not a goal. Each new insight creates a new layer of potential insights.

6. The organization's results reflect me and my performance. If I want to change the results, I have to change myself first. This is particularly true for me, the owner and CEO, but it is equally true for every employee.

So to make the changes that will lead to great performance, I recommend focusing on goals, expectations, contexts, actions, and learning. Lee Thayer, a humanities professor at the University of Wisconsin, has another way of saying pretty much the same thing. He argues that since performance is the key to organizational success, management's job is to establish the conditions under which superb performance serves both the company's and the individual's best interests.

CEOs need to focus first on changing themselves before they try to change the rest of the company. The process resembles an archaeological dig, or at least it did for me. As I uncovered and solved one problem, I almost invariably exposed another, deeper problem. As I gained one insight and mastered one situation, another situation arose that required new insight and more learning. As I approached one goal, a new, more important, but more distant goal always began to take shape.

own product line as well as for Palmer. The new plant came on line in 1987. Palmer has come back to us several times since to increase the size of its orders even further.

SUCCESS—THE GREATEST ENEMY

The pace of change increased after Palmer. Now that all of Johnsonville's people expected and wanted some degree of responsibility for strategic decisions, we had to redefine Point A, our current situation. The new level of involvement also led us to a more ambitious view of what we could ultimately achieve—Point B, our vision and destination.

We made additional changes in our career-tracking system. In our early enthusiasm, we had played down the technical aspects of our business, encouraging everyone to become a coordinator, even those who were far better suited to technical specialties. We also had some excellent salespeople who became coordinators because they saw it as the only path to advancement, though their talents and interests lay much more in selling than in coaching. When they became coordinators, we lost in three ways: we lost good salespeople, we created poor coordinators, and we lost sales from other good salespeople because they worked for these poor coordinators.

A career team recommended that Johnsonville set up dual career tracks—one for specialists and one for coordinators—that would enable both to earn recognition, status, and compensation on the basis of performance alone. The team, not the senior coordinators, agreed to own and fix the compensation problem.

Everyone at Johnsonville discovered they could do considerably better and earn considerably more than they had imagined. Since they had little trouble meeting the accelerated production goals that they themselves had set, members raised the minimum acceptable performance criteria and began routinely to expect more of themselves and others.

Right now, teams of Johnsonville members are meeting to discuss next year's capital budget, new product ideas, today's production schedule, and yesterday's quality, cost, and yield. More important, these same teams are redesigning their systems and structures to manage their continuing journey toward Point B, which, along with Point A, they are also continually redefining. Most important of all, their general level of commitment is now as high or higher than my own.

In fact, our greatest enemy now is our success. Our sales, margins, quality, and productivity far exceed anything we could have imagined in 1980. We've been studied and written about, and we've spent a lot of time answering questions and giving advice. We've basked in the limelight, telling other people how we did it. All the time we kept telling ourselves, "We can't let this go to our heads." But of course it had already gone to our heads. We had begun to talk and brag about the past instead of about what we wanted for the future. Once we saw what we were doing, we managed to stop and, in the process, learn a lesson about the hazards of self-congratulation.

When I began this process of change ten years ago, I looked forward to the time when it would all be over and I could get back to my real job. But I've learned that change *is* the real job of every effective business leader because change is about the present and the future, not about the past. There is no end to change. This story is only an interim report.

Yet another thing I've learned is that the cause of excitement at Johnsonville Sausage is not change itself but the process used in producing change. Learning and responsibility are invigorating, and aspirations make our hearts beat. For the last five years, my own aspiration has been to eliminate *my* job by creating such a crowd of self-starting, problem-solving, responsibility-grabbing, independent thinkers that Johnsonville would run itself.

Two years ago, I hired a new chief operating officer and told him he should lead the company and think of me as his paid consultant. Earlier this year, he invited me to a management retreat, and I enjoyed myself. Other people owned the problems that had once been mine. My whole job was to generate productive conversations about Johnsonville's goals and to communicate its vision.

On the second evening of the retreat, I was given a message from my COO. There was a special session the next morning, he wrote, and added, "I want you there at 8:15." Instinctively, it made me mad. Johnsonville was my company; I built it; I fixed it; he owed me his job. Who the hell did he think he was giving me orders like a hired consultant?

Then, of course, I laughed. It's not always easy giving up control, even when it's what you've worked toward for ten years. He wanted me there at 8:15? Well, good for him. I'd be there.

Ralph Stayer is the CEO of Johnsonville Foods, Inc., where he has further refined the system described here by developing a customer-based definition of value and by reorganizing management into three teams—a product-to-market team, a sales-and-marketing team, and a support-services team. In the five years since this article was written,

Johnsonville has doubled in size and tripled in profitability. Two years ago, Stayer published his ideas in book form (Flight of the Buffalo, Warner Books, 1993). He now spends 75% of his time consulting to companies like Frito-Lay, BMW, and McDonnell Douglas, helping them build customer satisfaction and develop value-creating strategies.

3

The Center-Cut Solution

TIMOTHY W. FIRNSTAHL

I OWN FIVE SUCCESSFUL restaurants in Seattle, but I recently came very close to owning none. My five restaurants gross about $10 million a year; employ 300 to 400 people, depending on the season; and, through most of the 1980s, produced a decent profit on a small margin. In the early 1990s, however, I found myself with the same problems so many other businesses have faced in recent years—declining income, growing expenses, operating losses. I had to cut costs drastically or go under. There are lots of ways to address this predicament, and I chose a common one: downsizing.

Now, the conventional approach to downsizing is to eliminate frills and peripherals. My trouble was that except for waste, which I also attacked, I *had* no peripherals. I had to cut at the center. Instead of lopping off limbs, therefore, I cut off the head of my company. Remarkably enough, it worked.

SQUEEZING THE JUICE OUT OF RESTAURANTS

Things started going sideways in a serious way when I opened Sharps Fresh Roasting restaurant in December,

1990. Opening night saw Seattle's worst snowstorm in 40 years. I had two customers, cops who came in to get out of the cold. The next night I had three customers—the same two cops had brought their boss. Seattle was a sheet of ice, and business was nil for weeks.

Next came the Persian Gulf War. Everyone was glued to CNN and uninterested in my brand new restaurant. After that, the recession hit Seattle full force. Boeing began laying people off. Then my landlord, a former restaurant owner himself, told me my new concept was all wrong. "Why don't you just do another Von's?" he kept asking.

Von's was my downtown restaurant. It had a polished mahogany interior, a ceiling covered with Seattle artifacts like taxi doors and water skis, and a thoroughly northwest menu featuring fresh salmon, Alaska king crab, and prime beefsteaks; but it was still basically a city saloon. Sharps was a bold suburban experiment, my contribution to restaurant history, and I was beginning to have some serious doubts. Was it boring? Did it surprise and delight the customer? Had I gone too far? Not far enough?

I was bleeding so badly that my other four restaurants, though still in the black—or perhaps I should say in the gray—couldn't make up the shortfall.

My business was dying, and its death would certainly bring on my own economic demise as well. Personal loan guarantees would see to that. I had been in the restaurant business for 25 years, I had worked as hard as I knew how, I had innovated, delegated, and empowered, I had struggled through earlier crises and basked in the sunshine of great success; and now I was going to lose everything unless I could come up with some powerful magic to turn my company around.

The truth of the matter is that restaurants have been in a bind for some time. That's how I found myself experimenting with the new Sharps concept in the first place.

Food costs have been rising. Labor costs have increased markedly since Congress raised the minimum wage and eliminated tip credits as a means of offsetting wage expense. Health costs too have been spiraling out of control. Worse yet, customers' incomes have shrunk. Today, both husband and wife have to work to match the earning power just one person had 30 years ago.

On top of it all, the foundation on which fine dining has prospered for 60 years has crumbled. Ever since the repeal of Prohibition in 1933, most restaurants have relied on the sale of spirits to offset their very small margins on food. This formula no longer works. For two highly commendable reasons—increased health aware-ness and stricter enforcement of the laws against drunk driving—restaurants sell a lot less alcohol than they used to.

In my particular case, I'm afraid I can add lousy cost control to the equation. We were just not managing expenses in a way that brought dollars to the bottom line. In fact, waste and theft often frustrate management and destroy restaurants. In our case, I estimated they were costing up to 9% of our gross revenues.

So I found myself in the jaws of a vice. My costs were rising, and my customers, by eating at home, were demanding lower prices. Charging $15.50 for 8 ounces of salmon would simply no longer do. I knew I would have to abandon that plateful of expensive protein so dear to American restaurants.

I also knew I would have to focus harder than ever on service, excitement, variety, and quality.

The heart of the Sharps Fresh Roasting concept fol-lowed directly from that analysis. If expensive protein wasn't the answer, then I'd try *inexpensive* protein—or at least less expensive protein. But how do you make less expensive protein tasty? How do you get top round to taste like prime rib? The answer we came up with was slow roasting.

Sharps takes five meats—beef, lamb, pork, chicken, and turkey—fruitwood smokes them, roasts them for three-and-a-half hours, then lets them coast in a slow oven for 18 hours more. This process (with some proprietary refinements) produces meat so filled with juice and flavor you can hardly tell the difference between the lean cuts we serve and the more expensive, fattier cuts you might order in a steak house. Our meats are not only healthier, they cost half as much as the food in traditional American-fare restaurants. That means we can price entrees under ten dollars—a magic number if you're out to attract suburban customers—and still recapture some of the margin on lost liquor sales. Sharps, I figured, would meet the public's demand for low-cost, high-quality dining.

What's more, I calculated, slow roasting would meet some of the other imperatives as well. It cuts waste, for example, and, by reducing the variety of raw materials, helps to ensure freshness. Service speed is another plus. With roasts ready to slice for immediate use, we get quicker service and higher customer turnover. Simplicity and efficiency also keep labor costs down. With less total culinary work than standard restaurants, Sharps uses more semi-skilled help.

Best of all, spit roasting makes a great spectacle. I always try to make my restaurants visually interesting, and it's never easy. Grocery stores do better food displays, galleries are better with art, and revolving tower-top restaurants will beat your view every time. So at Sharps, we've got an 8-by-20-foot roasting works right in the middle of the dining room with an ornate smoking oven, lots of polished machinery, and stainless-steel spits turning huge slabs of meat and 60 chickens at a time. It was as close as I could come in Seattle to a front-row seat in Henry VIII's kitchens.

But all of this together was still not enough.

The war and subsequent recession were killing us. After six months, Sharps still wasn't breaking even, and my other restaurants were earning only marginal profits. Operating costs were starting to come out of my own savings. I couldn't close Sharps; doing so would make me immediately liable for the $1 million I had borrowed to open it. And I didn't want to borrow more money— even if the banks would let me have it, which I seriously doubted. Anyway, deep down I still thought the Sharps concept was great. I just needed to cut my overhead and improve my cash flow so I could prove it.

Restructuring and positive cash flow had to be my top priorities. Yet bad publicity about cutbacks would hoist a red flag. I needed a blueprint to reestablish cash flow and adjust strategy while keeping my employees, customers, purveyors, the banks, and the media happy.

CONTEMPLATING MY OWN KREMLIN

It was one of those perfect summer days with an infinite blue sky, wispy clouds, and a cooling breeze. The sun danced on the water, the kids were turning cartwheels on the lawn, and I was brooding about Mikhail Gorbachev. Recent news reports detailing the disintegration of the Soviet Union rang unhappy bells with me. Gorbachev was presiding over the dissolution of his empire; I was presiding over the dissolution of mine. But there was more to it than that. There was a similarity I was missing, a subliminal parallel between Gorbachev's situation and my own that kept tugging at the edge of my awareness.

In all of history, the USSR was the world's largest centralized management system. Down to the last detail, everything was planned at the center, directed from the center, reported to the center. Situation-specific local management was disallowed. Information systems took precious time converting data to a fatuous pap and then filtering it up the bureaucratic ladder. In the end, the system grew so top heavy, expensive, cumbersome, and unresponsive that it simply collapsed.

But what did the fall of Communist Russia have to do

with a Seattle restaurateur? The answer that came to me that lovely summer afternoon was: almost everything.

Several years earlier I had empowered our frontline employees with a program and company credo called WAGS—We Always Guarantee Satisfaction. It gave food servers the authority and power to make immediate amends to customers for slow service, confused orders, overcooked meat, that sort of thing, by giving away food or drinks or even picking up a check.

Now it suddenly occurred to me that I had failed to extend this same kind of power and responsibility to my local managers. WAGS had done wonders to increase repeat business and employee commitment and, by proactively identifying problems before customers even had a chance to complain about them, to help us find and correct the causes of each system failure.

But where food servers had the power to take action on their own initiative, my line managers—bar managers, restaurant managers, kitchen managers, general managers—were still firmly subordinate to corporate headquarters when it came to payroll, menus, marketing, product development, accounting, training, hiring, and general decision making, just about everything except reservations and breathing. We were still operating under an antiquated line-staff system as obsolete as the centralized communist approach. What a revelation. How could I have missed such an obvious connection?

Centralization *breeds* stagnation. Hierarchies *invent* complexity, the enemy of efficiency. Bureaucracy revels in red tape and politics. It was true in the Soviet Union, and it was true at Satisfaction Guaranteed Eateries.

Here was my silver bullet. Like the Soviets, we were overstructured, overmanaged, and overhead overburdened. So, like Gorbachev, I would slash my center and liberate the company. Indeed, I would go him one better. I would transfer virtually all power and responsibility to my line managers and simply eliminate my corporate headquarters. I would fire my whole corporate staff.

It was ingenious, bold, and unconventional. It was also terrifying. But all those salaries were guzzling desperately needed cash.

KILLING CORPORATE

I think business wisdom in its plainest sense might be defined as discovering what *really* works. Once leaders have tried out a lot of personal hypotheses and tested a range of ideas from books and school, wisdom gradually forms to point them toward high return-on-investment strategies and behaviors.

Young organizations are inefficient because they're still learning. But because new companies usually don't have much cash, nascent entrepreneurs compensate for their lack of experience by watching every dollar. The trouble starts when a business begins making money. Resources finally exist for experimentation. The company's principals try all kinds of things. They've read widely and want to road test the management theories they have worked so hard to learn. This is generally a mistake. The company wasted considerably less money when it was brand new and resource poor.

Such, I realized, was the case with me. I could see the seeds of my current problem in an insight I'd had years ago when I was first wrestling with the need to delegate and figured out that the company could no longer afford to have me as the hero in every arena and that I had to get some help. Good advice, but I went overboard. From running a chain of restaurants by myself, making so many decisions and micromanaging so many people that I used to dictate letters and memos even while driving, I had progressed slowly to a corporate headquarters with a staff of 17 people. I had a product development department and a director of special events and 4,000 square feet of office space. Talk about centralization. I had the restaurants reporting to corporate headquarters in ways that would make a commissar feel right at home.

A company like mine can roll along for years with

silly job positions and too much overhead—the result of too much money and too little hardship. But a day of reckoning always comes, and now mine had arrived with a flourish. I was torching 10% of my personal cash assets every month. Two-thirds of all my bank accounts had already burned, so I had to move quickly.

I needed a detailed plan. This was not simply a question of putting the company on a strict diet. I was going to kill our corporate headquarters, and that meant rethinking and restructuring everything we did. It also meant I had to trace the implications of every change all the way to their final outcome.

Moreover, I had to get everything right the first time. Trial and error is a fine way to learn when you have the luxury of time and security. But layoffs make people nervous, and layoffs followed by chaos, indecision, and experimentation make people run for cover. If I was going to hold onto my employees, my bankers, my purveyors, and my customers, I had to make these sweeping changes all at once, without warning, and I had to make the whole thing swing into working order overnight. The experimenting had to take place in my mind and on paper, not in the restaurants.

Procrastination plagued me. How was I going to complete this huge project, keep it confidential, satisfy all stake holders, and do my regular work? Clearly, I would have to concentrate my energies. Reluctantly, I quit the school board and the Young Presidents Organization. I even decided to give up my occasional Sunday skiing. After reorganizing my life I had an open calendar and a clear desk. I had focus.

Procrastination still plagued me. I gave myself stern lectures about the dire circumstances and the need for action and courage. I reminded myself that I had years of experience to draw upon. I told myself that, like most entrepreneurs, I understood my business and knew what to cut without doing fatal damage. I *required* myself to believe in my own accumulated wisdom.

I also began carrying a loose-leaf binder with me wherever I went. It allowed me to record my thoughts instantly and served as a constant reminder of the urgency of my situation. At last, I started work in earnest. For five months I worked on the plan in every spare moment, seven days a week. Nights, weekends, and early mornings were devoted to figuring out how to save my company. And, finally, the answer began to unfold.

FILLING IN THE BLANKS

In the beginning, I had nothing but blank pages, but I began adding tabs like Timing, Cash Flow, Electronics, and Personnel Changes. I even had a section on Personal Changes and Self-Motivation. I'd go to the office at 3:30 most mornings, put on coffee, and set to work. Usually I started with the numbers, so I'd turn to the Pro Forma section of my binder where I was putting together all my projected income and expense figures. I needed to save at least $225,000 off the top—in addition to the 9% I needed to recoup by cutting waste and increasing efficiency—and I took it one piece at a time.

For example, what happened if I eliminated my special events (mostly banquets) director? It saved $25,000, I noted in the pro forma. But it also meant I had to talk to the various restaurants about a banquet process and give each of them systems for booking, planning, billing, and staffing. That too went into the pro forma. It also required some notes in the Electronics, Accounting, and Assets Location sections. But more responsibility for those managers also meant higher rewards and incentives, which sent me to the Salaries section and then back again to the pro forma.

And then of course I had to ask myself if it would work. Handled by my special events director, the banquet process had been very tidy, but if local managers were going to make banquet decisions on the spot, the whole thing would be messy and hard to track. Would it be a good tradeoff? I decide that it would. It would take special events out of my control and put more power and responsibility into the hands of the managers in the restaurants. And messy or not, that was precisely what I wanted to happen.

Eventually I had a 25-category, 300-page notebook. Uppermost in my mind throughout was the elimination of corporate headquarters and its bureaucracy, which weighed us down and threatened to capsize our ship, so I named the emerging plan after my goal for line management: 100% Power and Responsibility, "100% PAR" for short.

We would still need a central office, I reluctantly concluded, because we'd still need a company accountant to do our taxes and write certain corporate checks. And then of course I would need a desk somewhere. But I would call this trimmed central office the "workroom" to underscore the message: headquarters is dead. The buck doesn't pass. *Line management* is this company's engine. We're putting 100% of our power and responsibility at the edge, the cutting edge, and 0% at the center. Once and for all, we're putting an end to the silliness of corporate staffers pontificating to the line managers who actually serve the company's customers every day.

Besides, doesn't the very word "corporate" have a nasty ring to it? And isn't "corporate" traditionally the scapegoat for most company ills, real or imagined?

Killing corporate would eliminate that scapegoat and emphasize line responsibility. It would also force new company procedures to replace at least some of the missing staff. This too would be a positive turn.

Among other things, I was eager to do away with the masking effect of home office accounting. Shipping off invoices to corporate for processing blurs their significance. They come back in effect sanitized, devoid of the emotional content that might otherwise spur line managers to higher efficiency.

The better approach, I decided, would be to do as much accounting as possible at the local level. It would give restaurant managers a far better grasp of how their revenue dollars were used. Analyzing and approving bills in-house would dramatize the fact that all management decisions incur expense.

Moreover, I wanted to put the fear of restaurant-death into my managers. Nothing is so wrenching as not having enough money to pay bills. A CEO can talk himself blue in the face about controlling costs, but a confrontation with insufficient cash to meet expenses is truly memorable. Now unit management would begin to see and feel the tenuous life thread of cash flow.

Beginning again with my pro forma, I pursued these changes through my binder to Accounting, Electronics, Training, Salaries (I'd have to upgrade my restaurant bookkeepers and give them more money), and so back to the pro forma. Every change had implications that branched again and again, every branch had an impact on costs, one way or the other, and I had to capture everything.

To replace the biggest staff functions of all—planning, problem-solving, and decision-making—I began picturing a weekly meeting where managers would discuss company headaches and opportunities. I wanted them to see problems not as mistakes, a word that puts people on the defensive, but as targets for everyone's input. Our fundamental rule would be, "No one is wrong or right, everyone is a resource." Including me. The resource concept would be the foundation of our weekly meetings. I decided to call this new collaborative process "ally management."

While I was convinced that ally management could successfully run the company and replace the corporate staffers, there were still the practical problems of communication and decentralizing accounting. Without central accounts, my managers were going to need their own computers and accounting software. And without the central office as a clearinghouse for information, they were going to need some efficient means of staying in touch with each other and with me.

By asking hundreds of questions and consulting several outside experts, I was able to plan our own small electronic revolution. The workroom would get a state-of-the-art voice-mail system. Computers in the restaurants would be altogether upgraded and reprogrammed for in-house accounting and rapid processing of profit-and-loss calculations, which I wanted to start producing weekly. The computers would be interconnected with modems, eliminating the corporate mainframe (for which I'd paid $150,000 just seven years earlier). All the restaurants and the central workroom would be linked by fax machines. I would carry a mobile phone so I could be reached at any time. And we'd produce our own menus in the workroom with a laser printer and a high-speed, high-volume copier.

This was hardly an impressive list by the standards of a billion-dollar corporation, but for us it was a dazzling array of gadgets. Except they were not gadgets at all, of course, but tools—an important distinction in my mind. Our computer and electronic updating was late, perhaps, but we weren't just buying wizardry for the fun of it. Our needs were specific, the prices were finally right, and the goal was strategic—100% power and responsibility to line managers. I now had a reason to believe that electronic tools for quick communication and greater line control would radically change my business.

I went on tracking the theoretical cash-flow effect of 100% PAR with my evolving pro forma. For weeks on end, I worked at translating my plans into hard numbers. Meticulous review of our profit-and-loss statements—the most intense financial study of my life—helped me see more and more new possibilities. I crunched numbers and redid the pro forma until it made financial sense. I was discovering how to make my business work, and the paper results were encouraging. If I could indeed slice 9% from our operating costs, then those savings along with the cuts in our corporate staff would see me through while I perfected Sharps Fresh Roasting.

MANAGING MORALE

The loose-leaf-binder-and-pro-forma exercise also convinced me that, despite the urgency of the situation, I could not phase in 100% PAR overnight. Hiring experts to upgrade our in-house computers; installing faxes, modems, and phone systems; training line managers in computers and accounting—all of this would take time.

And despite the positive impact of empowerment, ally management, and the electronic revolution, I knew that reconfiguring the company would trouble employees, especially managers. I was afraid they would think that we were going into Chapter 11.

To counter negative thinking, I began working on a variety of big promotions for immediate activity and cash-flow impact. Since promotional money was something we didn't have, I had to find it. I wrote dozens of 25-page presentations that included detailed descriptions of possible events, scrupulous explanations of expected product or publicity benefits, and itemized budgets. Then I hit the streets, presenting my proposals to potential sponsors. The process was exhausting, but one in ten did agree to sponsor a program. I wound up with a glassware giveaway promoted by a soft drink company through a radio station, parasail sky races for the Special Olympics that started at one of my restaurants and ended at another, reggae bands celebrating a new beer, comedy nights and rock-and-roll concerts for the benefit of the Northwest Homeless Fund. The restaurants would be busy and so would the managers. That ought to undercut any fear of Chapter 11.

Another main concern was our suppliers. Layoffs

make purveyors extremely anxious, and just one of them going COD would launch a domino effect. If my suppliers began insisting on cash, that would scare the banks. And if word then got around that the business was in trouble, that in turn could frighten off customers, sealing our fate with purveyors and sending our employees out looking for new jobs. It was the restaurant chain that Jack built. Unless I could keep everyone comfortable and at ease through a major downsizing and what some might perceive as a foolhardy restructuring, nothing could prevent the chain reaction that would finish me *off*. I had done all I could in terms of cash flow and customer activity. The final piece of preparation was the plan itself, carefully reasoned, thoroughly documented, and totally reassuring—or so I hoped.

I began writing a formal package to distribute on what I had come to think of as Just-Do-It Day, when I would reveal 100% PAR to everyone at once in 60 pages of numbers, explanations, and projections. I wrote five different presentations for the various interested parties: managers, employees, purveyors, bankers, and the press. I included several pages about coming strategies and events. I described plans for new menus, a new smart-drink non-alcoholic beverage line we were introducing to bolster bar sales, a summer Dungeness crab festival, a new bar game, and the introduction of Family Sundays to spark what is traditionally our slowest day. I explained how the company's restructuring would enhance cash flow, open the door for new growth, and allow further development of the Sharps concept. The overall picture was full of good news and hopeful signs, which I tried hard to communicate. I was scared to death.

Just-Do-It Day was all over in eight hours. I bounded out of bed and delivered the 200 packets I had stacked on my office desk. Next I drove to every restaurant and explained the changes to my managers, posting copies of the plan for everyone else. I mailed descriptions of 100%

PAR to banks, purveyors, and the press. I spoke to each member of my corporate staff in person, trying to soften the blow with severance pay and a full explanation of my thinking. Some of them tried to bargain, some were angry, and a few even congratulated me and said I should have done it all months earlier. In one case, I found *myself* in tears.

Altogether, I laid off the corporate president; the operations manager; the directors of marketing, training, product development, and special events; three of six accountants; three secretaries; and, in the restaurants, five bar managers. When the day was over, the center of my company was gone and with it my own support system, the people who ran my errands and kept me company. The place felt like a morgue.

ALLIES AND BENEFITS

On the other hand, my line managers had new responsibilities and powers, new salary packages, and new bonus incentives based on a percentage of cash flow. The plan paid additional dividends quickly.

The pared-down version that went to the media led one newspaper to do an upbeat story for the front page of its business section.

The thoroughness of the package I sent my bankers helped me persuade them to give us a 90-day principal reprieve during our slowest months.

The new, lean workroom allowed us to move from 4,000 square feet to 800, with an 80% reduction in rent. It now houses our central filing, prints menus, writes payroll checks, does taxes, and gets almost as much done as before at about one-third the cost. I was part of the improvements too: my new office overlooks an alley.

We moved quickly ahead with the electronic revolution—voice mail, carry phones, modems, sophisticated PCs—and started using all of it. (I made half of each restaurant manager's salary increase contingent on mastering the new PCs and the accounting packages that we got to go with them.)

The crowning touch was ally management, which has worked better and produced more benefits than I had dared to hope. Its first challenge was cost control, a problem we still had to solve or lose the business. At the first session of the ally management meeting—the general managers of the five restaurants and I meet every Thursday from ten to four—I simply opened the topic of cost control and sat back with pen and paper to take notes. It was an uncomfortable test for me. Costs really had me worried, so I desperately wanted to take charge as I always had in the past and get things moving quickly. I had to force myself to be patient. The others began trading ideas, and I wrote them down. The meeting became a forum for self-instruction.

In the course of the next couple of hours, we came up with several dozen simple ideas for limiting costs—everything from holding a hellfire stop-theft meeting with employees to putting the hand-held liquor dispenser in a container overnight to see if it was leaking. Over the weeks that followed, the list grew to 30 pages, and we now review and alter our cost control sheets once a week. There is always some addition or improvement.

As managers started coming up to speed on their new accounting software, a whole new set of ideas began to surface. Responsibility for his own labor costs brought home to one manager the inefficiency of using a $12-an-hour cook to peel potatoes. To discourage waste and theft, another began teaching his employees that the typical restaurant profit margin is 4%, not the 25% many of them assumed. Someone else noticed that buying supplies in small amounts increased their perceived value and encouraged conservation.

I was astonished at how rapidly we brought costs into line. In less than a year, we achieved the 9% total savings

I had targeted in the pro forma. (Savings at individual restaurants have ranged from 5% to 12%.)

Yet soon I would like to tear up these commendable cost control sheets and start over. If that seems an odd thing to do, consider the benefits of having to recreate all that expertise. Information goes stale. It takes new insights to hold one's own attention.

Ally management's second challenge was product development. Here too, the necessity to innovate educates managers better than corporate force-feeding.

The most pressing item on the product development agenda was the ailing apple of my eye, Sharps Fresh Roasting. Clearly it needed something more to surprise and delight customers, but I still loved its ingenious new concept. Moreover, I had personally guaranteed its million dollar debt.

We started our comeback using ally management for recipe refinement. We invented 40 new items based on our five roasts of lamb, beef, pork, chicken, and turkey: Bubba's Enthusiastic Jerk Chicken, Satay Pork, Grandma's Old Fashioned Chicken Dinner, No Sin Turkey (7 of calories from fat), Jack Daniel's Old No. 7 BBQ Beef, and Rio River Red Pork, to name a few.

We also attacked the decor. We are a stone's throw from SeaTac International Airport, so someone came up with the idea of calling the bar The Bent Prop. We combed rural airports and airplane graveyards all over the Northwest and came up with two hundred airplane propellers that had been bent in bad landings. We hung them from the ceiling.

We worked hard getting restaurant critics interested. One writer did two articles about our recipes. In all, Sharps was reviewed and highly recommended five times. Revenues began increasing month by month. A year later, Sharps Fresh Roasting is the gold mine I always believed it could be, and I've starting selling franchises. My landlord—the man who originally insisted Sharps was a bad idea—bought two.

BELIEVING OUR OWN STORY

It was ally management that rescued the fresh roasting concept, and I think it can save us from a national epidemic of restaurant deaths. It was also ally management that solved the cost problem I'd struggled with in vain for 20 years. I'd tried bonuses, praise, threats, outside consultants, classes, tapes, videos, and seminars. Nothing had worked very well or for very long. Now, without Herculean effort, we've achieved the best cost control results we've ever had. From 1991 to 1992, cash flow went from negative to positive for a 200% turnaround, and I've recouped more than half the cash lost during our negative cash flow period. What happened? How did all this come about? Here's my analysis.

Information is a hot topic—organizing it, processing it, storing it, accessing it. But these activities, in my estimation, may not be what matters most. In the marketplace, information's role is to stimulate action. You might even say that knowledge not acted upon is worthless. With this in mind, I maintain that information's most important feature is believability. If I don't believe it, I won't act on it.

This is the strength of 100% PAR and ally management. Because we create all our information ourselves from scratch, we believe it. Because we believe it, we're ready to act on it, much more ready than we would be to act on the advice of a business school professor, however distinguished, or, for that matter, on a directive from the CEO. And action, in my opinion, is the cardinal rule of management.

The crux of ally management is both subtle and obvious. It provides a forum for line managers and allows them to participate in shaping company destiny. It gives them incentives very much like the owner's—a percentage of cash flow, defined as net profit with depreciation added back in and principal payments against debt subtracted out. It helps them act.

I see quicker company change, more powerful motivation, and a much more confident and hopeful culture. We have achieved the best cost control numbers in the history of the company. We have reduced the time it takes to produce end-of-the-month financial statements from ten days to three. We have done away with our bureaucracy and turned business around in a down market. In the process, we have reestablished a basic capitalist principle: making money.

All this because our managers are managing themselves.

*The drastic reorganization described in **Timothy W. Firnstahl**'s article turned his restaurants around and put his company solidly in the black. As Firnstahl explains it, the need to cut the organization down to its bare bones required him to focus on the essence of the business—the roaster concept. He closed one of his five restaurants, sold one, converted two to fresh roasting, sold two franchises, and changed the company name from Satisfaction Guaranteed Eateries to Grand Roasters Ltd. The original restaurant, now called Sharp's Roaster and Alehouse, which posted a 1993–1994 loss of $50,000, returned a profit of some $150,000 in 1994–1995. As a whole, the company's profits have doubled.*

Tim Firnstahl is now working on a diet book for people over 40, based on the appealing idea that people need to get enough to eat, but without much fat or an awful lot of calories. The recipes range from chile rellenos to Florentine vegetable stew and provide an abundance of what Firnstahl calls "amplifiers" (cabbage, turnips, potatoes, broccoli) combined with flavoring elements—usually meat stocks that are virtually fat and calorie free.

4

Managing without Managers

RICARDO SEMLER

IN BRAZIL, WHERE paternalism and the family business
fiefdom still flourish, I am president of a manufacturing
company that treats its 800 employees like responsible
adults. Most of them—including factory workers—set
their own working hours. All have access to the company books. The vast majority vote on many important
corporate decisions. Everyone gets paid by the month,
regardless of job description, and more than 150 of our
management people set their own salaries and bonuses.

This may sound like an unconventional way to run a
business, but it seems to work. Close to financial disaster
in 1980, Semco is now one of Brazil's fastest growing
companies, with a profit margin in 1988 of 10% on sales
of $37 million. Our five factories produce a range of
sophisticated products, including marine pumps, digital
scanners, commercial dishwashers, truck filters, and mix-
ing equipment for everything from bubble gum to rocket
fuel. Our customers include Alcoa, Saab, and General
Motors. We've built a number of cookie factories for
Nabisco, Nestlé, and United Biscuits. Our multinational

competitors include AMF, Worthington Industries, Mitsubishi Heavy Industries, and Carrier.

Management associations, labor unions, and the press have repeatedly named us the best company in Brazil to work for. In fact, we no longer advertise jobs. Word of mouth generates up to 300 applications for every available position. The top five managers—we call them counselors—include a former human resources director of Ford Brazil, a 15-year veteran Chrysler executive, and a man who left his job as president of a larger company to come to Semco.

When I joined the company in 1980, 27 years after my father founded it, Semco had about 100 employees, manufactured hydraulic pumps for ships, generated about $4 million in revenues, and teetered on the brink of catastrophe. All through 1981 and 1982, we ran from bank to bank looking for loans, and we fought persistent, well-founded rumors that the company was in danger of going under. We often stayed through the night reading files and searching the desk drawers of venerable executives for clues about contracts long since privately made and privately forgotten.

Most managers and outside board members agreed on two immediate needs: to professionalize and to diversify. In fact, both of these measures had been discussed for years but had never progressed beyond wishful thinking.

For two years, holding on by our fingertips, we sought licenses to manufacture other companies' products in Brazil. We traveled constantly. I remember one day being in Oslo for breakfast, New York for lunch, Cincinnati for dinner, and San Francisco for the night. The obstacles were great. Our company lacked an international reputation—and so did our country. Brazil's political eccentricities and draconian business regulations scared many companies away.

Still, good luck and a relentless program of beating the corporate bushes on four continents finally paid off. By

1982, we had signed seven license agreements. Our marine division—once the entire company—was now down to 60% of total sales. Moreover, the managers and directors were all professionals with no connection to the family.

With Semco back on its feet, we entered an acquisitions phase that cost millions of dollars in expenditures and millions more in losses over the next two or three years. All this growth was financed by banks at interest rates that were generally 30% above the rate of inflation, which ranged from 40% to 900% annually. There was no long-term money in Brazil at that time, so all those loans had maximum terms of 90 days. We didn't get one cent in government financing or from incentive agencies either, and we never paid out a dime in graft or bribes.

How did we do it and survive? Hard work, of course. And good luck—fundamental to all business success. But most important, I think, were the drastic changes we made in our concept of management. Without those changes, not even hard work and good luck could have pulled us through. (See "Ricardo Semler's Guide to Stress Management.")

Semco has three fundamental values on which we base some 30 management programs. These values—democracy, profit sharing, and information—work in a complicated circle, each dependent on the other two. If we eliminated one, the others would be meaningless. Our corporate structure, employee freedoms, union relations, factory size limitations—all are products of our commitment to these principles.

It's never easy to transplant management programs from one company to another. In South America, it's axiomatic that our structure and style cannot be duplicated. Semco is either too small, too big, too far away, too young, too old, or too obnoxious.

We may also be too specialized. We do cellular manufacturing of technologically sophisticated products, and

There are two things all managers have in common—the 24-hour day and the annoying need to sleep. Without the sleeping, 24 hours might be enough. With it, there is no way to get everything done. After years of trying to vanquish demon sleep and the temptation to relax, I tried an approach suggested by my doctor, who put it this way: "Slow down or kiss yourself good-bye."

Struck by this imagery, I learned to manage my time and cut my work load to less than 24 hours. The first step is to overcome five myths:

1. *Results are proportional to efforts.* The Brazilian flag expresses this myth in a slightly different form. "Order and Progress," it says. Of course, it ought to say, "Order *or* Progress," since the two never go together.

2. *Quantity of work is more important than quality.* Psychologically, this myth may hold water. The executive who puts in lots of hours can always say, "Well, they didn't promote me, but you can see how unfair that is. Everyone knows I get here at 8 A.M. and that my own children can't see me without an appointment."

3. *The present restructuring requires longer working hours temporarily.* We think of ourselves as corks on a mountain stream headed for Lake Placid. But the lake ahead is Loch Ness. The present, temporary emergency is actually permanent. Stop being a cork.

4. *No one else can do it right.* The truth is, you *are* replaceable, as everyone will discover within a week of your funeral.

5. *This problem is urgent.* Come on. The real difference between "important" and "urgent" is the difference between thoughtfulness and panic.

Those are the myths. The second step is to master my eight cures:

1. Set an hour to leave the office and obey it blindly. If you normally go home at 7:00, start leaving at 6:00. If you take work home on weekends, give yourself a month or two to put a stop to this pernicious practice.

2. Take half a day, maybe even an entire Saturday, to rummage through that mountain of paper in your office and put it in three piles.

Pile A: Priority items that require your personal attention and represent matters of indisputable importance. If you put more than four or five documents in this category and are not currently the president of your country, start over.

Pile B: Items that need your personal attention, but not right away. This pile is very tempting; everything fits. But don't fall into the trap. Load this stuff on your subordinates, using the 70% test to help you do it. Ask yourself: Is there someone on my staff who can do this task at least 70% as well as I can? Yes? Then farm it out. Whether or not your subordinates are overworked should not weigh in your decision. Remember, control of your time is an exercise in selfishness.

Pile C: Items that fall under the dubious rubric "a good idea to look at." One of the most egregious executive fallacies is that you have to read a little of everything in order to stay well-informed. If you limit the number of newspapers, magazines, and internal communications that you read regularly, you'll have more time to do what's important—like think. And remember to keep your reading timely; information is a perishable commodity.

3. In dealing with Pile A, always start with the most difficult or the most time-consuming. It also helps to have a folder for the things that *must* be done before you go home that day and to make a list of the things that simply cannot go undone for more than a few days or a week. Everything else is just everything else.

4. Buy another wastepaper basket. I know you already have one. But if you invited me to go through that pile of papers on your desk, I could fill both in a trice. To help you decide what to toss and what to save, ask yourself the question asked by the legendary Alfred P. Sloan, Jr.: "What is the worst that

can happen if I throw this out?" If you don't tremble, sweat, or grow faint when you think of the consequences, toss it.

This second wastebasket is a critical investment, even though you'll never be able to fill both on a regular basis. Keep it anyway. It has a symbolic value. It will babysit your in-basket and act like a governess every time you wonder why you bought it.

5. Ask yourself Sloan's question about every lunch and meeting invitation. Don't be timid. And practice these three RSVPs:

"Thanks, but I just can't fit it in."

"I can't go, but I think X can." (If you think someone should.)

"I'm sorry I can't make it, but do let me know what happened."

Transform meetings into telephone calls or quick conversations in the hall. When you hold a meeting in your office, sit on the edge of your desk, or when you want to end the discussion, stand up from behind your desk and say "OK, then, that's settled." These tricks are rude but almost foolproof.

6. Give yourself time to think. Spend half a day every week away from your office. Take your work home, or try working somewhere else—a conference room in another office, a public library, an airport waiting room—any place you can concentrate, and the farther away

from your office the better. The point is, a fresh environment can do wonders for productivity. Just make sure you bring along a healthy dose of discipline, especially if you're working at home.

7. About the telephone, my practical but subversive advice is: Don't return calls. Or rather, return calls only to people you want to talk to. The others will call back. Better yet, they'll write, and you can spend ten seconds with their letter and then give it to the governess.

Two ancillary bits of phone advice: Ask your assistants to take detailed messages. Ask them always to say you cannot take the call at the moment. (Depending on who it is, your assistants can always undertake to see if you can't be interrupted.)

8. Close your door. Oh, I know you have an open-door policy, but don't be so literal.

---

we work at the high end on quality and price. So our critics may be right. Perhaps nothing we've done can be a blueprint for anyone else. Still, in an industrial world whose methods show obvious signs of exhaustion, the merit of sharing experience is to encourage experiment and to plant the seeds of conceptual change. So what the hell.

PARTICIPATORY HOT AIR

The first of Semco's three values is democracy, or employee involvement. Clearly, workers who control their working conditions are going to be happier than workers who don't. Just as clearly, there is no contest between the company that buys the grudging compliance of its work force and the company that enjoys the enterprising participation of its employees.

But about 90% of the time, participatory management is just hot air. Not that intentions aren't good. It's just that implementing employee involvement is so complex, so difficult, and, not uncommonly, so frustrating that it is easier to talk about than to do.

We found four big obstacles to effective participatory management: size, hierarchy, lack of motivation, and ignorance. In an immense production unit, people feel tiny, nameless, and incapable of exerting influence on the way work is done or on the final profit made. This sense of helplessness is underlined by managers who, jealous of their power and prerogatives, refuse to let subordinates make any decisions for themselves—sometimes even about going to the bathroom. But even if size and hierarchy can be overcome, why should workers *care* about productivity and company profits? Moreover, even if you can get them to care, how can they tell when they're doing the right thing?

As Antony Jay pointed out back in the 1950s in *Corporation Man*, human beings weren't designed to work in big groups. Until recently, our ancestors were hunters and gatherers. For more than five million years, they refined their ability to work in groups of no more than about a dozen people. Then along comes the industrial revolution, and suddenly workers are trying to function efficiently in factories that employ hundreds and even thousands. Organizing those hundreds into teams of about ten members each may help some, but there's still a limit to how many small teams can work well together. At Semco, we've found the most effective production unit to consist of about 150 people. The exact number is open to argument, but it's clear that several thousand people in one facility makes individual involvement an illusion.

When we made the decision to keep our units small, we immediately focused on one facility that had more than 300 people. The unit manufactured commercial food-service equipment—slicers, scales, meat grinders, mixers—and used an MRP II system hooked up to an IBM mainframe with dozens of terminals all over the plant. Paperwork often took two days to make its way from one end of the factory to the other. Excess inventories, late delivery, and quality problems were common. We had tried various worker participation programs, quality circles, kanban systems, and motivation schemes, all of which got off to great starts but lost their momentum within months. The whole thing was just too damn big and complex; there were too many managers in too many layers holding too many meetings. So we decided to break up the facility into three separate plants.

To begin with, we kept all three in the same building but separated everything we could—entrances, receiving docks, inventories, telephones, as well as certain auxiliary functions like personnel, management information systems, and internal controls. We also scrapped the mainframe in favor of three independent, PC-based systems.

The first effect of the breakup was a rise in costs due to duplication of effort and a loss in economies of scale. Unfortunately, balance sheets chalk up items like these as liabilities, all with dollar figures attached, and there's nothing at first to list on the asset side but airy stuff like "heightened involvement" and "a sense of belonging." Yet the longer term results exceeded our expectations.

Within a year, sales doubled; inventories fell from 136 days to 46; we unveiled eight new products that had been stalled in R&D for two years; and overall quality improved to the point that a one-third rejection rate on federally inspected scales dropped to less than 1%. Increased productivity let us reduce the work force by 32% through attrition and retirement incentives.

I don't claim that size reduction alone accomplished all this, just that size reduction is essential for putting employees in touch with one another so they can coordinate their work. The kind of distance we want to eliminate comes from having too many people in one place, but it also comes from having a pyramidal hierarchy.

PYRAMIDS AND CIRCLES

The organizational pyramid is the cause of much corporate evil, because the tip is too far from the base.

Pyramids emphasize power, promote insecurity, distort communications, hobble interaction, and make it very difficult for the people who plan and the people who execute to move in the same direction. So Semco designed an organizational *circle*. Its greatest advantage is to reduce management levels to three—one corporate level and two operating levels at the manufacturing units.

It consists of three concentric circles. One tiny, central circle contains the five people who integrate the company's movements. These are the counselors I mentioned before. I'm one of them, and except for a couple of legal documents that call me president, counselor is the only title I use. A second, larger circle contains the heads of the eight divisions—we call them partners. Finally, a third, huge circle holds all the other employees. Most of them are the people we call associates; they do the research, design, sales, and manufacturing work and have no one reporting to them on a regular basis. But some of them are the permanent and temporary team and task leaders we call coordinators. Counselors, partners, coordinators, and associates. Four titles. Three management layers.

The linchpins of the system are the coordinators, a group that includes everyone formerly called foreman, supervisor, manager, head, or chief. The only people who report to coordinators are associates. No coordinator reports to another coordinator—that feature of the system is what ensures the reduction in management layers.

Like anyone else, we value leadership, but it's not the only thing we value. In marine pumps, for example, we have an applications engineer who can look at the layout of a ship and then focus on one particular pump and say, "That pump will fail if you take this thing north of the Arctic Circle." He makes a lot more money than the person who manages his unit. We can change the manager, but this guy knows what kind of pump will work in the Arctic, and that's worth more. Associates often make higher salaries than coordinators and partners, and they can increase their status and compensation without entering the "management" line.

Managers and the status and money they enjoy—in a word, hierarchy—are the single biggest obstacle to participatory management. We had to get the managers out of the way of democratic decision making, and our circular system does that pretty well.

But we go further. We don't hire or promote people until they've been interviewed and accepted by all their future subordinates. Twice a year, subordinates evaluate managers. Also twice a year, everyone in the company anonymously fills out a questionnaire about company credibility and top management competence. Among other things, we ask our employees what it would take to make them quit or go on strike.

We insist on making important decisions collegially, and certain decisions are made by a companywide vote. Several years ago, for example, we needed a bigger plant for our marine division, which makes pumps, compressors, and ship propellers. Real estate agents looked for months and found nothing. So we asked the employees themselves to help, and over the first weekend they found three factories for sale, all of them nearby. We closed up shop for a day, piled everyone into buses, and drove out to inspect the three buildings. Then the workers voted—and they chose a plant the counselors didn't really want. It was an interesting situation—one that tested our commitment to participatory management.

The building stands across the street from a Caterpillar plant that's one of the most frequently struck factories in Brazil. With two tough unions of our own, we weren't looking forward to front-row seats for every labor dispute that came along. But we accepted the employees' decision, because we believe that in the long run, letting people participate in the decisions that affect their lives will have a positive effect on employee motivation and morale. (For an example, see "Ricardo Semler's Guide to Compensation.")

We bought the building and moved in. The workers designed the layout for a flexible manufacturing system, and they hired one of Brazil's foremost artists to paint the whole thing, inside and out, including the machinery. That plant really belongs to its employees. I feel like a guest every time I walk in.

I don't mind. The division's productivity, in dollars per year per employee, has jumped from $14,200 in 1984—the year we moved—to $37,500 in 1988, and for 1989 the goal is $50,000. Over the same period, market share went from 54% to 62%.

Employees also outvoted me on the acquisition of a company that I'm still sure we should have bought. But they felt we weren't ready to digest it, and I lost the vote. In a case like that, the credibility of our management system is at stake. Employee involvement must be real, even when it makes management uneasy. Anyway, what is the future of an acquisition if the people who have to operate it don't believe it's workable?

HIRING ADULTS

We have other ways of combating hierarchy too. Most of our programs are based on the notion of giving employees control over their own lives. In a word, we hire adults, and then we treat them like adults.

Think about that. Outside the factory, workers are men and women who elect governments, serve in the army, lead community projects, raise and educate families, and make decisions every day about the future. Friends solicit their advice. Salespeople court them. Children and grandchildren look up to them for their wisdom and experience. But the moment they walk into the factory, the company transforms them into adolescents. They have to wear badges and name tags, arrive at a certain time, stand in line to punch the clock or eat

RICARDO SEMLER'S GUIDE TO COMPENSATION

Employers began hiring workers by the hour during the industrial revolution. Their reasons were simple and rapacious. Say you ran out of cotton thread at 11:30 in the morning. If you paid people by the hour, you could stop the looms, send everyone home, and pay only for hours actually worked.

You couldn't do such a thing today. The law probably wouldn't let you. The unions certainly wouldn't let you. Your own self-interest would argue strongly against it. Yet the system lives on. The distinction between wage-earning workers and salaried employees is alive but not well, nearly universal but perfectly silly. The new clerk who lives at home and doesn't know how to boil an egg starts on a monthly salary, but the chief lathe operator who's been with the company 38 years and is a master sergeant in the army reserve still gets paid by the hour.

At Semco, we eliminated Frederick Winslow Taylor's segmentation and specialization of work. We ended the wage analyst's hundred years of solitude. We did away with hourly pay and now give everyone a monthly salary. We set the salaries like this:

A lot of our people belong to unions, and they negotiate their salaries collectively. Everyone else's salary involves an element of self-determination. Once or twice a year, we order salary market surveys and pass them out. We say to people, "Figure out where you stand on this thing. You know what you do; you know what everyone else in the company makes; you know what your friends in other companies make; you know what you need; you know what's fair. Come back on Monday and tell us what to pay you."

When people ask for too little, we give it to them. By and by, they figure it out and ask for more. When they ask for too much, we give that to them too—at least for the first year. Then, if we don't feel they're worth the money we sit down with them and say, "Look, you make x amount of money, and we don't think you're making x amount of contribution. So either we find something else for you to do, or we don't have a job for you anymore."' But with half a dozen exceptions, our people have always named salaries we could live with.

We do a similar thing with titles. Counselors are counselors, and partners are partners; these titles are always the same. But with coordinators, it's not quite so easy. Job titles still mean too much to many people. So we tell coordinators to make up their own titles. They know what signals they need to send inside and outside the company. If they want "Procurement Manager," that's fine. And if they want "Grand Panjandrum of Imperial Supplies," that's fine too.

their lunch, get permission to go to the bathroom, give lengthy explanations every time they're five minutes late, and follow instructions without asking a lot of questions.

One of my first moves when I took control of Semco was to abolish norms, manuals, rules, and regulations. Everyone knows you can't run a large organization without regulations, but everyone also knows that most regulations are poppycock. They rarely solve problems. On the contrary, there is usually some obscure corner of the rule book that justifies the worst silliness people can think up. Common sense is a riskier tactic because it requires personal responsibility.

It's also true that common sense requires just a touch of civil disobedience every time someone calls attention to something that's not working. We had to free the Thoreaus and the Tom Paines in the factory and come to terms with that fact that civil disobedience was not an early sign of revolution but a clear indication of common sense at work.

So we replaced all the nitpicking regulations with the rule of common sense and put our employees in the demanding position of using their own judgment.

We have no dress code, for example. The idea that personal appearance is important in a job—any job—is baloney. We've all heard that salespeople, receptionists, and service reps are the company's calling cards, but in fact how utterly silly that is. A company that needs business suits to prove its seriousness probably lacks more meaningful proof. And what customer has ever canceled an order because the receptionist was wearing jeans instead of a dress? Women and men look best when they feel good. IBM is not a great company because its salespeople dress to the special standard that Thomas Watson set. It's a great company that also happens to have this quirk.

We also scrapped the complex company rules about travel expenses—what sorts of accommodations people were entitled to, whether we'd pay for a theater ticket, whether a free call home meant five minutes or ten. We used to spend a lot of time discussing stuff like that. Now we base everything on common sense. Some people stay in four-star hotels and some live like spartans. Some people spend $200 a day while others get by on $125. Or so I suppose. No one checks expenses, so there is no way of knowing. The point is, we don't care. If we can't trust people with our money and their judgment, we sure as hell shouldn't be sending them overseas to do business in our name.

We have done away with security searches, storeroom padlocks, and audits of the petty-cash accounts of veteran employees. Not that we wouldn't prosecute a genuinely criminal violation of our trust. We just refuse to humiliate 97% of the work force to get our hands on the occasional thief or two-bit embezzler.

We encourage—we practically insist on—job rotation every two to five years to prevent boredom. We try hard to provide job security, and for people over 50 or who've been with the company for more than three years, dismissal procedures are extra complicated.

On the more experimental side, we have a program for entry-level management trainees called "Lost in Space," whereby we hire a couple of people every year who have no job description at all. A "godfather" looks after them, and for one year they can do anything they like, as long as they try at least 12 different areas or units.

By the same logic that governs our other employee programs, we have also eliminated time clocks. People come and go according to their own schedules—even on the factory floor. I admit this idea is hard to swallow; most manufacturers are not ready for factory-floor flextime. But our reasoning was simple.

First, we use cellular manufacturing systems. At our food-processing equipment plant, for example, one cell makes only slicers, another makes scales, another makes mixers, and so forth. Each cell is self-contained, so products—and their problems—are segregated from each other.

Second, we assumed that all our employees were trustworthy adults. We couldn't believe they would come to work day after day and sit on their hands because no one else was there. Pretty soon, we figured, they would start coordinating their work hours with their coworkers.

And that's exactly what happened, only more so. For example, one man wanted to start at 7 A.M., but because the forklift operator didn't come until 8, he couldn't get his parts. So a general discussion arose, and the upshot was that now everyone knows how to operate a forklift. In fact, most people can now do several jobs. The union has never objected because the initiative came from the workers themselves. It was their idea.

Moreover, the people on the factory floor set the schedule, and if they say that this month they will build 48 commercial dishwashers, then we can go play tennis, because 48 is what they'll build.

In one case, one group decided to make 220 meat slicers. By the end of the month, it had finished the slicers as scheduled—except that even after repeated phone calls, the supplier still hadn't produced the motors. So two employees drove over and talked to the supplier and managed to get delivery at the end of that day, the 31st. Then they stayed all night, the whole work force, and finished the lot at 4:45 the next morning.

When we introduced flexible hours, we decided to hold regular follow-up meetings to track problems and decide how to deal with abuses and production interruptions. That was years ago, and we haven't yet held the first meeting.

HUNTING THE WOOLLY MAMMOTH

What makes our people behave this way? As Antony Jay points out, corporate man is a very recent animal. At

Semco, we try to respect the hunter that dominated the first 99.9% of the history of our species. If you had to kill a mammoth or do without supper, there was no time to draw up an organization chart, assign tasks, or delegate authority. Basically, the person who saw the mammoth from farthest away was the Official Sighter, the one who ran fastest was the Head Runner, whoever threw the most accurate spear was the Grand Marksman, and the person all others respected most and listened to was the Chief. That's all there was to it. Distributing little charts to produce an appearance of order would have been a waste of time. It still is.

What I'm saying is, put ten people together, don't appoint a leader, and you can be sure that one will emerge. So will a sighter, a runner, and whatever else the group needs. We form the groups, but they find their own leaders. That's not a lack of structure, that's just a lack of structure imposed from above.

But getting back to that mammoth, why was it that all the members of the group were so eager to do their share of the work—sighting, running, spearing, chiefing—and to stand aside when someone else could do it better? Because they all got to eat the thing once it was killed and cooked. What mattered was results, not status.

Corporate profit is today's mammoth meat. And though there is a widespread view that profit sharing is some kind of socialist infection, it seems to me that few motivational tools are more capitalist. Everyone agrees that profits should belong to those who risk their capital, that entrepreneurial behavior deserves reward, that the creation of wealth should enrich the creator. Well, depending on how you define capital and risk, all these truisms can apply as much to workers as to shareholders.

Still, many profit-sharing programs are failures, and we think we know why. Profit sharing won't motivate employees if they see it as just another management gimmick, if the company makes it difficult for them to see how their own work is related to profits and to understand how those profits are divided.

In Semco's case, each division has a separate profit-sharing program. Twice a year, we calculate 23% of after-tax profit on each division income statement and give a check to three employees who've been elected by the workers in their division. These three invest the money until the unit can meet and decide—by simple majority vote—what they want to do with it. In most units, that's turned out to be an equal distribution. If a unit has 150 workers, the total is divided by 150 and handed out. It's that simple. The guy who sweeps the floor gets just as much as the division partner.

One division chose to use the money as a fund to lend out for housing construction. It was a pretty close vote, and the workers may change their minds next year. In the meantime, some of them have already received loans and have begun to build themselves houses. In any case, the employees do what they want with the money. The counselors stay out of it.

Semco's experience has convinced me that profit sharing has an excellent chance of working when it crowns a broad program of employee participation, when the profit-sharing criteria are so clear and simple that the least gifted employee can understand them, and, perhaps most important, when employees have monthly access to the company's vital statistics—costs, overhead, sales, payroll, taxes, profits.

TRANSPARENCY

Lots of things contribute to a successful profit-sharing program: low employee turnover, competitive pay, absence of paternalism, refusal to give consolation prizes when profits are down, frequent (quarterly or semiannual) profit distribution, and plenty of opportunity for employees to question the management decisions that affect future profits. But nothing matters more than those vital statistics—short, frank, frequent reports on how the company is doing. Complete transparency. No hocus-pocus, no hanky-panky, no simplifications.

On the contrary, all Semco employees attend classes to learn how to read and understand the numbers, and it's one of their unions that teaches the course. Every month, each employee gets a balance sheet, a profit-and-loss analysis, and a cash-flow statement for his or her division. The reports contain about 70 line items (more, incidentally, than we use to run the company, but we don't want anyone to think we're withholding information).

Many of our executives were alarmed by the decision to share monthly financial results with all employees. They were afraid workers would want to know everything, like how much we pay executives. When we held the first large meeting to discuss these financial reports with the factory committees and the leaders of the metalworkers' union, the first question we got was, "How much do division managers make?" We told them. They gasped. Ever since, the factory workers have called them "maharaja."

But so what? If executives are embarrassed by their salaries, that probably means they aren't earning them. Confidential payrolls are for those who cannot look themselves in the mirror and say with conviction, "I live in a capitalist system that remunerates on a geometric scale. I spent years in school, I have years of experience, I am capable and dedicated and intelligent. I deserve what I get."

I believe that the courage to show the real numbers will always have positive consequences over the long term. On the other hand, we can show only the numbers we bother to put together, and there aren't as many as there used to be. In my view, only the big numbers matter. But Semco's accounting people keep telling me that since the only way to get the big numbers is to add up the small ones, producing a budget or report that includes every tiny detail would require no extra effort. This is an expensive fallacy, and a difficult one to eradicate.

A few years ago, the U.S. president of Allis-Chalmers paid Semco a visit. At the end of his factory tour, he leafed through our monthly reports and budgets. At that time, we had our numbers ready on the fifth working day of every month in super-organized folders, and were those numbers comprehensive! On page 67, chart 112.6, for example, you could see how much coffee the workers in Light Manufacturing III had consumed the month before. The man said he was surprised to find such efficiency in a Brazilian company. In fact, he was so impressed that he asked his Brazilian subsidiary, an organization many times our size, to install a similar system there.

For months, we strolled around like peacocks, telling anyone who cared to listen that our budget system was state-of-the-art and that the president of a Big American Company had ordered his people to copy it. But soon we began to realize two things. First, our expenses were always too high, and they never came down because the accounting department was full of overpaid clerks who did nothing but compile them. Second, there were so damn many numbers inside the folder that almost none of our managers read them. In fact, we knew less about the company then, with all that information, than we do now without it.

Today we have a simple accounting system providing limited but relevant information that we can grasp and act on quickly. We pared 400 cost centers down to 50. We beheaded hundreds of classifications and dozens of accounting lines. Finally, we can see the company through the haze.

(As for Allis-Chalmers, I don't know whether it ever adopted our old system in all its terrible completeness, but I hope not. A few years later, it began to suffer severe financial difficulties and eventually lost so much market share and money that it was broken up and sold. I'd hate to think it was our fault.).

In preparing budgets, we believe that the flexibility to change the budget continually is much more important than the detailed consistency of the initial numbers. We also believe in the importance of comparing expectations with results. Naturally, we compare monthly reports with the budget. But we go one step further. At month's end, the coordinators in each area make guesses about unit receipts, profit margins, and expenses. When the official numbers come out a few days later, top managers compare them with the guesses to judge how well the coordinators understand their areas.

What matters in budgets as well as in reports is that the numbers be few and important and that people treat them with something approaching passion. The three monthly reports, with their 70 line items, tell us how to run the company, tell our managers how well they know their units, and tell our employees if there's going to be a profit. Everyone works on the basis of the same information, and everyone looks forward to its appearance with what I'd call fervent curiosity.

And that's all there is to it. Participation gives people control of their work, profit sharing gives them a reason to do it better, information tells them what's working and what isn't.

LETTING THEM DO WHATEVER THE HELL THEY WANT

So we don't have systems or staff functions or analysts or anything like that. What we have are people who either sell or make, and there's nothing in between. Is there a marketing department? Not on your life. Marketing is everybody's problem. Everybody knows the price of the product. Everybody knows the cost. Everybody has the monthly statement that says exactly what each of them makes, how much bronze is costing us, how much overtime we paid, all of it. And the employees know that 23% of the after-tax profit is theirs.

We are very, very rigorous about the numbers. We want them in on the fourth day of the month so we can get them back out on the fifth. And because we're so strict with the financial controls, we can be extremely lax about everything else. Employees can paint the walls any color they like. They can come to work whenever they decide. They can wear whatever clothing makes them comfortable. They can do whatever the hell they want. It's up to them to see the connection between productivity and profit and to act on it.

Semco thrives, with an average annual growth rate of about 17 percent, but **Ricardo Semler** has added a new dimension to the business, a logical extension of the structural ideas in the second of these two articles. In Brazil, the practice of outsourcing support services is called third-party management. Semco, through joint ventures with two U.S. companies (Cushman & Wakefield and Johnson Controls) now makes a business of managing these third-party providers and the employees who work for them. Logically enough, this business, probably unique to Brazil, is called fourth-party management. It works more or less like this, to take just one example:

Semco now manages all support services for Brazil's second largest bank. Seventy-five former bank employees in charge of such things as data systems, building maintenance, security—indeed, everything except pure banking and banking services—still work at the bank but are on Semco's payroll. Through them, Semco manages the 650 people who actually perform these support services but are employed by third-party vendor companies. The savings to the bank are considerable, in large part because Semco has reduced the outsourced payroll from 850 people to 650, and Semco gets half those savings as its principal fee.

Fourth-party management now accounts for 35% of Semco's business and is growing at an annual rate of about 25%.

Four years after the first of these two articles, Ricardo Semler told the Semco story in an updated, more detailed form in a book called Maverick, The Success Story behind the World's Most Unusual Workplace (Warner Books, 1993).

5

Why My Former Employees Still Work for Me

RICARDO SEMLER

I OWN A manufacturing company in Brazil called Semco, about which I can report the following curious fact: no one in the company really knows how many people we employ. When we walk through our manufacturing plants, we rarely even know who works for us. Some of the people in the factory are full-time Semco employees; some work for us part-time; some work for themselves and supply Semco with components or services; some work for themselves under contract to outside companies (even Semco's competitors); and some of them work for each other. We could decide to find out which is which and who is who, but for two good reasons we never bother. First, the employment and contractual relationships are so complex that describing them all would take too much time and trouble. Second, we think it's all useless information.

Semco has long been a laboratory for unusual employment and management practices. What we're now engaged in might be called a radical experiment in unsupervised, in-house, company-supported satellite production of goods and services for sale to Semco itself and to other manufacturers by employees, part-time employees, ex-employees, and people who have never had any connection with Semco whatsoever (but who work on our premises and on our equipment). This is not at all the same thing as outsourcing. This is a borderless system of short-term, noncontractual task assignment often using Semco's own fixed assets, some of it in Semco plants and some dispersed at a dozen sites that don't belong to the company.

This satellite program, as we call it, sounds chaotic, can be frustrating, and is in some ways uncontrollable. It requires daily leaps of faith. It has serious implications for corporate culture. It has destroyed any semblance of corporate security. And, for the three years it has been in place, it seems to be working very well. Since 1990, 28% of Brazilian capital goods manufacturers have gone bankrupt. In 1990, 1991, and 1992, Brazilian gross industrial product fell by 14%, 11%, and 9%, respectively. Capital goods output has fallen back to what it was in 1977. But in this same period, Semco's overall sales and profits have remained intact, and I attribute the difference first and foremost to our satellite production.

Ever since I took over the company 12 years ago, Semco has been unorthodox in a variety of ways. I believe in responsibility but not in pyramidal hierarchy. I think that strategic planning and vision are often barriers to success. I dispute the value of growth. I don't think a company's success can be measured in numbers, since numbers ignore what the end user really thinks of the product and what the people who produce it really think of the company. I question the supremacy of talent, too much of which is as bad as too little. I'm not sure I believe that control is either expedient or desirable.

I don't govern Semco—I own the capital, not the company—but on taking over from my father, I did try to reconstruct the company so that Semco could govern itself on the basis of three values: employee participation, profit sharing, and open information systems. We've introduced idiosyncratic features like factory-floor flex-time, self-set salaries, a rotating CEO-ship, and, from top to bottom—from the owner to the newest, greenest maintenance person—only three levels of hierarchy.

You might say that what we practice is an extreme form of common sense: "common" because there's nothing we do that thousands of other people didn't think of ages ago, "extreme" because we actually do it. Another way of looking at Semco is to say that we treat our employees like responsible adults. We never assume that they will take advantage of us or our rules (or our lack of rules); we always assume they will do their level best to achieve results beneficial to the company, the customer, their colleagues, and themselves. As I put it in an earlier article in the *Harvard Business Review* (see the preceding chapter), participation gives people control of their work, profit sharing gives them a reason to do it better, information tells them what's working and what isn't.

With rare exceptions, this approach has been successful. We've had two or three strikes, but they were quickly settled, especially once the strikers saw that we would neither lock them out of the plant nor suspend their benefits during the work stoppage. (They were able to plan ongoing strike tactics while eating lunch in the company cafeteria.) We've had a few employees take wholesale advantage of our open stockrooms and trusting atmosphere, but we were lucky enough to find and prosecute them without putting in place a lot of insulting watchdog procedures for the nine out of ten who are honest. We've seen a few cases of greed when people set their own salaries too high. We've tried a few experiments that we later backed away from. We've had to accept occasional democratic decisions that management disliked, but we learned to swallow hard and live with them.

On the whole, as I say, our approach has worked. Loyalty is high, quality is excellent, and sales and profits are surprisingly good for a manufacturing company in one of the world's most lunatic business environments. But in Brazil no state of the economy is permanent. Few last long enough to be called temporary. Surviving the ups and downs of the Brazilian economy is a little like riding a Brahma bull. It is even more like riding a Brahma bull in an earthquake. Some of the worst jolts come not from the bull but the landscape.

In 1990, the jolt that sent us into our present experiment came from the minister of finance, who, believing Brazil's inflation was simply the result of too much money being used for too much speculation, seized 80% of the country's cash and introduced an extended period of economic bedlam. Employers could not meet payrolls. Consumer spending vanished. Business spending shuddered to a halt. Bankruptcies soared. Industrial output plummeted.

At Semco, we had several months of zero sales. After all, what company was going to buy machinery with a ten-month delivery when it didn't know if it could last out the week? Worse yet, back orders were canceled, or we found that our customers had gone out of business. Our marine division alone had $1.5 million of receivables that we couldn't hope to collect and $4 million worth of products that shipbuilders could no longer pay for. We had to rent warehouse space just to store all the unsold goods.

We cut costs. We organized workers into teams and sent them out to sell replacement parts directly to ships and restaurants. We cut down on coffee breaks, locked up the copiers, canceled orders for new uniforms, turned off all the lights we could find, scrimped on telephone calls. None of it was enough, and anyway, I don't really believe in cost-cutting. I like to think we don't waste money even when we've got it. And who can say how many sales we lose when we play Scrooge with the travel money or penny-pinch the phone bills?

Finally, we called the workers together in groups of 100 and discussed what we should do. They came up with lots of ideas, and we tried them without success until we reached a point where no one had anything else to propose and neither did we—except for two unhappy alternatives: cut pay or cut work force. We thought we could avoid layoffs by cutting salaries 30% across the board until business picked up again. But a lot of people were already struggling with bills and rents and mortgages and wanted us to start laying people off instead, so that those who stayed could at least survive. We went on searching desperately for a third way out.

And then suddenly the shop-floor committee came to us and said, "Okay, we'll take a 30% pay cut, but on three conditions." The first was that we increase their profit sharing by 15%, from just under 24% to just under 39%, until they got back up to their former salary levels. The second was that management take a 40% pay cut. And the third was that a member of the union committee would co-sign every check we wrote; because the workers wanted to be absolutely certain that their sacrifice would be worthwhile, they wanted to oversee each and every expenditure.

Well, at that moment, we *had* no profits to share, so there was nothing for us to lose and everything to gain. And by the second month, we were actually covering expenses. In their drive to save, the workers took on more and more of the former contract work. They did security and cleaning, drove trucks, even cooked the food in the cafeteria. No expense went unchallenged, and for four or five months, we made a small profit in the worst economic times any of us had ever seen.

But we kept on looking for a better solution.

In the first place, pure cost reduction has to be a temporary measure. What about training, research, new product development, and all the other seemingly peripheral activities that produce profits over the long haul? Those weren't responsibilities we could abdicate.

And what about those checks? The dual-signature scheme was working for the moment, but management couldn't permanently yield its power of the purse to a person chosen by the union without management input or approval.

Yet the explosion of energy, inventiveness, and flexibility we'd been witnessing was hugely attractive. And when we then added in several other factors—the need to cut our standing labor costs, the demands of Brazilian labor law, the dynamic example of our own peculiar Nucleus of Technological Innovation, which I'll come back to in a moment—what began taking shape was a radically new principle of organization.

THE THINKODROME AT THE FREE-FOR-ALL CORPORATION

Years ago, in the mid-1980s, three Semco engineers proposed a new kind of work unit. They wanted to take a small group of people raised in Semco's culture and familiar with its products and set them free. The new group would not have to worry about production problems, sales, inventory, equipment maintenance, delivery schedules, or personnel. Instead, they would invent new products, improve old ones, refine marketing strategies, uncover production inefficiencies, and dream up new lines of business. They would have no boss and no subordinates. They would pick their own focus, set their own agendas, and have complete freedom to change their minds. Twice a year they'd report to senior management, which would decide whether or not to keep them on for another six months.

The three engineers suggested we call the new unit the Nucleus of Technological Innovation (NTI) and somewhat predictably proposed themselves as its first three members. We bought their odd idea, and then we worked out an odd form of compensation to go along with it. Their guaranteed salaries went sharply down, but they would now share in the proceeds of their inventions, innovations, and improvements. They would receive a percentage of any savings they introduced, royalties on new products they devised, a share of the profits on their inventions, and they would also be free to sell consulting services on the open market. They might have done even better as truly independent entrepreneurs, but as NTI members, Semco would cushion them against disaster and give them the support of an established and well-equipped manufacturing operation.

By the end of their first six months, NTI had 18 projects under way, and over the next few years they uncorked such an array of inventions, changes, and refinements (one of my favorites is a scale that weighs freight trains moving at full speed) that NTI's members began to prosper mightily and Semco became unthinkable without their constant innovation and reform.

By 1990, we'd begun to feel that we'd like to NTI the entire company, liberate more creativity, tie compensation even more specifically to performance, loosen the ties that bound us all together, and scramble our overall structure. The 30% pay-cut-and-cost-reduction scheme had given us a breathing space of several months, but with the Brazilian economy in a bucket and no imminent prospect of recovery, we *had* to become permanently leaner and more flexible. At the same time, of course, we had a commitment to our work force that was central to the way we did business. That commitment had been our principal reason for trying to avoid layoffs.

For most other companies, there was another reason as well: Brazilian labor law protects laid-off workers by granting them several different forms of special compensation. The largest of these comes from an individual fund for each worker to which the employer contributes

8% of wages every month. When people are fired (or retire), they collect all this accumulated money, plus interest, in the form of a lump sum. Less substantial—but, unlike the 8% fund, a great problem for many employers—is severance pay itself, which is paid on the spot out of current income and which can amount to two years' salary in the case of workers with many years' seniority. By the end of 1990, a lot of Brazilian companies drifted slowly into bankruptcy rather than lay people off and go bankrupt overnight. With our finances still more or less intact, this widespread problem proved in our case to be an opportunity.

Semco's sales had gradually increased again, and we were making enough money to restore salaries to where they had been before the 30% cut. We took back our check-signing privileges. We were surviving in a crisis economy, but only just, and we began to face the fact that we had to cut our permanent staff and contract more of our work. We looked hard for a way of doing it without destroying the support system that Semco people lived on. It was here that NTI's free-form structure suggested a solution.

Instead of giving contracts out to strangers, we decided we could just as well give contracts to our own employees. We would encourage them to leave the Semco payroll and start their own satellite enterprises, doing work, at least initially, for Semco. Like NTI, these satellites could stay under our larger umbrella by leasing our machines, even working in our plant. Like NTI, they could also do work for other companies, again on our machines and in our factories. Like NTI, their compensation would take a variety of forms—contract payment, royalties, commissions, profit sharing, piecework, whatever they could think up that we both could live with. And like NTI, they could have some beginning guarantees. In particular, we would offer all of them some contract work to cut their teeth on, and we would defer the lease payments on all equipment and space for two full years.

This satellite program would have obvious advantages for Semco. We could reduce our payroll, cut inventory costs by spreading out raw materials and spare parts among our new suppliers, and yet enjoy the advantage of having subcontractors who knew our business and the idiosyncrasies of our company and our customers. Moreover, we would pick up the benefit of entrepreneurial motivation. Because of profit sharing, our employees already worked evenings and weekends when necessary, without any prompting from management. Being in business for themselves ought to raise that sense of involvement higher still.

But what in heaven's name were the advantages for our workers, who'd be giving up a secure nest at Semco for the risks of small business? And in the midst of economic bedlam? To begin with, of course, they all had the chance to make many times what they could earn at Semco—if the economy straightened out. Of course that was a big *if*. And should the recession persist, they might make less. But only assuming they continued to have a job at Semco, which was becoming an even bigger *if* with every day that passed. The fact was, they had distressingly few choices. And so did we.

We eased the transition in every way we could. We created a team of executives to teach cost control, pricing, maintenance, inventory management. To provide seed money, we gave people lay-off payments on top of severance pay and all the other legally required benefits. Many also made use of their 8% nest-egg funds. No one *had* to start a satellite. Some took their severance and left. Some managed to stay on the payroll for months or for good. But despite the difficulties, satellites sprang up quickly. White-collar workers were the first. Our tax accountants, human resource staffers, and computer programmers all went off on their own. Then blue-collar workers in food service and refrigeration systems followed suit.

Today, about half the manufacturing we once did in-house has gone to satellites, and we think we can farm out another 10% to 20% in the coming years. Best of all, to this day only one satellite has failed. Some are expanding and looking for partners. Some satellite workers have been rehired by the company, and a few have moved repeatedly back and forth between satellite and employee status as needs—theirs and ours—shifted. Some satellites have broadened their scope so greatly that most of their time—often right on our premises, remember—is spent with customers and production partners who have no other connection with Semco whatsoever.

In 1990, Semco had about 500 employees. Today, we have about 200, plus at least that many in our satellites, with another 50 or 60 people who work for a satellite and also work for us part-time. We have employees with fixed salaries. We have employees with variable salaries made up of royalties or bonuses based on self-set objectives like cash flow, sales, profits, production units, or any one of a dozen other measures. We have employees with both fixed and variable salaries. All our employees share in our profits.

On the satellite side, compensation may take the form of a fixed fee, an hourly stipend, a percentage of increased sales, a finder's fee, an honorarium, a retainer converting to an advance converting to a royalty, or even a simple win-or-lose commission. In one case, we had decided to kill a product-development project when one of our people picked it up from the table and said, "I'll take it. If you'll give me $1,000 a month, which will just pay my expenses, plus a 7% royalty for the first five years if I can make it work—I'll take it." So of course we gave it to him. The most we can lose is $1,000 a month, where we'd been spending $10,000 to $15,000 a month and getting nowhere. The most he can make is something like half a million, I'd guess, with the other 93% coming to Semco.

Once we posted a job for one engineer and got 1,430 résumés. We took them home in packs of a hundred, and then we interviewed for five months. In the end, we invited several dozen final candidates to a one-day seminar where we walked them through the entire company, opened our files, showed them everything we did, then asked them for proposals. We wound up hiring 41 engineers—one salaried employee and 40 satellite workers whom we paid on various forms of percentage-based commission.

In one of our plants, we've set aside a large room full of desks and computers to give everyone within our company sphere and, for all we know, a variety of guests and visitors from well beyond it, a place to sit and plan and ask questions and solve problems. We call it the Thinkodrome, and it's a busy, quiet place. That Semco survives at all we owe in large part to surrounding ourselves with people who look at everything we do and ask why we can't do it better or cheaper or faster or in some entirely novel way.

HUNTING THE FREE MARKET

Our ancestors laid out the ground rules of human teamwork several thousand generations ago, and they go like this: the woman with the keen eyesight is Chief Mammoth Finder, the guy with the strong arm and the long spear is Head Mammoth Killer, and the tribal elder with the special feel for herbs and spices gets to be Grand Mammoth Cook. For now. All these positions are temporary and to some extent self-selecting. If you want to be Chief Finder, go find some mammoths and the job is probably yours. But since everyone's well-being depends on your success, your status is also highly situational. Fail to find, and the job will pass swiftly and naturally to someone else.

Generally speaking, Semco's production process works along similar lines, both for satellite operations and for the work we do in-house. All work, including some aspects of management, goes to people with proven track records who want the jobs and can compete for them successfully. Satellite as well as in-house business units rise and fall on their merits alone—at least in theory.

This commitment to free-market principles was put to the test about a year into the satellite program, when our marine division found itself with a good deal of idle capacity. Marine's strategy was built on quality, not price—low volume but high margins. A shipbuilder seeking the very best performance and dependability in, say, a propeller system, tended to come to us. But with the economy in a straitjacket, orders had nearly disappeared.

On the other hand, our biscuit division, which designs and builds turnkey cookie factories for global giants like Nabisco and Nestlé, had two fairly big contracts in hand, one for about $2 million, another for $5.5 million, and was going to need a lot of skilled subcontracting. The portion of this work that marine could do would keep it occupied for four or five months, and marine's top manager (called a counselor at Semco) went ahead and figured the contracts from the biscuit division into his budget. But biscuit's purchasing people did not award the contracts to the marine division, which took too long to deliver, they said, and which charged too high a price for its exaggerated quality. They gave the contracts instead to satellite producers and outside contractors, including one of marine's archcompetitors. The fight that triggered was a bitter one, and the attempts of the interdepartmental management meeting to act as go-between did not make things easier. We were of two minds ourselves.

On the one hand, we were going to pay marine employees to sit around on their hands while another division paid outsiders to do work the marine employees could have done. And on the other hand, how could we ask biscuit employees, who share in their division's profits, to subsidize a business in trouble? Moreover, wouldn't the subsidy just postpone marine's inevitable reckoning with its own strategic predicament? In the end, we let biscuit have its way and endorsed the need to be as unforgiving toward our own business units as we would be toward outsiders. It was the right decision, of course. We finished the cookie factories on schedule, and the marine division—which decided to stick with its high-quality, high-margin strategy but to eliminate a number of products whose quality and cost were too high for the market—cut its staff by 70%, began farming out a lot of its work to satellites, and recovered its profitability.

CONTROL . . .

At the center of Semco is a group of six so-called counselors, and all of us take six-month turns as acting CEO. We also do six-month as opposed to yearly budgeting, because an annual budget tempts managers to postpone unpleasant decisions to the third and fourth quarters.

The budget cycles are January to June and July to December, but the CEO cycles begin in March and September. In other words, we avoid what other companies and shareholders think they want—responsibility nailed down to a single man or woman. Our CEOs don't wear themselves out trying to meet quarterly financial goals, and there's no one person to blame if the company goes down the drain. When financial performance is one person's problem, then everyone else can relax. In our system, no one can relax. You get to pass on the baton, but it comes back again two-and-a-half years later.

One consequence of this system is that we need to keep each other well-informed, which we do at regular weekly divisional meetings and biweekly interdivisional meetings. All these meetings are open and optional, and those who attend make decisions that those who don't may simply have to live with.

This self-selecting element in decision making is another consequence of the deliberate fragmentation of responsibility. Like our predecessors the mammoth hunters, the people who get responsibility are the people who seek it out and meet it. In fact, the actual, ad hoc control structure we work with from day to day builds on this principle and on two others that, together, create a kind of invisible order from the apparent chaos that characterizes the Semco environment.

The first principle holds that information is the ultimate source of virtually all power. For this reason, we try to make all of it available to everyone. All meetings are open. Designs and specifications are shared. The company's books are open for inspection by employees and for auditing by their unions. In short, we try to undercut and so eliminate the process of filtering and negotiating information that goes on in so many corporations. Meetings are chaired by the person who knows most about the subject under discussion rather than by the person who has the highest declared status or apparent income.

The second principle is that the responsibility for any task belongs to the person who claims it.

The third is that profit sharing for employees and success-oriented compensation for satellite enterprises will spread responsibility across the Semco map. With income and security at risk—and with information readily available—people try hard to stay aware of everyone else's performance.

To give an idea of how all this works in practice, let's take one of those turnkey cookie factories. The Big Cracker Company of Chicago wants a plant that will turn out a thousand tons a month of, say, butterscotch macaroons. To begin with, an independent agent will tell us of the project in return for a finder's fee. We will probably put the initial customer interface in the hands of a satellite company—four men who used to be on our payroll and now work for themselves. They'll go through the specifications with the customer, then they'll share that information widely, announce a meeting (to which anyone can come and no one is summoned), and chair the discussion (which will cover several unexpected proposals from unanticipated participants like the guy from refrigeration with a special point of view about handling butter and coconut). Someone, a group of employees or satellites, will take on the job of costing the project, and with this cost estimate in hand, a Semco counselor and biscuit-division coordinators will then set a margin and deliver the quote to Big Cracker.

A couple of times, we have even communicated this margin to the customer, because we thought it would be easier to justify, for example, a 12% net margin than to play the disingenuous game of claiming pencil-thin profits and no room for compromise. Our chief argument has been our profit-sharing program, since it seems so clear to us that people will work harder for more money and that a generous margin will therefore buy the customer much extra care and effort. But I'm afraid we've had only limited success with this approach.).

This margin-setting discussion often produces serious disagreements. In one case, we battled out the margin in a long, heated debate, and then the sales manager lowered it dramatically when he sat down with the customer. By Semco rules, that kind of last-minute capitulation is perfectly legitimate. Battle or no battle, he was with the customer, not we. Whoever holds the spear is completely in charge of bringing down the mammoth.

Let's say Big Cracker accepts our bid and the order comes in, 600 pages long. Let's also say we choose a coordinator for the project from outside the company, and let's call him Bob. Bob will go through the contract and decide how he wants to divide it up. He may get help from engineering. He will certainly get help from all the meetings he holds to make decisions, which he will chair and where he will lobby for the people he wants to do each job. Next, the biscuit division's purchasing department will negotiate contracts with the dozens of suppliers chosen. In 1991, we did about 70% of such a contract in-house. Today, that's down to 35% or 40%.

When Bob has put together a completion schedule and time chart, everyone will go to work—each contractor, employee, and satellite responsible to no single authority but answerable to everyone. At most companies, when something goes wrong the real responsibility falls between the cracks. At Semco, the fact that Bob is not an employee makes everyone react much faster when there looks like trouble.

. . . AND LACK OF CONTROL

Semco needs to maintain in-house just a limited number of functions—top management, applications engineering, some R&D, and some high-tech, capital-intensive skills that we do exceptionally well. We don't care how everything else gets done, whether by contractors or subcontractors, satellites or nonsatellites, former employees or total strangers or by the very people who do the same thing for our competition. None of that matters.

When we started, people warned me that all sorts of information about our company would get into the wrong hands, that we had to protect ourselves. I heard the same argument when we started distributing profit-and-loss statements to our employees. But it's a waste of time to worry about leaks.

First of all, we no longer know whose the wrong hands are. The competition used to be a company a mile away that made the same products we did, but now the competition comes from companies we've never heard of in Taiwan and Finland. Second, I've never seen a company overtake another because it had seen its 10K or even the specifications for a valve. Third, we want to be a moving target. We don't care about yesterday's information or last year's oil pump, which in any case the competition can buy, take apart, and study to its heart's content.

Finally, we don't think people give out much information anyway. I know. I've tried on numerous occasions to get a copy of, let's say, a pamphlet some company passed out to 1,000 employees, and nobody can lay their hands on one. The Chinese printed hundreds of millions of copies of Chairman Mao's *Little Red Book*, and still they're as rare as hen's teeth.

People also warned me about the loss of central goal setting and control. I admit that the lack of control is often hard to live with. But let's not compare Semco's circumstances with some ideal world where managers actually get to decide what people will do and when and how they'll do it. We have limited control over the day-to-day behavior of the people who make most of our components, but so do companies that do all their work in-house. At least none of our satellite people work nine to five and leave their problems at the plant when they go home at night—which means leaving them to management. We have motivation and responsibility working on our side. Our satellite workers are in business for themselves, so they'll work all night to complete an order to specification and on time. And if the order is late or fails to meet our quality standards, then we're free to give the next order to someone else. We can forget the witch-hunt and all the grief that goes into firing people or not promoting them.

As for planning and the control it presupposes, I think good planning is always situational. Thinking about the future is a useful, necessary exercise, but translating such conjecture into "Strategic Planning" is worse than useless. It's an actual barrier to survival. Strategic planning leads us to *make* things happen that fly full in the face of reality and opportunity.

For example, Semco is today in the environmental consulting business, which I could not have imagined five years ago. Our gadfly NTI group was looking at one customer's need for an environmentally active pump— a pump that would shred and process the material it moved—and saw that the company could reengineer its production line to do away with the pump altogether. Had we said, "We're in the pump business, not the environmental business," we might never have pursued that solution to the problem. As it was, we addressed the company's overall need, jettisoned the pump, and when it was all over, we'd also acquired a small environmental consulting firm to flesh out our own limited expertise. More recently, we've also entered into a joint venture with one of the world's leading environmental consulting groups. Today, the division represents about 14% to 15% of our total business and is growing at a rate of 30% to 40% per year.

The lesson this story teaches me is about the negative value of structure. Structure creates hierarchy, and hierarchy creates constraint. We have not utterly abandoned all control, but the old pyramidal hierarchy is simply unable to make leaps of insight, technology, and innovation. Within their own industries, pyramidal hierarchies can generate only incremental change.

Take dishwashers, one of Semco's businesses. Dishwashers are expensive to operate and messy to use, but over the last 50 years, dishwashers have changed hardly at all. What the customer wants is a machine that washes dishes silently, cheaply, and without any mess at all, which probably means without water. I've recently seen indications that such a thing may be possible, but the idea could never have come from a pyramid of Semco dishwashing executives. It was one of our satellites that brought us the idea. In fact, about two-thirds of our new products come from satellite companies.

What goes for planning goes equally for culture, vision, and responsibility. We find that fragmentation is strength in all these areas. Semco has no corporate credo, for example, and no mission statement. An articulation of company values or vision is just a photograph of the company as it is, or wants to be, at one given moment. Snapshots of this kind seem to hold some companies together, but they are terribly static devices. No one can impose corporate consciousness from above. It moves and shifts with every day and every worker. Like planning, vision at its best is dynamic and dispersed.

At Semco, so is responsibility. We have little control, even less organization, and no conventional discipline at all. People come and go whenever they like; many set their own compensation; divisions and units perpetuate themselves however they can; satellite companies work on our machines in our factories for us and others in a great confusion of activity; the system tying it all together is painfully loose—and this is *manufacturing*, much of it assembly-line manufacturing.

When I describe Semco to other manufacturers, they laugh. "What do you make," they ask me, "beads?" And I say, "No, among other things, we make rocket-fuel propellant mixers for satellites." And they say, "That's not possible." And I say, "Nevertheless . . ."

The point is simple but perhaps not obvious. Semco has abandoned a great many traditional business practices. Instead, we use minimal hierarchies, ad hoc structures, self-control, and the discipline of our own community marketplace of jobs and responsibilities to achieve high-quality, on-time performance. Does it make me feel that I have given up power and governance? You bet it does. But do I have more sleepless nights than the manufacturer who runs his business with an iron hand and whose employees leave their troubles in his lap every night? I think I probably sleep better. I know I sleep well.

We delivered our last cookie factory with all its 16,000 components right on time. One of our competitors, a company with tight controls and hierarchies, delivered a similar factory to the same client a year and two months late.

Semco thrives, with an average annual growth rate of about 17 percent, but **Ricardo Semler** *has added a new dimension to the business, a logical extension of the structural ideas in the second of these two articles. In Brazil, the practice of outsourcing support services is called* third-party management. *Semco, through joint ventures with two U.S. companies (Cushman & Wakefield and Johnson Controls) now makes a business of managing these third-party providers and the employees who work for them. Logically enough, this business, probably unique to Brazil, is called* fourth-party management. *It works more or less like this, to take just one example:*

Semco now manages all support services for Brazil's second largest bank. Seventy-five former bank employees in charge of such things as data systems, building maintenance, security—indeed, everything except pure banking and banking services—still work at the bank but are on Semco's payroll. Through them, Semco manages the 650 people who actually perform these support services but are employed by third-party vendor companies. The savings to the bank are considerable, in large part because Semco has reduced the outsourced payroll from 850 people to 650, and Semco gets half those savings as its principal fee.

Fourth-party management now accounts for 35% of Semco's business and is growing at an annual rate of about 25%.

Four years after the first of these two articles, Ricardo Semler told the Semco story in an updated, more detailed form in a book called Maverick, The Success Story behind the World's Most Unusual Workplace *(Warner Books, 1993).*

The Purpose at the Heart of Management

1

Tales from a Nonconformist Company

HAL ROSENBLUTH

IN MY EXPERIENCE, there are three perpetual business puzzles—change, people, and technology—and the trick is figuring out how to get them working for you instead of against you. My own approach is to try to control change—anticipate it, master it, exploit it—by putting people and technology at the head of my list of priorities.

Exploiting change is not a new idea at Rosenbluth Travel. It is very much the watchword of the 1990s, but it was the watchword of the 1890s too. When my great-grandfather, Marcus Rosenbluth, founded the company in 1892, he was responding to change on a grand, historic scale—the European immigration to America. For $50, his company provided steamship passage from a European port to New York, help with entry into the United States, and transportation from Ellis Island to Philadelphia.

But the business didn't stop there. Once they were settled and had jobs, a lot of those immigrants gave Marcus their savings—five and ten cents at a time—until they had $50 to bring over another member of the family. So in addition to running a travel agency, he also ran a savings bank of sorts and was licensed to do both. (Our first strategic business shift resulted from a change in the law that required us to give up one of the licenses. Marcus chose to stick with travel, a decision some of us in the family questioned until recently.)

The important thing about my great-grandfather is that, back in 1892, he had an insight about the business. He wasn't just in travel, selling tickets to people who wanted to cross the Atlantic. He was in family immigration, getting whole clans of people successfully settled in America. The original Rosenbluth Travel promoted the idea of bringing over one or two family members at a time, helped people through the bureaucratic maze on Ellis Island and on to jobs in Philadelphia, functioned as a depository for their savings, and then, by and by, sold the immigrating family a second ticket—and then a third. I don't know much about my great-grandfather Marcus, but I know from the way he ran his company that he was a smart businessman with a broad view of what it meant to serve people's needs.

My great-grandfather set standards of customer service and business insight that we still work hard to live up to. For one thing, we're still constantly redefining the business we're in. For several decades after the wave of immigration slowed, for example, Rosenbluth Travel was in the vacation business. Through two world wars, we were a one-office agency promoting mostly leisure travel, selling tour packages and developing a staff of area experts who knew their customers and hundreds of resorts and side trips.

Now, over the course of the past 10 or 12 years, we have once again completely transformed the way we think about what we do, how we do it—even why. It's been an exciting set of changes, and it has catapulted us from the largest travel agency in Philadelphia to one of the largest travel companies in the world.

The Boss's Son

In 1974, the day after I graduated from the University of Miami, I came to Rosenbluth Travel and went to work. I'd never planned to go into the family business—I'm not a great believer in nepotism—but my father was working too hard, I wanted to help out, and then, too, I figured I could probably make my mark in the travel business as well as in any other.

The fact is, as a child I often challenged conventional thinking. In grade school and high school, for example, when some teacher would go through that sarcastic routine about how maybe one of us thought he or she could do a *better* job (of teaching the class or running the country or developing the theory of relativity), I was always the wise guy in the last row who raised his hand.

So at Rosenbluth, I was fairly confident I'd be able to take some of the pressure off my dad and still devise ways to stand the industry on its head. I'm not sure my father shared that view. In fact, I think he probably wondered if I'd work out.

I think my father also understood that a lot of people might resent me just for being the boss's son—especially if I began moving up the ladder too fast—so I started as a gofer, running errands and stamping brochures. Then, after a year or so, I became an assistant vacation consultant and started actually selling travel. At first, they only let me sell tickets to New York and Washington—on the theory, I think, that if I screwed it up, people could always walk home—but eventually, I earned my wings and started doing real work. After another year or two, I started working in the meeting and incentive group, putting together conference packages and no-expense-spared incentive trips for our corporate clients' high achievers.

That was fun and creative, and I learned a lot. Once, for example, I booked the entire Queen Elizabeth II for a bar association cruise and put Rosenbluth at risk for about $1 million. Unfortunately, what I didn't anticipate was that every lawyer wanted first-class accommodations and nothing else would do. We sold 400 deluxe cabins the first day, and then for two months, we sold virtually nothing else, so the ship went out half empty. Luckily, we squeaked through without losing our shirts, and I learned a valuable lesson about the importance of getting into the mind of the customer.

In spite of some bad moments, however, I gradually managed to put my father's mind at ease. I got along with people. I avoided additional million-dollar risks. By 1978, I had even worked my way up to be head of the department, and the position carried the title of vice president. I seemed to be off to a good start.

CUSTOMER FOCUS TO A FAULT

In the course of those first few years at Rosenbluth, I earned my title by learning the travel business. Yet at the same time, I was still always questioning the status quo and observing the business with an eye to improvement.

What I saw was a tremendous focus on the customer, and it began to bother me that that focus so often created problems for our people. Everyone felt pushed to do heroic deeds for the client, which was fine in its way, except that the competition for hero status sometimes got a little out of hand. Booking agents competed. Vacation consultants fought over who got to sit at the desk nearest the entrance. People played up to the receptionist who directed calls. There was a lot of politics, a lot of scorekeeping, and a lot of stress.

Still, the company was doing well. At $20 million to $30 million in annual bookings, we were a very successful agency. Our customers were satisfied, and it was hard to argue with success. I just didn't like the way people treated each other. Our star performers could get away with murder, and did. Teamwork was nonexistent. I didn't believe that bitter competition among the staff would continue to yield success forever; sooner or later, people pass along that kind of stress, and I felt sure the ultimate object of that tension would be our customers. It was not a terribly pleasant place to work.

In the beginning, I did nothing. There wasn't much I could do. But once I was head of my own department, I started systematically getting rid of the prima donnas and the political manipulators. The whole organization took a dim view of my actions because the people I removed were seen as indispensable—even after they left and the company failed to fall apart. I knew I was doing the right thing, though no one else could see it. But I still wasn't satisfied.

CORPORATE TRAVEL, CORPORATE CHAOS

One day in 1978, I wandered into the area where a group of about 18 reservation agents did our business travel. They were sitting around three big tables covered with dog-eared airline-reservation books, each of them talking on two phones at once (corporate client on one, airline on the other) and writing out orders and sliding them into slots on a lazy Susan to be turned into tickets the next day and delivered.

We had no computers in those days. Until deregulation, the ticketing process had been comparatively simple. There were only two or three fares between any two points—first class, coach, economy—and an agent's job consisted of finding the airline with the most convenient arrival and departure times and of securing seats on those flights. The work was hard and constant, but there were not a lot of complications. Now, suddenly, air travel had been deregulated, and all the old rules were out the window. There were new airlines, new routes, dozens of new fares, and everything kept changing so fast that no one could keep up. The office was pure activity and noise.

I stood and watched for a while, then sat down in an empty chair and picked up a phone to help out. I stayed all day and came back the next. I loved it. In fact, in that room I fell in love with the company—or at least with the corporate travel agents and the way they worked together. There were no political squabbles. They worked hard, they worked *with* each other, they were a thousand miles from the petty backbiting I'd seen in other departments.

After a couple of days, I demoted myself from vice president to reservations agent and went into corporate travel full-time. We were a very close group. We'd ticket our brains out all day and then go to a tavern called the Top of the Twos every evening and talk about our dreams, our ambitions, our frustrations, and, believe it or not, about corporate travel.

In my father's and grandfather's time, corporate travel wasn't a lucrative field. Except for salesmen, business-people didn't do a lot of traveling—by train, you couldn't get to the Chicago office and back the same day—and those who did had ticket agents on their own payrolls or, more often, a secretary who called the railroad or airline and made a reservation. There wasn't much more to it.

But now predictability was gone, special new fares were appearing almost daily without warning (to avoid tipping off the competition), business customers were confused and frustrated, and yet most travel agents had their heads in the sand. Their reaction to the chaos seemed to be, "My God, deregulation? What a disaster! We're out of business!"

But our group dealt with the chaos all day, listened to the confusion and frustration of customers on the phone, and we drew just the opposite conclusion. We'd go to the Top of the Twos after work, and we'd say to each other, "My God, deregulation? What an opportunity! *We're in business!*" Being young and smart (and very confident), we figured we could take the confusion and turn it into a semblance of order for a marketplace yearning for some-body to tell it what the damned airfare really was.

FROM TRAVEL TO INFORMATION

The first step was computers. The airlines themselves were just starting to build their own computer reservation systems, and it wasn't much of a leap to see the difference that would make. Instead of getting the latest schedules and availabilities from an airline agent on one phone and passing it on to a customer on another, we'd have direct access to the reservation information we needed. It was a revolution. We'd be able to give customers better, faster service and get rid of half our telephones.

So I got the company to buy computers for everyone in corporate travel, we leased a couple of reservation systems—American's SABRE and United's APOLLO (in those days, travel agencies had to pay for access)—and we were off and running.

Or were we? We had the computers, but then so did a lot of other travel companies. What was our particular ace in the hole? Remember, I was no longer alone. I now worked with a whole roomful of people who, like me, were always questioning the status quo and working out ways to change it. We all wanted to do things no one else was doing—to do them first and do them better than anyone else who might come along.

Our first innovation, perhaps, was simply to take corporate travel seriously. Even before deregulation, we'd had some corporate accounts. Our first was with a Philadelphia division of General Electric. It had had four of its own staff people doing ticketing and reservations, but in 1970, it took a hard look at travel expenses, decided it could cut costs by using a travel company, and called Rosenbluth. The deal was simple: GE's four travel staffers moved into our offices and went onto our payroll, but they continued to handle all of that division's Philadelphia-based travel. For the division's other employees, nothing changed—they dialed the same extension and heard the familiar voices of their travel staffers on the other end of the line. But for management at both companies, the change was great. Rosenbluth made commissions on a couple million dollars worth of travel each year, while GE saved a bundle of money on salaries and benefits and got more efficient and more comprehensive service in the bargain.

We'd picked up a few more corporate clients over the years, but once we'd mastered the computers, we went after them wholeheartedly. Our capacity for teamwork was a great advantage: we weren't competing for clients but cooperating to offer them superior service. Enthusiasm was of course another big plus: we were the entrepreneurs at Rosenbluth, and we had a startup spirit that kept us working and thinking harder than most people normally do. Training was a third strength: we started as soon as computers came into the company and pursued it vigorously.

But I think our biggest competitive advantage was to understand that as deregulation changed the rules of travel, we were no longer in the travel business so much as we were in the information business. Where there had once been three or four different fares on any given route, most routes were now served by several airlines, each with dozens of different fares, for a total of several million fares across the country. And many of those fares changed every day.

Since business travelers couldn't possibly cut their way through this thicket of information far enough to figure out what they ought to be paying, we simply guaranteed them the lowest fare between any two points. (We compared all the fares when we did each booking, then laboriously double-checked them when we wrote each ticket.) Then we sold companies on the idea of managing their travel costs and of letting us help them do it.

As an overall strategy, it worked. In 1981, we opened the first reservation center in the United States, which was staffed with more than one hundred people. In 1985, we took on our biggest corporate client yet, Du Pont, and became a national company instead of a large local agency with offices only in greater Philadelphia and Allentown. In 1978, corporate travel represented about 25% of total Rosenbluth bookings of $20 million. By 1990, corporate travel was 92% of total annual bookings of $1.3 billion. Once again, we'd capitalized on the old Rosenbluth tradition started by my great-grandfather of reconceiving, redefining, and recreating our business.

PUTTING PEOPLE BEFORE CUSTOMERS

Of the three business puzzles I mentioned earlier—change, people, and technology—"people" is the most important. No business can ever get technology and change to work in its favor unless it has the enthusiastic support of its own staff. In practice, getting people on the company's side is a matter of putting the company on *their* side. (For a very literal example, see "The North Dakota Connection.")

When corporate travel began to expand, everyone at Rosenbluth was working long hours, productivity was growing by leaps and bounds, and we were taking on new business without increasing our staff. I could see that nothing was too much for these people I worked with. But I could also see that they were spending most of their waking lives—some 10 or 12 hours a day—at work.

When people are excited and happy about what they're doing, they can handle that kind of schedule, sometimes for quite a while, but once the glow wears off or when the job has a lot of problems, overwork can have an awful effect on people's lives and on their marriages and families. For that matter, if a job experience is generally negative, the hours don't make much difference—even part-time people will be miserable to live with. In either case, it's not fair or reasonable for a

THE NORTH DAKOTA CONNECTION

Over and over again, I hear corporate leaders lament the shortage of qualified, motivated people. We've had the same problem at Rosenbluth Travel. But in the summer of 1988, we stumbled across a partial solution to our talent shortage. Oddly enough, it grew out of a shortage of an altogether different kind—a drought.

One evening in July that year, my wife and I got to talking about the drought in the U.S. Farm Belt. Crops were being destroyed, communities devastated, families driven off their land. We had read that people were cursing the sun, and to us that seemed horrible. As a country, we Americans respond very well to natural disasters; unfortunately, it does seem to take rubble and injuries to get us mobilized. The drought was ruining farmers too slowly to jolt people into action.

The next morning, I got together with a number of colleagues to think about something we could do to help. We have always kept elaborate records on individual customer patterns and preferences, and we had an immediate need for a great deal of data-entry work. So our short-term answer to the challenge was to set up a data-entry facility somewhere in the Farm Belt to provide some temporary jobs.

We called the Department of Agriculture and asked what part of the country had been hardest hit by the drought. North Dakota, they said. A couple of our associates went to Bismarck and asked which part of the state most needed help. State officials pointed to a couple of areas, one of which centered on Linton, a town of about 1,500 people in south central North Dakota, about 60 miles from Bismarck.

Our plan was to hire 20 people full-time for three or four months (we had about 35,000 customer profiles to input) and inject a little money into the local economy. We sent out a bunch of computers along with technology people and trainers. They rented space from a farm-equipment dealer, borrowed tables and chairs from the churches, and put an ad in the paper. When roughly 80 people responded, the first thing we did was change our plan. In order to spread the jobs around and have the broadest possible effect on the community, we hired 40 people part-time instead of 20 full-time, and we were careful to hire no more than one person per family. We also deliberately favored people who lived on farms, figuring that farm families would spend their salaries in town, benefiting towns-people as well as themselves, while money earned in town was a lot less likely to make its way out to rural areas.

We trained our new associates to

do data entry, and they learned so quickly and so well that we found more data for them to input after the initial customer profiles were done. After a couple of months, I decided to fly out to North Dakota to see the operation for myself. I knew the project was going well, but I never dreamed how well. There was no turnover, no absenteeism, and virtually no errors. What's more, the town of Linton and its people were the salt of the earth—warm, decent, friendly people who'd just been waiting for a chance to show what they could do.

Based on what we'd seen so far, and given the growing number of computer functions that were not location-specific, we decided to make the Linton office permanent. Over the following months, we added a number of accounting, customer-service, and airline-liaison tasks to Linton's responsibilities, and we began hiring more people. Once we'd acquired a fiber-optic link, we added reservations as well, and today our Linton agents handle ticketing for business travelers all over the country.

As a result of this growth, our Linton operation now employs almost 100 people full-time and has taken over the entire farm-equipment dealership—17,000 square feet, with almost 200 workstations. Over the coming year or so, we will hire another 100 people in the Linton area.

One unexpected problem has been how to pay our Linton associates on a scale comparable to what we pay people elsewhere without upsetting the social fabric of the town. (Due partly to the lower cost of living, salaries in Linton are generally lower than in many other parts of the country.) We already pay more than most other businesses in Linton—and we're by far the largest employer—so a jump in our pay scales would make it tough for other local companies to compete. We've solved the problem by keeping wages near the Linton norm and giving big bonuses at Christmas, which seems to satisfy everyone's needs, including our need to reward people for their work.

Before we opened our Linton facility, I had no particular expectations one way or the other. We just went there to try to do some good. It was pure good fortune that what we found was a well-educated, dependable, honest work force with superior skills and an old-fashioned, puritan work ethic—not to mention operating expenses at least a third lower than in most other parts of the country.

Now we're making an effort to get other corporations to share our good fortune. Several times a year, we invite other companies to come out and spend a few days seeing for themselves what the people of Linton can do. We have also built a $1 million conference center outside the town, and the companies that book it go home with a good feeling about North Dakota.

I've heard that there are academics writing papers about giving the Great Plains back to the buffalo. Yet the people who live there have roots in their farms the same way I have roots in the travel business. The worst thing that could happen—for them and, frankly, for Rosenbluth Travel— would be for those people to give up and leave their homes. The plains don't need abandonment, they just need a second source of income that's not agriculturally dependent. We can demonstrate convincingly that the companies providing that income opportunity will reap great benefits.

company to take that much of a person's life and give nothing back but money.

As I watched people knocking themselves out for Rosenbluth Travel, I suddenly realized that it was my responsibility to make their lives more pleasant. In simple terms, that meant giving people the right working environment, the right tools, and the right leadership. It meant eliminating fear, frustration, bureaucracy, and politics. Of course, it meant decent compensation—and bonuses when the company did well—but it also meant helping people develop as human beings. It meant opening their eyes to new ways of looking at the world and new ways of working and interacting with everyone they dealt with every day.

What it all boiled down to—I understood this for the first time during that period of rapid expansion—was that the people in a company have to come first, even ahead of the customers.

This is not to say that customers don't matter, since obviously they matter very much. It's just so easy to put a sign in a window or a line in your brochure that says the customer comes first, whereas in fact, if your people aren't happy with their jobs, the customer will never be uppermost in their minds. When they ought to be focusing on the customer, they'll be thinking about their own frustrations.

We believe that only if our people are first in our eyes will they be able to put the customer first in theirs. In other words, to put someone else first and mean it, you have to know what it feels like on the receiving end.

This philosophy governs not only our "associate" policies (I threw out the term "employee" years ago) but also the way we treat each other. Aside from outright dishonesty, for example, we have only one absolute taboo—setting up other associates for failure. If one of us made fantastic promises to a prospective corporate client, for instance, it would put colleagues down the line in a position where they couldn't deliver. That sort of thing not only frustrates people (and gives them a bad experience to take home at night); it compromises the whole organization's reputation for selling reality. We encourage everyone to sit down with clients and brainstorm about the future, but that's a far cry from misrepresenting our real capacities today.

Brainstorming about the business is, in fact, an indispensable activity at Rosenbluth and has the status of policy. Since I'm not the only person who likes to question the status quo, we give everyone regular opportunities to review executive performance and tell us how they would run the company. It's been a hugely successful program in generating new ideas, and if constructive criticism is a gift, then in my office it tends to be Christmas every day.

Moreover, since information is now our stock-in-trade, we see to it that our front-line service providers have access to all they need. We realized early on that if we expected our people to manage the business, they had to know what they were doing and why. They have to understand our margins, our financial needs, and our competitive strategy, as well as our computer systems and work procedures.

In the area of compensation, the people-first philoso-phy means a general understanding that when the com-pany does well, everyone does well, and when it doesn't do well, we start tightening belts from the top down. Last year was the best year we'd ever had, so nearly everyone received a bonus. The combination of war and recession made January and February of 1991 the worst two months in the company's history, so our executives started cutting back their own salaries, and they were soon joined by any number of associates who volun-teered to take time off without pay.

For that matter, our executives get relatively modest salaries in the first place. Most of their pay is based on profitability. In certain other parts of the company, on the other hand, we have what we call a Pay-for-Quality program, based 60% on accuracy, 20% on professionalism (which means going the extra mile for colleagues), and 20% on productivity (but only if the other two criteria are satisfied). We invented Pay-for-Quality as a way of compensating our reservation agents more fairly. They were on the front line with clients day after day and needed the nerves of an air traffic controller and the brains of a magna cum laude, but we'd been paying them as if they planted flowers. That wasn't right, and it cer-tainly didn't fit the new philosophy. Now our emphasis on quality has evolved into a formal total-quality manage-ment initiative, to the point that even our ticket delivery people are learning statistical process control and measur-ing things like on-time deliveries and the number of indi-vidual customers not in when deliveries are made.

The best part is that Pay-for-Quality has increased indi-vidual take-home pay by 32% and reduced the total pay-roll by 4%. Because people are doing things right the first time, we've been able to eliminate the positions needed to rework mistakes. In addition, turnover has declined, training costs have dropped, human resource expenses have gone down, and productivity has improved.

In training, too, we've put people first. Right from the start, I've chosen our training staff on what I call the kindergarten principle—which basically comes from the fact that I loved my kindergarten teacher, Miss Goldberg. She was creative and exciting, she made me want to learn, and she made me eager to get back to first grade that next fall.

We look for instructors like Jane Goldberg because our trainers are going to have an immense, lasting effect on our people and their skills, whether the subject is information retrieval, time management, or a topic with little or no direct relevance to the job, like financial planning, nutrition, or defensive driving.

And there was one more thing that occurred to me later: in kindergarten we had fun. Our present director of training believes that most of the fun has been taken out of learning by the fourth grade, and he's been able to show that retention rises steeply when people have a good time learning. So, among other things, we've invented "television" game shows like Rosenopoly and Travel Jeopardy as instructional tools, and the people in class play them with a lot of shouting and laughter and applause. It's corny, but they have fun—and they remember what they learn.

What we have is a hierarchy of concerns: people, service, profits. We focus on our people, our people focus on service, and profits result—a by-product, you might say, of putting our associates ahead of our customers. I know it sounds simplistic, but I know it works.

COMPUTERS TO SERVE CUSTOMERS

The final business puzzle is technology. I've described our early acquisition of computers and of airline reservation systems. In fact, the airlines regularly supply two distinct computer systems to most travel companies. The so-called front-room system is the one the reservation agent uses to find flight and price data, make the reservation, and get a seat. There is also, however, a so-called back-room system that agencies lease from an airline to do their accounting, analyze their bookings, manage their customer base, and perform any other computer jobs that need doing.

When we first started guaranteeing the lowest airfares to our customers, we quickly saw that a front-room link to two airlines was not enough, despite the fact that each system supposedly listed every flight and fare on every carrier. The trouble was the inevitable time lag between a new fare going into effect and that same new fare getting listed in a competitor's front-room system. Often, an airline's own front-room system was incorrect because, in order to keep some attractive new fare secret, the company would advertise it in newspapers before putting it into their system where the competition would see and maybe match it.

Since we knew the different systems spoke to each other haltingly, we went out and leased every airline system we could find (close to a dozen altogether) and put them all in one big room where we could extract their secrets one at a time and compare them.

It was laborious. The work cried out to be done electronically, but computerizing the search-and-compare operation presented problems. Every airline's reservation system contained a bias toward its own flights—it listed them first, it made them easy to book, and, all too often, it led agencies to give their clients those flights without even looking for better alternatives. Overcoming that bias and introducing a bias of our own—in this case, price—could only be done with a large independent system, not with any system we leased from an airline. After all, how could we use an airline's technology and an airline's programmers to help us reorganize flight information to eliminate that airline's advantage, perhaps even to steer revenue to other carriers? It didn't sound like a promising opportunity for teamwork.

The only answer was to buy our own mainframe and build our own back-room system. It was an expensive alternative, but it would make us independent and give us a freedom no one else yet had.

We put together our first private reservation data system in 1983 and called it READOUT—Rosenbluth's Exclusive Airfare Directory of Unbiased Tariffs. We made a commercial that showed a man calling a bunch of different airlines and agencies looking for the lowest airfare to Chicago and getting a bunch of different answers. Then he calls Rosenbluth, and because READOUT lists airfares in ascending order of price in one quadrant of the reservation agent's work screen, Rosenbluth tells him instantly what he wants to know. The word got around that Rosenbluth really *knew* what the lowest airfare was—and guaranteed it. Business boomed.

Price, however, was only one piece of the total picture. We believed that by collecting and analyzing company-specific data of many different kinds, we could help corporate managers change travel from a necessary but uncontrollable aggravation to a manageable expense. There was plenty of information floating around, but no one yet had turned it into the kind of usable knowledge that a company could act on.

From READOUT, we moved on to a relational database we called VISION. Then we added applications that permitted us to upload data into corporate mainframes and that allowed our customers to dip into our system in search of certain kinds of information.

In 1983, Du Pont corporate headquarters did a thorough study of its nationwide travel costs and decided it could purchase travel less expensively from a single agency than from different agencies all over the country. Du Pont executives interviewed travel companies over several months to find one they could work with and finally chose Rosenbluth.

From our point of view, it was a marriage made in

heaven. We already knew we had to go national. Our innovations in the consolidation of business-travel purchasing were creating a trend in the industry that made a lot of sense, and we needed to capitalize on it before someone else did. But we couldn't afford to speculate—our margins were too slim. The Du Pont contract allowed us to make an acquisition or open a new office in major Du Pont cities with our principal client already on board. It was a path to national expansion, and the path was client driven.

Moreover, as we spread into new cities, we were also able to expand the services we offered to our other corporate clients. By serving more and more of their facilities, we were able to give them more and more information about their travel patterns and to cut their travel costs even further.

As we began opening more offices, we implemented another critical innovation that prepared us well for national expansion: we linked all our offices electronically. It would have been cheaper to use stand-alone equipment and ship magnetic tapes around the country, consolidating information where needed, but we were hell-bent on getting information to our clients instantaneously. Normally, it took an agency 45 to 75 days to supply a corporation with its own travel data, but a company can miss a lot of opportunities in that much time. Now that our clients can tap into their own travel data in our mainframe—we call it USER-VISION—they can make a decision on Tuesday and see its effects on Thursday. We've become strategic partners with our clients, another logistical arm of their organizations.

CONSTRUCTING AIRFARES FROM THE GROUND UP

In the early 1980s, even before we signed our contract with Du Pont, it dawned on us that we could play a significant role in airfare construction—a move that has since revolutionized the industry.

Clearly, an airplane seat is as perishable a product as one can find. It's not like a can of peas that's still there on the shelf tomorrow if you don't open it today. When a plane leaves the gate, the value of an empty seat drops suddenly to nothing, and the revenue lost can never be recaptured. Working in the room with all those reservation systems, we saw that the airlines were already shaping their fares to fill those unused seats. Yield management, as they called it, had been growing ever since deregulation, and ultimately we figured we'd see planes with no two passengers paying the same price for seats.

But if every seat was going to be managed for maximum yield, why couldn't a travel agency negotiate its own managed fares? We started talking to airlines, offering to fill more of those empty seats if they would reduce the price of their tickets to our clients. We developed systems to track the movement of people from one airline to another, and we were able to show carriers the point of intersection between lowered price and increased revenues.

At the same time, we restructured our commissions to eliminate the inherent conflict of interest within our industry. If Rosenbluth historically made a 10% commission on bookings, then we'd been making $30 on a $300 ticket. But if negotiated seats were now available for $250, why would we want to sell them and make only $25? The solution was to get a higher commission on a less expensive ticket, and then everyone would win. We'd earn more money on lower fares, our clients would save on each ticket purchased, and the airline would increase its total revenues. The key to the whole scheme was having an independent statistical database that showed the airline it could make more money selling cheaper tickets.

Over the years, we have negotiated fares on thousands of routes across the country. I'm not a trained negotiator, and I do very little of the actual negotiating. Most of it's done by colleagues who share my conviction that the greatest strengths we bring to the table are integrity, statistics, long-term vision, and the desire to establish mutually beneficial relationships.

In fact, building mutually beneficial relationships—with our clients, suppliers, and, most importantly, with our associates—has been the key to our success in everything we've done. Since all the problems and opportunities of change rest ultimately on human foundations, fitting people together with technology, tasks, goals, common benefits—and other people—is the jigsaw puzzle that makes or breaks a company.

Change has been Rosenbluth's strength and hallmark. As long as our focus doesn't waver from the people who make it occur, we'll continue to succeed.

Sales at **Hal Rosenbluth**'s *company, now called Rosenbluth International, have grown to $2.5 billion annually, making it the third largest travel management company in the world after American Express and Carlson Wagonlit. Rosenbluth International has operations in 18 countries in South America, Europe, and Asia and joint ventures in Russia and China. The company's 3400 "associates" work with a totally electronic travel and ticketing environment. The North Dakota contingent has grown to 400 people—185 in Linton and more*

than 200 in Fargo—who do reservations and customer service plus a big share of the company's accounting. The Customer Comes Second and Other Secrets of Exceptional Service *(William Morrow, 1992), by Hal F. Rosenbluth and Diane McFerrin Peters, has been a business best-seller in the United States and was translated into Spanish and Chinese.*

2

The Turnaround Value of Values

JOHN THORBECK

IN THE TEN YEARS since I left business school, I've played a critical role in achieving higher sales, lower costs, and bigger profits at three companies. Indeed, if you take it at face value, my résumé looks brilliant:

AS MARKETING DIRECTOR at the Aspen Skiing Company from 1980 to 1983, I managed to increase skier days, which had been declining for several years. I also created the Aspen Foundation to raise money for local causes, and I helped to found the Aspen Winternational, a combination of ski racing and winter carnival that put Aspen on the World Cup circuit and attracted worldwide television coverage every March.

AS HEAD OF MARKETING from 1983 to 1987 at Timberland, a small boot company in New Hampshire, I fought and won a battle between my strategy of selling higher quality boots and shoes at higher prices and an opposing view, championed by the sales department, that we should sell less expensive footwear in army-navy stores and discount outlets. I also waged and won an uphill fight to sponsor the Iditarod sled dog race and identify Timberland with Alaska's frontier ruggedness and endurance. All in all, my marketing strategy helped carry the company from $37 million in annual sales to $110 million.

AS CHIEF EXECUTIVE OFFICER from 1987 until early last year at G.H. Bass & Company, a shoe manufacturer in Maine, I took a company with declining sales, factory closures, big losses, and plummeting morale and turned it around quickly and dramatically, once again by focusing on quality, customers, and the top end of the market.

NOW I'M THE CEO and an owner of the Geo. E. Keith Company, which dates back to 1758 and is not only the oldest shoe manufacturer in the United States but probably also the finest. Like Bass, Geo. E. Keith had fallen on hard times after a period of real greatness early in this century. I've owned it only since March 1990, but I have already begun carrying out a plan to bring it back to the top of an upscale market.

Yet the truth is, behind this string of successes featuring quality focus, innovative marketing, and record profits, I could also put together quite a different kind of personal history, and privately I often do.

In Aspen, for example, a lot of townspeople opposed my marketing schemes, hated the company, and were suspicious of me. Aspen is a pretty combative place, but the Skiing Company, well handled, could have played a unifying role. Establishing the Aspen Foundation was an excellent beginning—today it grants nearly $2 million a year to local non-profit groups. But despite a few good ideas, what I did best was to isolate myself from people in the company and in the community.

At Timberland, what I've called a battle with sales was

actually more like a war. The brothers who owned the company were at odds (one of them compared a typical management meeting to a day in Beirut), and I entered the brawl with such a will that I eventually got fired.

By the time I arrived at Bass, I had learned that confrontational innovation isn't the best way, or even a good way, to manage. Mind you, I'd had pretty good results with it, but my ex-employers had a way of describing me as "controversial" even before they mentioned my wonderful numbers. I approached that new job in a much more sensitive and cooperative spirit. Yet there is still one broad sense in which Bass too was more failure than success for me, despite the company turnaround. For all my success in grasping the company's values and competence and using them to rebuild, I was only beginning to discover a larger point—the coherence *between* values and competence, the spirit that makes organizational values and competence meaningful beyond their mere application to a product or paycheck.

Over the past ten years and three jobs, I've learned that healthy organizations are coherent communities whose personalities, capabilities, and attitudes are consistent with their acts, while unhealthy organizations either lack this coherence or, as in Bass's case, aspire to it against overwhelming opposition, sometimes from the market or some other source but all too often from management. There is no more powerful service a CEO can perform than to communicate coherence and give a company permission to express its latent or suppressed aspirations.

The corollary to this lesson is that you cannot impose an individual's will on an organization without endangering its health. This doesn't mean there's no place for leadership; it means only that leadership can't be independent of the community, that leaders have to understand their organizations and lead them places they are capable of going.

LOSING SIGHT OF THE FOREST FOR THE SHOES

When I stepped in as CEO in 1987, G. H. Bass &
Company was 111 years old. It had begun as a boot and
moccasin maker to loggers in the Maine woods, and the
founder's mission statement—"We will make the best
shoe for the purpose for which it's intended"—was simple, clear, and had a kind of awkward charm. In that
backwoods spirit, Bass continued to make a number of
best shoes for rugged purposes. It made the boots
Charles Lindbergh wore crossing the Atlantic. It made
footwear for Admiral Byrd's expedition to the South Pole
and boots for the U.S. Army's Tenth Mountain Division
in World War II. Since the 1930s, it also made the
world's most famous loafer, the Bass Weejun (short for
"Norwegian slipper," the import from Norway that
inspired it).

But when I took over, that history had been largely
forgotten, and the company had lost its way. During the
previous four years, Bass had lost $72 million—$46 million in 1986 alone. It had also closed six of eight domestic factories, though it was still making, by my count,
620 different models of 17 different categories of shoes, a
good indication of how far it had wandered from its original mission statement. Far from making the best shoe
for a few specific uses, Bass now seemed determined to
make several shoes of varying quality for every purpose
anyone could possibly name. The company had a massive inventory.

It took a lot of guts to make me CEO. At Timberland,
I had played a part in one of the few marketing success
stories in recent U.S. shoe business history, but I was
only 35 years old, had never been a CEO, had only four
years of industry experience, and had never in my life
had more than six people reporting to me. But Phillips-
Van Heusen had just acquired Bass from Chesebrough-
Pond's, which had been trying to unload it for two years,

and CEO Larry Phillips and COO Bruce Klatsky wanted
to take a chance on me. For one thing, Klatsky was only
39 himself, so in principle he liked young executives.
For another, Klatsky and Larry Phillips believed that
what Bass needed was marketing, not sales or manufacturing, and I was certainly all marketing. I believed marketing direction was all a business really needed.

Conversely, all three of us knew from the start that we
disagreed on strategy. Over the previous 10 to 20 years,
large clothing retailers had been dropping brand names
and moving more and more toward private labels, which
they usually bought directly from manufacturers in Asia.
With no confidence that even a well-established trade-
mark insured them against this private-label threat, Larry
Phillips and Phillips-Van Heusen concluded that the traditional business of selling brand-name apparel through
department stores had little future. Their counterstrategy
was to set up their own direct links to customers
through factory outlets.

Phillips and Klatsky thought these same general
ground rules applied to footwear and wanted to expand
Bass's factory-outlet business aggressively. They also figured that with Bass's reputation for quality, direct discount retailing would be a quick way to recover their
purchase price.

My opposing view was that brands dominated the shoe
market and always would. Shoes were not a commodity. I
thought we should revive Bass's reputation for quality
and reestablish our relationships with major retail stores.

In spite of our differences, the three of us got along
well. I believed they would come around to my point of
view in time, that I could convince them with results.
They believed I could set a new direction, boost morale,
revise the product line, and reposition the brand, and
they were perfectly happy to let me pursue a high-
quality, full-price wholesale strategy while they continued to push factory-outlet sales.

My first day on the job, a Monday morning in November 1987, I called together the senior executives in the main office in Falmouth, Maine. "We've got to make some changes," I told them. "Let's try to make them together." It was a brief, guarded meeting.

Afterward, the senior vice president for manufacturing took me aside and suggested I pay a visit to the factory in Wilton, Maine, where the company had started. No CEO had been there for four years, he told me. He and I made the one-hour drive the next day, and I received another guarded welcome from the workers and supervisors there. They had good reason. None of them had received a raise for four years, and they knew management had already closed all but two of the Bass factories in the United States.

But one of the few good things about companies in trouble is that they're nervous about the status quo and primed for change. We began with a long list of conventionally drastic steps. We cut $9.3 million in costs, some of it by closing down a design office in Italy and a warehouse and distributorship in Canada. We liquidated $21 million in inventory. I changed a lot of senior management and switched the sales representatives from straight commission to salary and bonus, which led 20 of 30 of them to quit.

From conventional changes, I moved quickly to changes that were more fundamental. I cut 620 design patterns to 200 and 17 footwear categories to 6. I asked the people on our product-development team to make a superior product in three of those categories, and I told them not to worry about price. We needed to make a statement about Bass quality to retailers and consumers even if the shoes didn't sell. We also needed to make a statement about manufacturing quality to our own employees, who for years had continued to make good shoes as a matter of pride, perhaps, but not as a matter of company policy.

I sensed that people were ready to rise to the occasion, and it was an invigorating feeling. I moved up the introduction date of the new line by six months, and we planned Bass's first advertising campaign in four years—12-page inserts in *Vogue* and *GQ*. We were offering 11 new models at prices over $100, about twice what Bass had ever charged for a pair of shoes. We launched the new line in the spring of 1988, delivered shoes in the fall, and all that time I held my breath.

LITTLE VICTORIES

Company vision and philosophy are pretty lofty terms. I had no grand vision when I started. Later I thought I could see that most of the changes I made were the right ones for Bass, but at the time it was largely an accident. I had come in with the idea that I was going to impose direction and, by the force of my personality, by sheer authority and the demands of the market, I was going to transform the company. I wasn't interested in philosophy, I just wanted to sell some shoes and prove a point to Phillips-Van Heusen.

It took me a year to realize that the issue of vision was perhaps transcendent. At the outset, I was just a marketing guy with no experience in manufacturing. I had never been in charge of finance, personnel, or data processing, and it was clear to me that I was never going to know more about those areas than the people already in place. The question for me, I realized, was how to bring all these people together.

On one of my first days on the job, I asked for a copy of every report used in management. The next day, 23 of them appeared on my desk. I didn't understand them. The manufacturing reports were written in manufacturing language, the finance reports in finance language, and the sales reports in sales language. Manufacturing talked about hand-sewn shoes from Wilton and cemented shoes from Brazil. Sales information was organized by individual salesperson and dollars rather than by product or geography. Financial information was accounting-driven not customer-driven. Each area's reports were Greek to the other areas, and all of them were Greek to me. Since we had to start cutting costs and products, we were going to have to do a lot of talking, but until we had a single market-driven language, we weren't going to have any common management information to talk about.

We spent the next year throwing out the old separate languages and translating the databases into market terms. We had reduced our production to six categories of shoes—for example, all loafers were now part of the Weejun collection and all boat shoes belonged to the Outdoor collection—so we built our language around those categories.

I also put together a Monday morning management meeting where we just talked about the business, informally and frankly. I knew right from the start I was going to have a hard time finding things to get excited about in those meetings, so I focused hard on little victories.

A little victory might be a report from sales that a particular account had accepted the $100 shoes, even if they'd taken only a hundred pairs. One important little victory was being named "Western Maine Business of the Year" in 1988. All right, Western Maine is only Franklin and Oxford counties, but it mattered a lot to people who'd been afraid of closure. Another important little victory was making a special pair of Weejuns for President Bush and having him send us a thank-you note and a picture of himself examining our new upgraded shoes. That meant a lot.

Maybe my favorite was a wildly successful United Way campaign in the company. We went from less than 50% participation the year before to 73%, and contributions quadrupled. We made quite a big deal out of that—it showed that we were a company that could set goals and then exceed them.

The psychology behind the little victories was to lower expectations but create believers. I told everyone the new line was not going to save the company and that I didn't want us focused on one big sales result. I wanted us all to concentrate on things that were more immediate and continuous—little week-to-week victories rather than a single, great triumph. I needed believers. I hired some, I created some, and I found a lot more already on the payroll, most of them in Wilton. Very gradually I became a believer myself, but to my own surprise, a believer not so much in marketing as in vision and community. I started to believe in G. H. Bass & Company as a cohesive organization with consistent strengths and purposes.

TRACKING DOWN HISTORY

Bass's owners did not share that belief, and that difference came to epitomize our strategic disagreement. The owners had seen tastes change and cost pressures rise as the shoe business moved steadily toward lower cost and higher fashion. They'd seen athletic shoes steal the casual market from loafers, and they'd watched offshore production run away with 90% of domestic shoe consumption. Not surprisingly, they had come to take a dim view of Bass's traditional, expensive product. As far as they could make out, the "Made in Maine" label was a cost albatross. For Chesebrough-Pond's and now for Phillips-Van Heusen, the old strengths were weaknesses.

But I now thought we could resell those old strengths to customers, to the owners, and, for that matter, to the company itself. Since I'm not much interested in businesses that have to be reinvented every year, I wanted to reassociate the name with quality and build a product line more enduring than season-to-season fashion. In order to capture that sense of continuity, however, we had to recapture the company's past. We began resurrecting stories about George Henry Bass, who founded the company in 1876, and about the shoes we made for Admiral Byrd and Charles Lindbergh. We advertised as "The look that never wears out," and we put that line about "The best shoe for the purpose" right on every box.

Of course, corporate history is tricky. As an external, cosmetic reference, history is just hype. History can also be a form of escape, a way of turning your back on the present by invoking a comfortable past and clinging to it. But as a statement of company values, of a company's inherent way of doing things, history can be powerful.

People want to be associated with something larger and more enduring than themselves. For most of this century, however, our view of progress has been a resolute march away from the old toward the modern, usually defined in terms of high volume and low cost. Yet organizations that turn their backs on their history and traditions are often turning their backs on their values, on their need for vision and purpose, and on their own particular competence.

I wanted to know more about Bass's personality, values, and history because I wanted to match them with new business opportunities. Quantitative measures drove U.S. business for most of this century, but we're no longer a mass-market society, and an exclusive reliance on market share is an anachronism. What drives successful businesses today is market responsiveness, and yet it wasn't as simple as saying that market values would determine the right direction for Bass to take. To motivate Bass toward a new future, we had to understand its past, honor its strengths, and build on them. To make Bass into the kind of company I wanted it to be, we had to know who we were.

In March of 1988, I hired a new director of marketing

to manage the process of making history relevant. As I saw it, our job was not so much to recapture Weejun popularity as to tie Bass quality to contemporary tastes. I also hired a corporate identity consultant to redo our packaging and our image, but we needed facts to work with. The company was like grandma's attic. We knew there were a lot of interesting stories up there, but we had to dig them out. I decided to hire an archivist as well. Over the summer of 1988, he put together a company history, a kind of family album, partly from interviews, partly from company documents and clippings that one of the secretaries in Wilton had spent years collecting and cataloging in her spare time. The idea was not to produce advertising copy but to identify the company's personality, values, and idiosyncrasies and then try to match them with the new market realities.

The archivist helped to uncover four specific qualities I knew we could use in turning the company around.

First, amazingly enough, the values of the company were still closely connected to the Bass family, who had sold the company in the 1970s. The culture and ethos of the organization were still those of a proud family shoe company that was centered in a small town. The work force had simply never acknowledged that the real owner was now a distant corporate giant.

A second important company quality was loyalty, expressed at that time in a willingness to accept adversity. Our employees were loyal even in hard times, which relates back to the small-town values. Cynics will say they had no choice, that there simply weren't any other jobs, but that's not quite true. There were paper mills within 25 miles that paid more—double and triple what we were paying at the Wilton factory—so there must have been something about Bass that kept people there.

Third was a persistent belief that Bass was the best, even though, in fact, many competitors had passed us by. For the people in Wilton, Bass still stood for superior quality—or at least the potential for superior quality. Either way, quality was still a Bass hallmark in their minds.

Finally, Bass had a number of key employees who had been with the company for decades. They were informal leaders of a kind, enjoyed great respect in the organization, and helped bring stability to an unstable situation. They were also the people who carried the company's oral history. Back in the 1950s and 1960s, for example, Weejuns were sold by allocation—each retailer got only so many pairs. Demand always exceeded supply. The older work force still basked in that glory, like a baseball team that had won a pennant 30 years before. So the redirection of the company toward higher quality and a traditional, classic product line rang true for them.

There was, in short, a set of historical organizational values that we could use to make a coherent whole out of manufacturing, marketing, sales, and accounting. What I found at Bass was a company whose management focused almost entirely on costs, placed no value in work, and ignored the company's history. What we managed to create or, rather, rejuvenate, was a company that knew its strengths and how to use them. And all we had to do was give it permission to be itself. Bass wasn't just a name on shoes. It was a community.

SUCCESS AND FAILURE

In the spring of 1988, we presented the new product line to 20 department stores all over the country.

We had projected initial orders of 30,000 pairs, but they ran twice that, and our first-season sales were 150,000 pairs. From a loss of $46 million on sales of $150 million in 1986, we took the company to a $16 million profit on sales of $180 million in 1988. And we did it on the basis of premium quality, which meant we had taken the company back to something approximating its original condition. The basic Bass competence had been a handicap, and we'd turned it back into an asset.

This should be the happy ending. But I tell this story as if I'd been the owner, and of course I was not. In reality, I represented a corporation in New York whose strategy and values matched Bass's in some ways and differed hugely in others. Phillips-Van Heusen was as eager as Bass to save brand names in shoes and clothing, for example, and Larry Phillips and Bruce Klatsky approved of most of my initiatives. They were skeptical about magazine advertising, and they thought I was moving too fast in changing sales compensation, but they never said no to anything I did. And they never mentioned company history one way or the other.

Where we parted ways completely was on the question of factory outlets. Their plan was to trade on the grand old Bass name and its reputation for quality, greatly expand our discount outlets, and make a ton of money. One of the reasons I moved so quickly on the new line of $100 shoes was to produce results that would show them we could make as much or more on genuine quality, a strategy with two additional advantages: it wouldn't wear thin when customers woke up to the fact that cheap Bass shoes were cheaply made, and it would give our own work force a shot in the arm.

For a while, Phillips and Klatsky were willing to tolerate both strategies—wholesale quality and retail discounts—but in the long run that dual strategy sent incompatible messages both to customers and to employees. Since they refused to believe we could be wholesale-driven, and since they couldn't cajole me into spending more time and energy on retail, Larry Phillips decided to have the retail stores report directly to the retailing division of Phillips-Van Heusen. He let me keep wholesaling for myself, but I became the CEO of less than a whole company.

Our differences of opinion grew so serious that Phillips-Van Heusen hired a strategy consultant to come in and review the principal issue: were shoes commodity-oriented like apparel, or was a brand-name, wholesale strategy viable? The consultant did a six-month study, and in my opinion he validated the strategy I favored, but it made no difference. As far as Bass was concerned, Phillips-Van Heusen simply ignored the implications of his report. Eventually I resigned.

It's very tempting for me to say that Phillips-Van Heusen was wrong and leave it at that. The company had a chance to fill a lucrative, upscale market niche by reinvigorating a long-standing Bass heritage, and it chose not to.

The problem with this seductive line of reasoning, of course, is that the strategy decision was ultimately theirs to make. For all my talk about coherence, I had failed to include the owners in my picture of the Bass community. And because I was trying to take the company someplace its owners simply wouldn't let it go, my lasting gift to Bass was frustration. There is a big gap between the picture I painted for the work force and the actual strategy it now pursues.

BUILDING SHOES TO A STANDARD, NOT A PRICE

In my present job as CEO of Geo. E. Keith, I've pared down the community and eliminated the opportunity for strategy conflict by owning the company. My experience at Bass had convinced me that my strategy could work. It had also convinced my friends F. Warren Hellman and John Pasquesi of the investment firm of Hellman & Friedman in San Francisco, who calculated that even my aborted efforts at Bass had created more than $150 million in value. Together we looked for a midsize company to buy, something with annual sales on the order of $50 million.

We couldn't find one, but we did eventually find Geo.

E. Keith Company, the tiny, declining remnant of the 200-year-old and once world-famous Keith shoe dynasty. In the first half of this century, it sold premium-quality shoes under its own Walk-Over brand name in 102 countries. At its peak, some 6,000 employees in 9 factories made 1,200 different models and a total of 20,000 pairs of shoes a day.

By the time we found it, production had dropped by more than 95% and annual sales stood at $12 million, but the company had never cheapened its product or gone offshore. Every shoe still spent five days on the last (the shoe form), and welt construction was still standard even for women's shoes (most manufacturers cement them). The company kept its inventory records in big, old-fashioned ledgers and submitted its quarterly financials to the bank in longhand. Two hundred workers still made Walk-Overs for 200 to 300 of the 6,000 retail stores that once carried them (including, still, Barneys in New York and J. Simon in London), but the company's principal business was now top quality private-label shoes for a handful of retailers and brands, among them Brooks Brothers, Cole-Haan, Marshall Field, and L.L. Bean.

I never looked at Geo. E. Keith as a broken-down company. I looked at the industry as a whole and wondered how Keith had survived at all when scores of others had gone under. The answer lay in its history and its values, which we could resurrect as a key to reinterpreting the brand and the company itself. No one had ever heard of Geo. E. Keith, but this Rip van Winkle company was still making the finest footwear in America.

I met the workers my first day and told them it was their workmanship that drew me. I told them they could be proud of their quality and promised them an ambitious, quality-driven strategy. I felt good about that meeting. The place had a good feel to it. When I came in the next morning, a Wednesday, I poured myself a cup of

coffee and went back into the factory. No one was
there. The factory manager had sent everyone home
until Monday because there were not enough orders
in production.

So my work was cut out for me, but at least I had a
company whose history I could honor and build on. I am
not a sentimentalist by any means. I don't want to go
back in time and re-create a once-great company in its
former glory. But I do believe in character, and formerly
great companies often have all the character needed for
building a great future on the foundation of their past.

The George E. Keith for whom the company was
named was a fifth generation descendent of the first
Keith shoemaker. An enormously innovative man, he
introduced the first brand-name shoes in the United
States, was the first shoe manufacturer to bypass jobbers
and do his own wholesaling, became the first U.S. shoemaker to open his own stores in Europe, established one
of the first employee health programs in the world, and
was one of the first businessmen anywhere to make use
of multimedia advertising (in 1906, when movies were
still a novelty, the company made a promotional film
about its factories and distributed it nationwide). But
most important, George E. Keith and his company made
an early commitment to quality, and they reaffirmed that
commitment every time the market seemed to demand
lower prices and a lesser product. When other companies did whatever they could to cut costs during the
Depression, the Geo. E. Keith Company decided to build
its shoes just a little bit better than before

"Quality only will count" and "The victory of quality"
were typical company war cries. So was the idea of building shoes "to a standard not a price." Shortly after
George E. Keith died, his son Harold told his assembled
retailers, "I want you to always remember that this is not
an ordinary business, but an institution with a heart,
with broad principles and high ideals. It is a monument,

the foundation of which George E. Keith laid, and he laid it square and straight and true."

Grand words about a mere businessman, but then he was talking about the man who once said, "There is an honor in business that is the fine gold of it; that reckons with every man justly; that loves life; that regards kindness and fairness more highly than goods or prices or profits. It becomes a man more than his furnishings or his house; it speaks for him in the hearts of everyone."

If we can't rebuild a profitable, thriving company with values like those as our raw material, then I haven't learned as much about coherence as I think I have.

*The Geo. E. Keith Co. closed its doors in December 1994, the victim of a poor economy, the loss of its biggest customer, and, **John Thorbeck** insists, some early errors in judgment. As Thorbeck sees the failure, he bit off more than he could chew in attempting "the world's first leveraged startup turnaround"—trying to give the Walk-Over brand a fresh lease on life while seeking to turn around the production of private-label shoes, all under the burden of a great deal of debt. Walk-Overs were doing relatively well, with gradually increasing sales through Nordstrom's, Macy's, and Federated Department Stores, among others. But in a poor economy, shoes are one of the first purchases people postpone, and private-label sales declined sharply. When lackluster sales figures led to disagreements among the company's financial backers— and when the company's biggest single customer rejected Thorbeck's innovative proposal to use Geo. E. Keith's on-shore location and short lead times to make small test runs of new designs that would later be produced in quantity abroad—the company could not survive.*

"It is embarrassing," says John Thorbeck, "to speak grandly about

ideals and principles while commanding a sinking ship, but in fact I've lost none of my convictions. In the course of my career, I developed a set of business values very like the ones George E. Keith used to build and nurture an enormously successful company. I don't think the values were the problem. The problem was my own lack of tough-mindedness as I pursued them."

3

The Reluctant Entrepreneur

KEN VEIT

FOR YEARS, I'VE been reading about executives who
leave their jobs and go into business for themselves,
where they find contentment and learn the meaning of
life. Now that I've done it, I'm here to tell you it isn't
quite that easy.

I was on the corporate fast track for almost 30 years,
and now I own a retail store in a mall. The first experience had money, perks, and status. The second has 15-
hour days, unacceptable risk, no salary, no security, and,
just maybe, no future.

There is another side to the coin, of course. I have no
more soporific meetings, reports, and slide presentations.
I am also a better all-around executive now than I was in
my corporate days. I am more self-reliant. Most important, I have more business flexibility and more personal
freedom. But the experience so far has certainly not been
the idyll some former executives describe.

When I left graduate school in 1961, I took a job with
an insurance company, and over the next 28 years I was
promoted nine times and given annual raises averaging

15%. I became an actuary, a product-development wizard, and eventually a global strategist, negotiator, and diplomat. By 1985, I was international division president of one of the world's largest insurance companies.

Like most executives at my level, I had never actually sold an insurance policy. The customer interface never particularly interested me. What did interest me was penetrating new markets, opening offices, and buying and selling insurance companies. In 1985, for example, I bought a 40% interest in a Spanish company for $10 million, and three years later our Spanish partner offered to buy back our share for more than $100 million. I enjoyed that. I enjoyed most of what I did. Unlike a lot of executives, I didn't thirst to go out and build my own business and be my own boss.

On April 11, 1989, I was fired. The official version said, "Ken Veit has elected to retire and pursue outside interests," but that was nonsense. I loved my job. Anyway, what outside interests? All I did was work. I was allowed to retire as a courtesy and to preserve my medical benefits, but the truth of the matter is that I was achieving long-term gains at the cost of short-term losses. I was a builder in a time of containment and expense cutting, so they had no further use for me.

Severance was generous. I got full salary for 18 months and then a pension at 20% of my former base pay. Counting benefits and outplacement, the company spent roughly half a million dollars to make me go away. Sometimes I would wake up at night and think, "I have 28 years of experience. I've made millions for the company and have knowledge that will cost them millions more to duplicate in someone else. Yet they were willing to spend $500,000 for nothing—just to get rid of me."

I was outraged that they could have made such an incorrect judgment, wasted so much money, written off so much of value. Friends and colleagues assured me that with my experience and track record, some other insurance company would snap me up. I thought so too.

For 18 months, I averaged one hot prospect a month. I interviewed well, I was suitably eager, but the insurance industry was in disarray. My strength had been expansion, building new markets in new regions. Suddenly, no one was expanding. The industry was hiring only downsizers.

By late 1990, I had to choose: continue the search and hope the job market would improve or do something radically different. My finances were not inexhaustible. I had two college-age stepsons, the collapsing real-estate market had eaten up most of the liquidity in my house, and my principal asset—some 30,000 shares of unexercised stock options—had become virtually worthless when my former company lost its AAA rating and its stock price fell by 50%. Nevertheless, if I moved quickly, I still had enough to start a small but adequately capitalized business.

Opening a small business in a recession may seem a poor choice, but so was the alternative. And I did have some definite advantages. To begin with, I would not be starting on a shoestring. Also, unlike many new entrepreneurs, I had experience in every aspect of business. Indeed, I scored high on every index of potential entrepreneurial success. I was a workaholic. I did not give up easily. I thrived on challenge. I figured that running a small business involved meticulous planning, a great deal of negotiating, and a level head for coping with constant crises. As luck would have it, planning, deal-making, and crisis management were my strong suits. It's true I'd grown used to five-star hotels, limousines, and the Concorde, but I knew it wouldn't kill me to change my own light bulbs and lick my own stamps.

In short, I felt prepared for whatever small business had to offer.

I HAD BOUGHT AND sold enough insurance businesses to know that buying someone else's problems is extremely risky, especially in a small business where the buyer knows so much less than the seller and the margin for error is so tiny. This led me to franchising. In franchising, I could benefit from—rather than pay for—the earlier mistakes of others. I could also expect to draw on an established support system of the kind I'd grown used to as a corporate executive. I was wary of trying to run a small business without any help whatsoever. I investigated several franchises before settling on a relatively new company called Cartoon Corner.

The idea for Cartoon Corner came from the Disney stores, which had expanded into shopping malls all over the country. But the Disney stores sold only Disney products. If your passion was Bugs Bunny or Betty Boop, you were out of luck. Cartoon Corner, on the other hand, carried thousands of products featuring hundreds of cartoon characters from all of the studios.

For me, however, the special genius of Cartoon Corner was its marketing concept. The product was not primarily toys or children's clothing. The product was nostalgia, all our pleasant memories of a childhood full of Mickey Mouse and Snoopy. Moreover, since the studios had already spent millions promoting each cartoon character, every product in a Cartoon Corner store had instant name recognition. The need to advertise was minimal. In addition to the T-shirts, videos, games, novelties, and stuffed animals, about a quarter of a store's sales came from animation art, one of the hottest collectibles in the art world.

Still, I had no special knowledge of cartoons, and keeping track of more than 25,000 pieces of inventory, from postcards to jewelry, seemed an overwhelming task. Unlike many franchisors, who take your money and hand you a manual, Cartoon Corner offered an extensive training program followed by a surprising amount of ongoing support.

The management information system was state-of-the-art. In a business this trendy, one key to success is knowing which characters sell and which products are hot. The MIS left nothing to guesswork. It analyzed sales and integrated every operation of the stores, from purchasing and receiving to point-of-sale activities and inventory maintenance. It even had a complete general ledger accounting module. You still had to manage your personnel, of course, but the computer provided every possible tool.

I had listened to a lot of franchising schemes, and this one seemed to make sense. The franchise executives, in particular, impressed me. They were young and bright, and they had solid, thoughtful answers to my questions.

The company was operating several wholly owned stores in the Northeast, and these were doing quite well. The management team treated each of them as an experiment, discarding features that failed, incorporating those that worked into the other stores. After 2 1/2 years in operation, company leaders had already rebuffed two substantial acquisition offers from big corporations. They planned to franchise 100 stores over the next few years, then go public. If all went well, the Cartoon Corner chain could build a market valuation of $75 to $100 million by the mid-1990s.

It all sounded too good to be true.

IN MY FORMER JOB, planning had been a cloistered activity. Getting our hands dirty had no part in the process. We sat in our executive suites in near-clinical isolation, poring over numbers and designing grand strategic models. Management believed that if these models were sufficiently sophisticated, with enough variables to represent the key features of the real world, then our job as managers was, first, to construct sets of assumptions that would produce satisfactory outcomes and, second, to make those assumptions come true. In practice, of course, no set of assumptions can be controlled so nicely. Something always screws it up.

Variables vary. Luck intervenes. Our plans veered farther and farther from reality, until they lost most of their affinity with actual conditions and all of their relevance for action. When we reached this impasse, we either started over with new sets of assumptions or we refined the models.

Part of our problem was a tendency to confuse planning with forecasting. Forecasting begins with the need to produce acceptable numbers and works backward. It is a necessary activity, but it's not what I'd call planning. In my book, planning is about responses to what the real world dishes up.

With no experience of merchandising, customers, or credit, I now sat down to plan—or, rather, forecast—my future. Cartoon Corner's talented CEO had a wonderfully sophisticated computer model of a Cartoon Corner store. Since it is illegal for a franchisor to make projections for a potential franchisee, I persuaded him to let me use his model and put in my own assumptions about sales, payroll, rent, operating expenses, and much more.

This approach is full of pitfalls. It's easy to get caught up in the sophistication of the model. But with no retail experience, I had nothing to rely on except Cartoon Corner's data and industry averages.

I went on with my due diligence. I contacted the venture capitalists backing Cartoon Corner, who were putting up $1 million a year to finance its expansion. They were brusque but reassuring. Recognizing my vulnerability, I even went so far as to hire a consultant to evaluate the whole scheme independently before I signed on. Everything kept coming up green.

My wife and I were living in Connecticut at the time, but we were more than willing to leave. Cartoon Corner proposed a space in a new mall then under construction in Scottsdale, Arizona. It was a part of the country we had always liked, so I went out to investigate.

The new mall represented a fresh concept in retailing:

an entertainment mall. With so many department stores in financial trouble, the developers had decided to challenge the notion that a shopping center must have anchor stores. Instead it would have a million-gallon, shark-filled aquarium with a 450-foot walk-through acrylic tunnel, seven movie theaters (including an IMAX with a six-story screen), a sound-and-light show, a musical fountain that shot water 90 feet in the air, a dozen restaurants and night clubs, and an amusement center with a high-tech miniature golf course and a space-flight simulator. America West was installing a departure lounge with luxury buses that would shuttle back and forth to the Phoenix airport. Finally, Omni Hotels planned to build a five-star hotel on an adjacent piece of land.

Clearly, this was meant to be one of the leading tourist attractions of the Southwest. In addition to all of the entertainment features, there would be 240 retail stores—not the usual shops found in regional malls everywhere but exclusive European boutiques, art galleries, antique dealers, museum-quality stores. The creative genius behind the mall had previously performed a similar miracle in Canada, while the builder was one of the largest and most prestigious shopping-center developers in the United States.

The cost of my Cartoon Corner venture was to be about $300,000. Half of that was for fitting out the space, since everything, even walls, was the tenant's responsibility. When I learned that Cartoon Corner had negotiated a lease for me on such favorable terms that the developer was paying for 100% of the leasehold improvements, every red light in my internal warning system suddenly winked on. Why, I thought, would the developer give me a prime location on favorable terms and then pay all of the build-out expense? It was crazy. If the mall was the blockbuster it promised to be, I should be paying for the privilege, not the other way around.

But once again, the answer made sense. Having avoided the huge expenses associated with attracting major department stores, the developers were able to spend money attracting the specialty stores they wanted. I earned additional points by committing before the building was completed. Moreover, the developer was a shareholder in Cartoon Corner and so had an interest in my success. Finally, and most important, since I was one of its first five franchisees, Cartoon Corner itself had a particular interest in seeing me succeed. I was to be a bell cow, and as long as it was all above board, I certainly had no cause to complain.

I made several trips to Scottsdale before the end of the year. The mall was progressing splendidly, and in early December, my wife and I found a beautiful house in Paradise Valley. It was more expensive than our reduced finances would really allow, but it was a repossessed property that had been on the market for some time, and the bank was willing to give us a sweetheart deal. In fact, by buying this house with almost nothing down, we could use our cash to pay for all of the remaining franchise costs. It was better than buying a much less expensive house, putting a large deposit down, and financing the store through a Small Business Administration loan as originally planned. In effect, it was near-permanent financing of inventory at a rate of 10%. It felt as good as any multimillion-dollar deal I'd ever made in the corporate world.

If we hit the sales of $400 per square foot that the company hinted at (some Cartoon Corner stores were doing even better) and held our expenses to normal levels, I would take home something in the low six-figure range. Moreover, because of our instant product recognition, there would be little of the ramping up most new stores experience. However, being an old hand at marking down optimistic plans, I cut the sales projection to $350 per square foot and increased the expenses.

Together with my pension, this would still give us a very comfortable lifestyle. Not so grand as before, perhaps, but I had been traveling nearly 200,000 miles a year since 1981, and I was happy to put the pseudo-glamour behind me.

I signed a franchise agreement on December 21, 1990 and closed on the house the following week. We would not move in until March, but our first mortgage payment wasn't due until March 1.

IN JANUARY, I BEGAN training at Cartoon Corner's headquarters in Woburn, Massachusetts. It went extremely well. Along with one other franchisee, I was taught everything they thought I should know about retailing, computer systems, strategy, and products.

In early February, I went to Scottsdale to finalize the lease and hire a manager. The mall was scheduled to open in late March. My actuarial training and experience had taught me to put faith in numbers, conservatively derived, and so far the numbers looked better and better. It was true that the Gulf War had put the economy temporarily on ice, but over the long term, surely, the numbers would hold up.

Over the coming months, I was to learn for myself the truth of an observation once made by Denis Healey, the former British chancellor of the exchequer. For planning purposes, he wrote, "The precision of numbers often bears no relation to the facts."

When I arrived in Scottsdale, I learned that the mall's opening had been pushed back two months. The building was finished, but a number of planned stores had been put on hold. However, the developer assured me that the mall was still 80% leased, with 50% of the stores to open in May. And the entertainment features were still moving forward, though the aquarium would probably not open until the fall. I could feel the ground starting to shift.

I took another look at the numbers. It was too late to back out. In the soft real-estate market, I'd be crucified if I tried to sell the house we'd just bought. I compared the costs of backing out with the risks of going forward. I negotiated substantial rent concessions, redid the financial plan at $300 per square foot for the first year, cut expenses, and decided it was all still feasible.

Before I had recovered from this setback, however, Cartoon Corner announced it was going into liquidation. This seemed impossible, but it was true. The recession had cut into cash flow severely. Management was having no trouble signing up new franchisees, but it was taking longer than expected for the new stores to start producing revenues, and the costs of the franchise support systems were too high to handle without income. Cash out suddenly outstripped cash in as the Gulf War brought mall traffic to a virtual standstill all over the country.

At this point, Cartoon Corner's venture-capital backers reassessed the feasibility of hypergrowth in a recession, spotted better opportunities elsewhere, and pulled the plug. It all happened so fast, there was no time for them to try raising money from other sources.

Once again, I looked at the numbers. I had been through most of the training and received most of the value from my franchise fee. (I certainly was not going to get any of it back.) My sunk costs were more than $100,000, and, of course, there was the house. There were two major risks in going forward on my own: my inexperience at retailing and the loss of support provided by the franchising organization, chiefly volume discounts. On the positive side, there would no longer be a monthly franchise fee to pay.

I put a $25,000 value on the cost of my likely mistakes of inexperience, and I assumed a 3% reduction in gross margin due to the loss of volume discounts and other franchise support. Offsetting this was the 6% saving on franchise fees. In addition, I could save at least

$10,000 by purchasing some of my initial inventory from Cartoon Corner's corporate stores at liquidation prices.

On balance, all this was a wash. What *wasn't* a wash was that I was now in this thing alone. For the first time in my life, I realized uncomfortably, I was truly on my own—no staff support, no colleagues to confer with, no larger organization to help absorb the business blows that were bound to come.

Since every cloud has its silver lining, one of the first results of Cartoon Corner's collapse was a chance to acquire the franchise's most profitable store at a fraction of its actual value. Since I didn't have the cash to take advantage of this opportunity—and since it would have been insane to attempt to run two stores on opposite sides of the country—I began looking for a partner. Two candidates with excellent experience were excited about the financial prospects. Both backed out when they realized they would actually have to live in New Jersey.

Another possible joint venture popped up when one of Cartoon Corner's former vice presidents offered to go into partnership with me to do catalog sales of animation art. In lieu of severance, the company had given him its list of art buyers, and he proposed that we offer my inventory to his market. Since there was little risk and great potential reward, I was delighted.

MY WIFE AND I arrived in the Arizona desert in mid-March to a week of steady rain. It turned out to be especially for my parade. I'd no sooner landed than I learned that the mall's grand opening in May had been downgraded to a "Preview Opening," with only 25% of the stores ready for business.

This led to more negotiations, further rent concessions, and another revision of my first-year sales forecast to $250 per square foot. If we went through the summer with a skeleton staff, we might just make it until the real opening in the fall. Even so, it didn't appear that I would make enough the first year to cover my huge mortgage payments on the house. The catalog sales now became critical.

This roller-coaster alternation of bad news, good news, bad news was exhilarating and educational, but it was very hard to live with. Now the roller coaster suddenly gave way to a kind of entrepreneurial skydiving, and I discovered the world of small business free-fall.

Three new blows fell in rapid succession. First, my prospective joint venture partner in catalog sales suddenly changed his mind and decided to go it alone. Second, an important supplier of animation art abruptly cut me off because an existing customer in Scottsdale was also moving into the new mall, and the supplier wouldn't sell to both of us. Third, my bank unexpectedly pulled an important plug.

Although the developers were paying for the leasehold improvements, I had to pay the general contractor first and then apply for reimbursement. To do this, I needed a 30-day bridge loan. My bank first told me there would be no problem; but when they learned of the additional delays at the mall, they got cold feet. I wound up defaulting on my obligation to the general contractor. For someone who used to prepay his credit cards before leaving on a trip, this was a terrible humiliation. Fortunately, my contractor generously carried me until the developers paid off.

"Anxious Nights" would make a good title for those two months. I was up at four o'clock most mornings, pacing the floors and worrying about all of the things that might go wrong. The things that did go wrong were worse. For example, the inventory I had purchased at liquidation prices was improperly packed and arrived with thousands of dollars worth of damage.

I was on the phone constantly, starting at dawn in Phoenix when offices were opening back east. In one month, I logged over 500 calls to straighten out orders,

negotiate credit, track down lost shipments. My combined personal credit-card limits exceeded $50,000, but
now I was pleading with vendors to ship a $250 order
and give me 30 days to pay.

I was used to long hours but not to weeks on end of
15-hour days. I had to think of everything, forget nothing, initiate anything I wanted done, and do most of it
myself. Somehow, everything was ready on time.

The day before the new mall's official opening, a customer wandered in and bought a Marvin Martian T-shirt
and a yo-yo. It took me and my manager 45 minutes to
process this transaction on the computerized register, but
already we were $21.09 ahead of plan.

We opened formally the next day, May 23, 1991. We
had a beautiful store in a prime location near the main
entrance to a spectacular mall. The general gaiety was
dampened only by the facts: a mere 20 stores of an originally planned 240 were open, and there were no theaters,
no restaurants, no aquarium, no hotel, no airline departure lounge, no miniature golf, and no space-flight simulator. The *Arizona Republic*'s feature article concentrated
on the emptiness.

Yet that first week was like Christmas. Thousands of
people poured in to see the long-awaited, sensational
new mall. Customers lined up before we opened in the
morning, and they banged on the doors after we closed
at night.

The second week was a quick dive back into reality.
Reactions to the store and the mall were still enthusiastic, but people had come to *see* the place, not to do any
serious shopping. The structure itself was clearly worth a
trip, and people said they loved it. Then they promised
to come back as soon as more stores were open.

THE SUMMER WAS ALL about hanging on. Scottsdale is
dead in the summer, anyway. Temperatures routinely exceed 110°, and everyone who can afford it goes someplace

cool. Our daily sales were often less than $100. The recession obviously hadn't ended. Customers would come in, look at everything, tell us how much they loved it all, and buy a postcard. From June to September, sales volumes for everything but art were running at 25% of the levels we needed to break even. Fortunately, art sales took off quickly and stayed relatively strong.

As it turned out, our amazing computer systems were amazingly problematic. We struggled to cope with machine malfunctions and our own inexperience. Since the computer refused to disgorge its financial secrets, I now plunged into the mysterious world of trial balances and audit trails and began to keep a parallel set of books by hand. I found that manual books have a purity and simplicity no computer can match. When you're balancing a critical account at five in the morning, for example, handwritten books never flash messages like "Reading Error Tape Drive E" and then shut off all further communication.

There was also the Christmas ordering to do. Projecting the needs for our first Christmas—with no retailing history or experience, in a new mall, in a continuing recession—was a laughable exercise. In the end, we placed approximately 100 purchase orders for more than $100,000 worth of merchandise. Unless sales improved markedly, I would have no capital to pay for all of this—and, of course, the banks would finance nothing at all.

I'd been told that the small businessperson never sleeps, but the mood swings were worse. When we had a good day or made a big sale, I got a terrific high. When we had a $100 day or lost what appeared to be a sure art sale, the downer that followed was awful. I discovered that retailers have no average days.

In a retail store with hundreds of small items, one postcard or yo-yo more or less hardly seems to matter. It is tempting to concentrate on the big-ticket transactions.

But it's the aggregation of innumerable small sales that spell success or failure. A clerk who used to work at a Disney store told me 50% to 60% of their walk-in customers buy something. Our rate was about 15%. I rearranged the merchandise, fiddled with pricing, and launched promotions until it dawned on me that the problem wasn't us but the mall.

We were in the Taj Mahal of Scottsdale. We didn't get shoppers, we got gawkers. If they were going shopping, they went to a mall with a wider variety of stores. An identical Cartoon Corner store in Ohio, operated by another former franchisee, was cranking out sales at nearly double our rate, and the only difference was the mall. The one in Ohio was fully occupied.

By the end of the summer, my bank account was dwindling fast. The lack of foot traffic was hurting us badly. However, animation art, which I had expected to start slowly, was selling a good deal faster than I'd forecast. Fantasy, escapism, and nostalgia were clearly the right commodities for a recession, and the animation cash flow kept us alive.

The mall did not fill up in the fall. Many stores put off their openings until closer to Christmas. An equal number canceled their openings entirely. The aquarium project lost its financing. America West went into Chapter 11. The planned hotel remained an empty lot. Customer traffic picked up a bit when the IMAX theater finally opened in late September, but most people still wanted to know when the mall was going to open "really." Plans for the grand opening were quietly merged into a "Christmas Celebration," avoiding a lot of unnecessary expense and embarrassment. I dropped my first-year sales estimate to $225 per square foot.

By Christmas, the mall was still only half full, and because we couldn't attract heavy traffic, holiday sales were badly below expectations. In early 1992, I lowered my projections for the first full year to $200 per square foot and sold off my excess inventory to the Ohio store. I renegotiated lease terms yet again.

In Scottsdale, the big tourist influx begins right after Christmas, so March is often as good as December for retail sales. It compensates for the dreadful summers. But at our mall, the tourist season was a flop. My first full year came in at $175 per square foot—less in total revenue than my former personal compensation package. Drawing no salary and paying only a fraction of what was called for in my lease, I was just breaking even. I now began surrendering my IRA accounts to pay the all-financing mortgage on my house. My income taxes were less than the year I graduated from college. One more time, I renegotiated my lease.

I OFTEN READ of executives making mid-life career changes and achieving satisfaction as entrepreneurs. True stories of success warm the American heart. But hard work and big risks don't always produce success. I began with well-above-average experience, a proven concept, and excellent capitalization, yet in my case, personal bankruptcy remains a distinct possibility. External factors will swing the balance.

But even if success eludes me, I have certainly had an extraordinary education. I have discovered that real planning is a learning process, not a means of control. It is the totality of what you intend to do proactively and reactively, along with an effort to envision the opportunities you want to take advantage of. Good planning needs to be done every day. It is more anecdotal than numerical.

I have learned to identify more with the customer, a lesson most executives would profit from. Corporate statements about customer service tend to be empty platitudes about striving for excellence and working to earn the public's trust, but real customer service is doing what customers want, not getting customers to do what you want.

I have relearned the value of dealing with people as human beings rather than computer blips or "parties of the first part." When I couldn't pay my general contractor and he said he'd extend me credit because he trusted me, I actually cried from relief after hanging up the phone. In a corporate setting, we would have dealt with the matter by calling our legal hired guns.

I have also come to understand better an important paradox. While little things taken individually rarely make any difference in the large sweep of events, their combined effect is decisive. This is true of elections, soil erosion, and dieting. It's also true of retailing, where it is thousands of small sales (and small expenses) that separate successful from unsuccessful enterprises. In the life of a corporate executive, the focus is on the big decisions that "really count." Meanwhile, the waste in most large corporations is terrible. A reorientation of thinking from macro to micro might pay enormous dividends for big companies. For small ones, it is a matter of life and death.

Entering the four-month summer doldrums after a slow Christmas and a pitiful tourist season, our business unexpectedly picked up. Last year we just sat here and baked in the heat. This year the first half of the summer has been a source of cautious optimism, proving to me once again that I've got my hands on a winning concept—if I can just hang on financially until the mall fills up.

But the cartoon business, like life, is full of surprises.

Our nearby Disney store, for example, is not so much competitive as complementary. We send each other customers. Despite Disney's cartoon superstars and name recognition, nearly half of my business comes from Warner Brothers characters. And now Warner Brothers has surprised me with a bombshell that could cost me my business. In August, as part of a plan to build more than a hundred of its own stores all across the country, Warner opened a cartoon store a mile from mine that is much bigger and with lower prices on many of the goods I carry.

This was certainly not in my plan. (In fact, a friend inside Warner had assured me they were *not* coming to Scottsdale.) But perhaps the most important lesson I've learned is that few plans are ever realized as conceived. Formal planning and forecasting are largely exercises in reading tea leaves. They must be done, or the business will operate aimlessly. Yet doing them does not increase their chances of coming true. Accuracy does not improve with the increased sophistication of mathematical technique or the increasing precision of input data.

For my business today, I redo plans and forecasts continuously, knowing full well that this alone does not make things happen. People do. In the end, success is determined by an accumulation of details, of individuals doing the right things, of small breaks one way or the other. Strategy is the synthesis of details. It is useless if expressed in overly general terms. This is more apparent in a small business, but it is just as true in large corporations.

I REMEMBER READING somewhere once that the first rule of management is always to look for the disquieting evidence. I think if I hired my old self now, as a consultant, the former Ken Veit would take a long, hard look at this storm of disquieting evidence, do a numerical analysis of revenue cost and reduced margins, and tell me to cut my losses. Pack it in.

But this is *my* money at risk. There's more at stake here than a year-end bonus; my life savings are pledged as part of lease guarantees. Like it or not, I am now a fully committed entrepreneur. Having tried and failed to find shelter in a franchise, I'm on my own, and I hate the idea of failing in what should be—still can be—a successful business venture. The mall is still far from full, and Warner

Brothers is making life difficult. Recognizing that I am at a point where any numerical analysis is likely to be of limited value, I now focus on how to survive.

Instead of giving ground to Warner Brothers, I have made a careful inventory of my resources. I've talked to customers about the things they like and dislike about the Warner Brothers store, and I've come up with a list of strategies that make the most of my smaller size and the greater flexibility available to an owner-operator. I can provide extraordinary service. I can customize my merchandise to suit Arizona and my customers. I can do promotions no corporate store manager would be allowed to do.

I can also lower prices by lowering costs by spreading fixed overhead over two stores. Even with sales at current levels, two stores would allow me to take advantage of volume purchasing, show a profit, and even take a salary.

In fact, I have found a space in a first-class mall in Phoenix. I have negotiated a lease, found an architect, hired a contractor, applied for financing, cursed my bank for turning me down, changed to a bank where the officers are also my customers, and secured an SBA loan. We open in November. If the second store works, I will open a third in Tucson.

Will I survive? I don't know. The risks are still immense, the chances for failure great, and luck is still high on my list of business needs. To tell the truth, I'll be happy if my luck just averages out, since it's been mostly bad so far.

There is a Chinese saying that lucky is better than smart because a lucky man can make money despite mistakes, whereas an unlucky man will lose money despite brains. Small business owners need a great deal of luck even if they do everything right. Uncertainty is our constant companion.

Ken Veit *and his Cartoon Corner live on. He opened his second store in late 1992, but in 1993 he closed his original store when the Galleria Mall went bankrupt—one of the worst financial disasters in shopping-mall history. Veit then opened four more new stores, all small, in different locations around Phoenix. The first two stores had cost him roughly $100,000 each to build and furnish, but he opened the four small stores for $5,000 to $6,000 apiece—plus the cost of merchandise.*

But problems and setbacks persist. One of the new stores was put out of business by shoplifters. He closed one at a downtown mall where only the restaurants did well. One attracted big spenders—but not enough of them to stay open. Through it all, Warner has offered brutal competition, cutting prices, flooding the market with art but simultaneously cutting off Veit's access to Warner Brothers' cells. Suppliers send "automatic" shipments of unordered goods. Customers try to return Christmas merchandise in June. Business bounces up and down unpredictably. Ken Veit sums it all up this way: "In a small business, every day, in every way imaginable, someone has his hand in your pocket, trying to take what is yours in order to solve his problem. Your natural reaction is to want to strike back. The most difficult aspect of survival

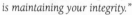

is maintaining your integrity."

Nevertheless, Veit and his (now) two stores survive. All in all, in fact, he figures he has broken about even. He's put about $300,000 into the business, but he's taken out about $150,000 and has roughly $150,000 in merchandise. He's now planning a new store in Tempe.

4

Development, Democracy, and the Village Telephone

SAM PITRODA

I WAS BORN IN 1942 and raised in a poor village in one of the poorest areas of rural India, a place with kerosene lamps and no running water. In 1980, at 38, I was a U.S. citizen and a self-made telecommunications millionaire. By 1990, I was 47 years old and nearing the end of nearly a decade back in India as leader of a controversial but largely successful effort to build an Indian information industry and begin the immense task of extending digital telecommunications to every corner of my native country, even to villages like the one where I was born.

That effort persists today at an increased pace, but it remains controversial. Some of the controversy has centered on me and my methods. Most of it focuses on the efficacy and logic of bringing information technology to people who are in global terms the poorest of the poor.

Common sense and accepted thinking about economic development have long held it ridiculous to supply Third-World villages with state-of-the-art technology. What subsistence farmers need is not high-tech science and complex systems, the argument goes, but immunizations, basic literacy, disease- and drought-resistant cereals and oilseeds, simple pumps, deep-drop toilets, two-phase electrification—all the "appropriate" technologies that the unsophisticated rural poor can use and understand.

I agree with this argument as far as it goes. Third-World farming villages need water, hygiene, health, and power, and the need is usually great. But the argument falls short in its definition of "appropriate." It ignores technology's profound social implications. And it comes dangerously close to consigning the Third-World poor to a life of third-rate capacities and opportunity. The policies of development agencies like the World Bank too often limit "appropriate technology" to the two-dimensional, twopenny solutions that bring the poor to the doorway of the modern world but not actually across the threshold.

For me, three facts about Third-World development stand out with great force. First, high technology is *already* an essential element in effective water sourcing, sanitation, construction, agriculture, and other development activities. Geohydrologic surveys are carried out from satellites. Bioengineering has revolutionized crop production. Appropriate technology has moved well beyond the water screw and the inclined plane.

Second, modern telecommunications and electronic information systems are thoroughly appropriate technologies even in those regions of the world that still lack adequate water, food, and power. The reason is simply that modern telecommunications is an indispensable aid in meeting basic needs. If a U.S. community needed, say, widespread immunizations or replacement of a power grid, would the telephone seem a vital or an irrelevant tool in getting the job done? Would the telephone seem more or less critical if the job were tied to a natural calamity such as flood or drought and required the mobilization of diverse resources over a broad area?

Third, as a great social leveler, information technology

ranks second only to death. It can raze cultural barriers, overwhelm economic inequalities, even compensate for intellectual disparities. In short, high technology can put unequal human beings on an equal footing, and that makes it the most potent democratizing tool ever devised.

IN 1942, THE VILLAGE of Titilagarh in the Indian state of Orissa, southwest of Calcutta, had a population of 6,000 or 7,000 and no electricity or telephones. My early education took place in one-room schools, and most of my classmates had no shoes or books. My family was of the *suthar* caste—lowly carpenters—yet my father was an ambitious man. He never learned English until I brought him to the United States to enjoy his retirement, but he did business with the English and used what opportunities he had to build a prosperous trade in lumber and hardware and to send most of his eight sons and daughters to high school and on to university. For 12 years, I lived with one or more of my brothers and sisters in towns and cities far from home and studied hard to get the kind of grades that would outweigh my origins. In 1964, I succeeded. I was only 21 years old, and I had never used a telephone. But my masters degree in physics, specializing in electronics, from Maharaja Sayajirao University in the city of Baroda in Gujarat state, gave me membership in a new technological caste that superseded the one I was born to.

My older brother and I decided that I should apply to a university in the United States to do postgraduate work, and my father readily agreed to give me $400 toward this education, expecting me in return to bring my brothers and sisters to the United States one by one as I made my way in the world. I applied to the University of Oregon and the Illinois Institute of Technology but did not apply for scholarships, on the theory that an expression of need might reduce my chances of getting in. I was accepted at both schools and chose Illinois. The state of Orissa gave me a travel grant of $600, just enough for a taste of every form of transport: a boat to Genoa, a train to London, an airplane to New York, and a Greyhound bus to Chicago.

I arrived in December, 1964, with my father's $400 in my pocket. Tuition for the first semester was $700. I paid half on account, found a cheap apartment to share with another Indian, and landed a job in a physical chemistry lab to earn my keep and the rest of my tuition. A year later, I had a master's degree in electrical engineering. I had not only learned to use a telephone, I had, in essence, learned to make one. More important still, I had learned enough to design an electronic telephone switch.

TELEPHONE SWITCHING IS what operators used to do by hand in the early days of the century. Using a board with cords and plugs, the operator created a manual connection between the telephone in the caller's hand and the phone being called across town. Voice transmission then took place by means of analog electrical signals derived from a vibrating diaphragm in one handset and translated back into sound waves in the other. The system was marvelously simple, but, by technological standards, dreadfully labor intensive. If all the calls in the United States were handled that way today, every U.S. citizen would have to be a telephone operator.

Fortunately, electromechanical switching appeared in the 1920s, allowing the system to locate and connect two phones entirely by means of electrical signals opening and closing metallic contacts. These switches were automatic, but they had moving parts, and any device that moves wears out. So, while they required no operators, they did need people to carry out routine maintenance and regular replacement.

Finally, in the 1960s, I myself was involved in the invention and evolution of digital electronic switching equipment, which has two huge advantages over its analog predecessor. First, without moving parts and able to perform its own automatic maintenance, it never wears out. Second, it uses microchips as its basic building blocks and therefore takes up very little space. A large metropolitan switching station for 50,000 phones once occupied a six-to-ten-floor building and needed hundreds of people to keep it operational. The same capacity can now be housed in one-tenth of the space and requires a staff of perhaps ten people to operate its computer and software controls. Indeed, the only serious remaining drawback is that digital switches still produce heat and must be air-conditioned to prevent overheating.

Over the next few years, I worked for GTE in Chicago, designing and refining digital switching equipment and analog-to-digital conversion technology. I was responsible for nearly 30 patents and enjoyed a prominent position at GTE's annual patents banquet in the late 1960s and early 1970s. I married an Indian woman I had met at the university in Baroda, started a family, brought my parents and most of my brothers and sisters to the States, and began to become a middle-class American.

But my father kept telling me I was too young to get into the habit of working for other people, and I was beginning to tire of pats on the back for the patents I'd won, so I quit. In 1974, with two local telecom entrepreneurs, I founded Wescom Switching Inc.—their money, my technical expertise—and we began manufacturing digital switching equipment that I designed. In 1980— six years and more than a dozen patents later—we sold out to Rockwell International. As part of the deal, I agreed to work for Rockwell for three years and undertook not to compete in telecommunications for five years. My 10% of the company came to roughly $3.5 million in cash.

I LEFT TITILAGARH in 1951 to go to boarding school in Gujarat; I left India in 1964 to go to graduate school in the United States; now, in 1980, I was a millionaire, and to my own surprise I felt nearly as much guilt as satisfaction. All my life, I had dreamed of wealth and success, but now I suddenly confronted the fact that I had walked out on India. The sheer immensity of India's problems, the huge gap between my luxurious U.S. suburb and the struggling poverty of villages like the one where I was raised, the selfishness of my own success so far, all of it weighed on my mind and set me off in pursuit of another American dream: the exploration of a new frontier and challenge. In my case, that challenge was to use telecommunications as an agent of change—a bridge between the First World and the Third.

As I began my new job as vice president at Rockwell, I began observing telecommunications at work in underdeveloped countries. What I saw disturbed me. On the whole, telecommunications was not so much closing as *widening* the gap between the rich countries of the north and the poor countries of the south. The First World, inventing and deploying new technology as if it were fast food, seemed headed in the direction of unlimited and universal information access. Even in the Second World, information technology had penetrated far enough to destroy the information monopoly that supported totalitarianism and to launch Eastern Europe toward the West. However, in the Third World, telecommunications and information technology remained an urban luxury, and an unreliable one at that. India had fewer than 2,500,000 telephones in 1980, almost all of them in a handful of urban centers. In fact, 7% of the country's urban population had 55% of the nation's telephones. The country had only 12,000 public telephones for 700,000,000 people, and 97% of India's 600,000 villages had no telephones at all.

What was worse, India, like most of the Third World, was using its priceless foreign exchange to buy the West's abandoned technology and install obsolete equipment that doomed the poor to move like telecom snails where

Europeans, Americans, and Japanese were beginning to move like information greyhounds. The technological disparity was getting bigger not smaller. India and countries like her were falling farther and farther behind not just in the ability to chat with relatives or call the doctor but, much more critically, in the capacity to coordinate development activities, pursue scientific study, conduct business, operate markets, and participate more fully in the international community.

Worse still, I was perfectly certain that no large country entirely lacking an indigenous electronics industry could hope to compete economically in the coming century. To survive, India had to bring telecommunications to its towns and villages; to thrive, it had to do it with Indian talent and Indian technology. In other words, there were two goals to work toward: telecommunications and other information technologies could not only help Indians create wealth in every walk of life, a telecom and information industry could also create wealth of its own. Unless we had both, we had no future as a nation.

Worst of all, I began to see that information technology played an indispensable role in promoting openness, accessibility, accountability, connectivity, democracy, decentralization—all the "soft" qualities so essential to effective social, economic, and political development. India needed the capacity to network people, ideas, and initiatives. Telecommunications was as critical and fundamental to nation building as water, agriculture, health, and housing, and without it, India's democracy could founder.

I BEGAN LOOKING for an entry into Indian telecommunications, a rigid bureaucracy with about a quarter of a million employees: one for every ten telephones.

In 1981, a friend in Bombay sent me a newspaper clipping reporting that Prime Minister Indira Gandhi had set up a high-level committee to review telecom development. I wrote to its chairman and asked for an interview. From my name and location, he concluded that I was an Italian-American with telecom products to peddle. I wrote back at greater length to say I had nothing at all to sell except the conviction that India possessed all the talent necessary to pursue telecommunications modernization on her own. He invited me to India. He could not absolutely promise me an appointment—and I would have to pay my own way—but he did ask me to come. Ultimately, I spent two hours with the entire high-level committee.

My message was that India should abandon electromechanical switching and move immediately toward digital systems for switching and transmission. My reasoning was twofold. First, electromechanical switching was ill-suited to the Indian climate and to Indian conditions. With few available telephones, most lines were intensively used, and electromechanical equipment was much more likely than digital to malfunction from overuse. (We later discovered that some public phones in India generate as many as 36 calls per hour at peak volume, compared with maybe 10 to 12 in the United States.) Electromechanical switches are also more vulnerable to dust and moisture. Analog transmission, finally, suffers over distance, while digital transmission is what gives those astonishingly intimate connections halfway around the world. In a country with low telephone density like India, distance—and therefore static—were nearly unavoidable.

Second, the development of digital technology would help build native industries in electronics, software, and related fields. Moreover, India needed one piece of digital equipment that no other country manufactured but that many developing nations could use: a small rural exchange. In the United States and Europe, the smallest exchanges built will accommodate 4,000 to 10,000 lines, and, in small towns and rural areas, these exchanges are installed and then deliberately underutilized. This kind of waste may be tolerable in a country where the number of small exchanges is tiny. In India, exchanges with a vast overcapacity would have to be installed in hundreds of thousands of villages, and waste on such a scale was unthinkable. Development of an efficient exchange for 100 to 200 telephones would not only solve India's problem, it would give the country a valuable high-tech export.

The committee was impressed—by my enthusiasm if nothing else—and suggested I meet the prime minister. Two weeks later, Mrs. Gandhi's office agreed to give me ten minutes of her time. Because I needed at least an hour to get my message across, however, I turned the offer down. New Delhi was full of people who had been waiting *years* to get ten minutes with the prime minister, but I really did need an hour. By pushing what few connections I could muster, I eventually got my background papers into the hands of two advisers to Mrs. Gandhi's son Rajiv. One of them spent several hours studying the file, and in November, after five months of trying, I got an hour with Mrs. Gandhi, her senior cabinet colleagues, the chief ministers of several Indian states, and Rajiv, whom I met for the first time that day but who was already an advocate for my point of view.

I began my slide presentation almost as soon as Mrs. Gandhi walked into the room. There was a lot of ground to cover, and I covered it as swiftly as I could. I summarized world telecom statistics and correlated telephone density to productivity, efficiency, prosperity, and gross national product in about 50 countries. I pointed out that only a handful of countries had achieved universal service and raised the possibility that it was not so much wealth that created telephone density as telephone density that created wealth. I reminded them that Indian telecom was characterized by high unsatisfied demand, low accessibility as well as density, poor connectivity, lack of dependability, substandard maintenance, superannuated technology, overcentralization, bureaucracy, bad management, and limited capital. I underlined India's reliance on imported equipment of traditional, not to say obsolete, design, and tied that equipment to poor service and system inflexibility. I laid out a program that emphasized rural accessibility, customer service, digital switching, and large-scale technological innovation and integration, all of it accompanied by privatization, deregulation, and organizational restructuring. I outlined plans for design, production, installation, networks, fax, E-mail, telex, and more. At the end, I spoke of resources and management and then offered three alternatives.

The first alternative—obviously unacceptable —was to do nothing at all and let the system limp along until it failed completely. The second was to pursue the present development plan, using imported technology to address some problems and ignore others. But the present policies meant that India would fall steadily farther and farther behind the developed world, with dire consequences for India's economy, government, and people.

My third alternative was to adopt radical new technologies, products, and programs, hire new people—in particular, a core group of young research-and-development engineers to develop new hardware and software—and set India on the path to universal telecommunications accessibility by the turn of the century. I suggested the creation of new organizations with the power to issue bonds and sell stock to raise massive sums of capital. I talked about large-scale manufacturing plants to meet domestic and export demand. I proposed a telecom commission to oversee regulatory requirements. I spoke of the need for a generational change in telecommunications thinking.

Prime Minister Gandhi listened attentively to the entire presentation, and when it was over, I answered a number of questions. In the days that followed, the word went out that the prime minister was interested in a plan to modernize Indian telecom, and I began three years of commuting between Chicago and New Delhi to put together a strategic framework, plan the program, give shape to an R&D entity for developing human resources and new technology, and lobby it all through India's parliament and intricate governmental bureaucracies.

LIVING IN THE United States for the most productive years of my life had altered my values and perceptions beyond recognition. My approach to business, and for that matter to life, had become performance oriented. But every few weeks I left Chicago for New Delhi and a set of standards and values that were feudal, hierarchical, and complex beyond belief. From my now thoroughly American point of view, India was in desperate need of modernization. And my frustrating efforts to install some of the modernizing mechanisms only underscored how badly the country needed technology to organize, simplify, economize, and create the infrastructure to meet basic human needs. I saw so much potential for technology's problem-solving capacity that even as I struggled through quagmires of social and political confusion, I was near to drowning in ideas and excitement.

Through all of it, Rajiv Gandhi was my ally. I saw in him a young, energetic, modern man, direct and honest, eager to explore telecom's role in Indian development. He and I had clicked at our first meeting and quickly became friends. Over the next few years, we fought together for dozens of administrative experiments and reforms using information technology—computerization of railways, for example, and of land records, which was vital to the progress of land reform. At the moment, however, we worked together for the creation of the Centre for Development of Telematics, C-DOT as it came to be known.

The battle was uphill. Every important decision had a political as well as an economic impact. For example, a few months after my meeting with Mrs. Gandhi, India signed a deal with a French multinational to manufacture a digital switching system, so those who stood to profit from this arrangement opposed our concept of an indigenous digital industry and labeled it redundant. One European CEO wrote a strongly worded letter to Mrs. Gandhi pointing out that his company had already spent $1 billion developing digital technology and questioning the wisdom of so massive an investment by the Indian government. Given India's limited resources and the vast needs of its people, that argument had wide political support.

In 1984, the breakup of the U.S. Bell System set in motion a process of deregulation and privatization around the world and gave our proposals the extra boost they needed. In August, C-DOT was registered as a nonprofit society funded by the government but enjoying complete autonomy. Parliament agreed to give us $36 million over 36 months to develop a digital switching system suited to the Indian network. An executive director was appointed, we found five rooms in a rundown government hotel, and we went to work using beds as desks.

A few months later, in October, 1984, Indira Gandhi was assassinated, and her son Rajiv became prime minister. He and I decided that I should press the initiative for all it was worth. Since I could not simply pull up stakes and move to Delhi—back in Chicago, my father was dying of cancer—I began spending about half my time in each city. I did not finally move to India with my wife and children until August, 1986, after my father's death. In the meantime, I continued to commute, now more often than ever.

From 1984 on, I was a principal adviser to C-DOT with a salary of one rupee per year, an arrangement I modeled on Roosevelt's dollar-a-year men during the New Deal. I wanted the chance to work for a cause, an Indian cause in particular, and I knew that in order to succeed, I had to place myself above the suspicion of greed or self-interest. In any case, what could I have earned? The top government salary at that time was

5,000 rupees per month—then about $400—and I was spending more than ten times that amount of my own money just on plane fare and hotels. In any case, it was an arrangement that no one in New Delhi understood. One day the deputy minister for electronics took me aside and said, "Mr. Pitroda, what is it you really *want* out of this?" My answer, "Nothing," puzzled him. Whether or not he believed me, my motives remained a subject of discussion in New Delhi for the next six years, with eventual dire results for me.

For the moment, however, activity was bliss. Our engineers were conspicuously young, and they never seemed to sleep or rest. Most had been ready to leave India when this opportunity came along. Now they threw themselves into India's future and worked with an energy that the underdeveloped world is not commonly supposed to generate.

From the outset, C-DOT was much more than an engineering project. It did of course test the technical ability of our young engineers to design a whole family of digital switching systems and associated software suited to India's peculiar conditions. But it was also an exercise in national self-assurance. Years earlier, India's space and nuclear programs had given the country pride in its scientific capability. Now C-DOT had the chance to resurrect that pride.

From the outset, consequently, I was interested in process as well as product. Technology may be complex, but human motivations and interactions are even more so. I knew India had great young engineers, and I believed there was nothing they couldn't accomplish if we challenged them and gave them a proper environment to work in. Part of our mission was to inspire a whole generation of young talent and thumb our noses at the nay-sayers, the political reactionaries, and the vested interests whose prosperity rested entirely on imports. I set impossible targets. I cheered people on. Knowing as I did that young Indians did well in the

United States, I tried to create an American work environment. I set about instilling a bias toward action, teamwork, risk, flexibility, simplicity, and openness. I was almost brutal in my determination to root out hierarchy and bureaucracy: I once shouted and made a thoroughly mortifying scene in order to get typists to stop leaping to their feet every time a manager entered their work space to use one of the two telephones we started out with. I did my best to shield our young engineers from bureaucrats, politicians, and business interests. At the same time, I opened our doors to the media, which responded with excitement, optimism, and the kind of hero worship that we hoped would attract more young people to technology careers.

By 1986, C-DOT had sprawling, chaotic offices, 425 employees (average age 25), and the drive, activity, and optimism of a U.S. presidential campaign. My methods had been highly unconventional for India and highly unpopular with a lot of the old guard, but within C-DOT we had accomplished wonders.

By 1987, within our three-year limit, we had delivered a 128-line rural exchange, a 128-line private automatic branch exchange for businesses, a small central exchange with a capacity of 512 lines, and we were ready with field trials of a 10,000-line exchange. Better yet, the components for all these exchanges were interchangeable for maximum flexibility in design, installation, and repairs, and all of it was being manufactured *in India* to the international standard: a guaranteed maximum of one hour's downtime in 20 years of service. We had fallen short on one goal—our large urban exchange was well behind schedule —but, overall, C-DOT had proved itself a colossal, resounding success. In addition to the four exchanges, we had licensed some 40 public and private companies to manufacture and market C-DOT products, and more than 100 businesses had sprung up to manufacture ancillary parts and components.

Moreover, these rural exchanges were small master-pieces of "appropriate" design.

As I mentioned earlier, even digital switching pro-duces heat, so switching equipment has to be air-condi-tioned in order to function dependably. But in the countryside, the Indian electrical grid is notoriously undependable, and we couldn't give villages exchanges that were certain to overheat the first time the electrical system went down. The solution was simple but inge-nious. First, to produce less heat, we used low-power microprocessors and other devices that made the exchanges work just slightly slower. Second, we spread out the circuitry to give it a little more opportunity to "breathe." The cabinet had to be sealed against dust, of course, but by making the whole assembly a little larger than necessary, we created an opportunity for heat to rise internally to the cabinet cover and dissipate. The final product was a metal container about three feet by two feet by three feet, costing about $8,000, that required no air-conditioning and could be installed in a protected space somewhere in the village and switch phone calls more or less indefinitely in the heat and dust of an Indian summer as well as through the torrential Indian monsoon.

Our 512-line exchange was designed for the some-what larger market town nearby, where it could handle intervillage and long-distance calls for a dozen villages or more. What now remained was to disseminate this new technology through the Indian telecommunications sys-tem and actually reach out to the towns and villages that needed it.

In 1987, I chaired a national conference that proposed the establishment of a new, streamlined, semiautonomous Telecom Commission to replace the old, heavily bureau-cratic Department of Telecommunications. Before the government could act on that proposal, however, Rajiv Gandhi appointed me adviser to the prime minister on

National Technology Missions, with the rank of minister of state. I had to give up my U.S. passport to take the job, but I couldn't turn down such a marvelous opportunity. The Technology Missions existed to marshal, motivate, and manage the efforts of more than ten-million people and lots of technology involved in meeting six basic human needs: drinking water, immunization, literacy, oilseeds, dairy production, and telecommunications.

Our specific goals were straightforward. Make clean, potable water available to about 100,000 problem villages in the amount of 40 liters a day per person and 30 liters a day per head of livestock. Immunize 20-million pregnant women and 20-million children every year. Teach 80-million people in the 15 to 35 age group— about 75% of adult illiterates—to read and write at a rate of 10 million each year. Increase oilseed production by as much as 18-million tons and reduce, eliminate, or reverse India's annual 10-billion-rupee import bill for edible oils. Increase dairy production from 44- to 61-million metric tons per year over eight years, raise dairy employment and incomes, and expand the number of dairy cooperatives by 42%. Last but hardly least, improve service, dependability, and accessibility of telecommunications all across the country, including rural areas.

The six mission directors worked for different ministries, so my job was to cheerlead, set agendas, and integrate the activities of ministries, state governments, national laboratories, and voluntary agencies. For two years, I traveled the country visiting tribal areas, villages, towns, cities, and state capitals. Every day I made two or three speeches, took part in half a dozen meetings, talked to scores of people, made dozens of phone calls (if a telephone could be found). I was doing my best to generate ideas, communicate goals and enthusiasm, fight red tape, clear obstacles, tie up loose ends, assess progress, mend bureaucratic fences, and bridge bureaucratic ravines. It became by far the most hectic period of my life, but I got swept up in the romance of making a difference and began working and traveling nearly around the clock. I saw enormous commitment from tens of thousands of people and solid resistance to change from entrenched interests. I began to sense an unholy alliance among many politicians, bureaucrats, and businessmen to stop people from taking power into their own hands through literacy and community-based programs—and through communication.

I was learning the ropes of development in action, and everything I saw strengthened my conviction that telecommunications lies at the very heart of progress. This is true in the political and social sense—people must be able to reach out to government, media, institutions, and allies if they're to make their voices heard—and it is true in the more practical sense that development depends on communication for logistical efficiency. Let me give two examples of what I mean.

One of our greatest assets in the oilseed and dairy missions was Dr. Verghese Kurien, chairman of the National Dairy Development Board and winner of the World Food Prize in 1989. In the 1950s, Dr. Kurien started the farm cooperative movement in India and in 30 years built it into a multimillion-dollar enterprise with a membership of one-million farmers in 50,000 villages. Forgetting for the moment the added years and extra toil it took to build such an organization by word of mouth and personal recruitment, aided only by a postal system famous for incompetence, just imagine the task of galvanizing this organization into concerted action without the ability to computerize membership roles or to contact members by phone or telegraph. In spite of that limitation, Dr. Kurien has succeeded in stabilizing oilseed prices by buffer-stocking large quantities of oil and in building a cooperative milk-distribution system that reaches 170 million people. Telecommunications makes the efforts of men and women like Dr. Kurien incalculably less onerous and more effective, which is one of the reasons a dozen agribusiness lobbies in New Delhi oppose the spread of rural telephones.

Another example comes from the drinking-water mission. One group in the Rural Development Ministry was pushing for the purchase of 40 imported drilling rigs at a cost of several million dollars. Unfortunately, there were two vital pieces of information that no one seemed to possess: first, the number of drilling rigs already in the country, and second, the length of time it took to drill a well and how long it took to move a drill from one village to another.

We found a UNICEF official who was able to tell us that India already owned 1,200 drilling rigs, and several weeks of research revealed that, on average, it took about ten hours to drill a well and roughly ten days to move a rig. These were not ten days of travel time but ten days of bureaucratic wrangling and communication disarray in picking a site, negotiating political priorities, and getting the equipment on the road for a trip of a day or two. If a proper telecommunications network allowed the ministry to improve its planning and coordination even enough to cut that time to *five* days, India would gain the equivalent of 1,200 new water-drilling rigs without importing a single one.

Yet many of those who asked such questions and argued in favor of such solutions were accused of promoting technology *at the expense* of development and, to add insult to injury, of not understanding the plight of the drought-affected poor.

The fact was that no one in India had previously investigated and articulated the role that information systems play in development. Once we started, the practice and the insight grew and grew. After two years at the Technology Missions, I was given a chance to shape that practice even more directly.

IN 1989, AFTER two years of debate and study, the government decided to reorganize Indian telecommunications and create the Telecom Commission recommended in our 1987 report. Rajiv Gandhi appointed me the commission's chairman.

I met for three days with the heads of all telecom companies in the country: service providers, manufacturers, laboratories, C-DOT, and others. Then I met with the leaders of 37 telecom unions and the telephone white-collar bureaucracy. At the moment I took over, Telecom had 500,000 employees managing five-million lines, and it took me nine months to get their leaders to buy into my plan to quadruple the lines by the year 2000 without adding to the work force.

Once the unions were on board, we faced three fundamental challenges: connectivity, accessibility, and rural expansion.

First, we replaced all our existing electromechanical long-distance exchanges with digital equipment manufactured in India on license from a French company. We set up two factories to manufacture fiber optics and built high-speed fiber-optic highways to connect the four largest metropolitan areas: Bombay, Delhi, Calcutta, and Madras. We connected 400 district headquarters to automatic dialing, increased our population of digital switching exchanges by 50%, expanded the capacity of switching-system manufacturers, and increased automation at the operator level. We launched a multimillion-dollar program to computerize telecommunications operations nationwide. We introduced international direct dialing to more than 120 countries.

In a country the size of India with only five-million phones, it is difficult to have a significant impact on telephone *density*. Quadrupling the number of lines still means only one telephone for every 50 people, compared with more than one phone for every two people in the United States. *Accessibility* is another matter. By providing more phones in public places, we could put millions of people within reach of telecommunications.

In most areas, coin-operated phones seemed a poor idea for any number of reasons, including the fact that they cost a great deal to manufacture. Instead, we equip ordinary instruments with small meters, then put these phones into the hands of entrepreneurs who set them up on tables in bazaars, on street corners, or in cafes or shops whose owners feel they attract customers. These telephone "owners," frequently the handicapped, take in cash from their customers but are billed only six times a year, with 20% to 25% discounted as their commission. The phones are in such constant use that, in most cases, the revenue is enough to support a family. We launched a drive to install 200,000 such phones in public places nationwide, creating more than 100,000 jobs along the way. Today, the small yellow signs indicating a public telephone can be seen all across India.

The third piece of the program was rural communication, close to my heart because of my own background, and I now set in motion an ambitious program that envisioned nothing less than universal telecommunications accessibility by the year 2000. For us, accessibility was to mean that every Indian citizen should live within three or four kilometers of a dependable instrument, a goal that may strike Westerners as trivial, though I believe it will alter the face of India.

Several years earlier, C-DOT had run a test in Karnataka state with hugely encouraging results. In one town of 5,000 people with almost no previous telephone service, business activity rose many times following installation of an automatic digital exchange for 100 lines. Suddenly, it was possible for a truck owner to chase his drivers, line up goods and labor by telephone, and monitor the movement of his vehicles. Local farmers could call nearby cities and get real prices for their produce. Artisans could speak to customers, machine operators could arrange for service and repairs, shopkeepers could order goods—all by phone and in real time. In the six months after the introduction of service, total bank deposits in the town rose by an impressive 80%.

There were also social benefits. The townspeople could call doctors and ambulances, order pumps and textbooks, call newspapers, speak to politicians, share experiences with colleagues, and organize community ceremonies and functions. One villager told me that when his father died seven years earlier, he'd had to send 20 messengers on trains and buses to inform relatives in nearby villages. More recently when his mother followed, the villager went to the local tea shop and phoned all 20 villages—instant, certain, and far less expensive.

One-hundred phones in a town of 5,000 is a laughable density to an American and a miracle by Indian standards. Among other surprises, we found considerable long-distance traffic not just to Delhi and Bombay but also to London and New York. The villagers, it seems, have relatives and friends in all four cities.

In 1989, we set a goal of installing one rural exchange a day. By 1993, Telecom was installing 25 rural exchanges every day, and the rate continues to accelerate. By 1995, 100,000 villages will have telephone service. By the turn of the century or very shortly after, almost all of India's 600,000 villages will be covered. Once in place, the village telephone becomes as critical as water, food, shelter, and health services. Once exposed, people in rural areas want a village telephone more than they want any other community service.

Of nearly equal importance for me, the community phone becomes an instrument of social change, fundamental to the process of democratization. With telecommunications networks now spreading across the Second and Third Worlds, I believe that no amount of effort can put information back in the hands of the few, to be isolated, concentrated, and controlled.

MY OWN EFFECTIVENESS with the Indian Telecom Commission ended in 1990. Rajiv Gandhi was defeated in parliamentary elections in November, 1989, and I came under political attack a short time later. Eventually I was accused of corruption. Businesses owned by my family in the United States were said to have profited by contracts I awarded while at C-DOT. A thorough investigation by the Comptroller and Auditor General of India turned up no evidence to support this allegation. Moreover, to my gratification, hundreds of scientists, colleagues, academics, and thousands of citizens came to my defense. But the strain was very great. My family moved back to the United States, and in October, 1990, I had a heart attack. A few months after quadruple bypass surgery in Delhi, I went back to work as chairman of the Telecom Commission, with high hopes that Rajiv Gandhi would be returned to office in the 1991 elections. When Rajiv was assassinated in May of 1991, I resigned from my job as chairman and rejoined my wife and children in Illinois. The only post I now held was adviser to the new prime minister on Technology Missions, the same position I had held under Rajiv Gandhi but resigned when he left office.

Though I don't think of my telecom work in India as finished, I have begun to alter my focus somewhat over the last two years. Specifically, I've been struck by the preconditions that the First World has set for Third-World development. Europe and North America built their economies with the help of coercion, work-force exploitation, child labor, and environmental plunder, but the First World has announced to the Third that these and other violations of human and ecological rights are quite unacceptable.

The developed countries are forcing human rights and environmental sensitivity on the world's poor, setting all kinds of new conditions and restrictions on economic growth. This is not fair, of course, but it is an excellent policy.

Still, the First World must understand that it is not likely to achieve this policy goal except with the help of telecommunications and other information technologies, for two simple reasons.

First, telecom makes abuses infinitely easier to monitor. It gives watchdog groups as well as the victims and witnesses of human and environmental outrage access to one another. Local stories become international news, and local events become global events. Just as information technologies helped make totalitarianism impossible in Eastern Europe, they can help destroy exploitation in the developing world.

Second, telecom helps to create wealth, and prosperity is everywhere a force for civilized behavior. Take child labor. It is poverty that puts children to work, and it is unskilled labor that children are able to perform. When telecommunications comes to the Third World, it brings with it new economic activity, new higher-paying jobs for parents, and new technologies that reduce the utility of unskilled child labor. Countless towns and villages in India can bear witness to telecommunications' electrifying effect on entrepreneurialism, employment, and the overall standard of living. On top of all that, of course, information technologies create their own skilled jobs.

The dreadful human and physical conditions that the industrial revolution created in the West are now avoidable. But it is not some fundamental improvement in human nature that makes such progress possible. Growth without freedom and responsibility can still take place. It is technology, and information technology in particular, that makes humane development feasible.

The fact is, the telecom revolution has hardly begun. In addition to new products, systems, and integrated services, we will soon have new information-based relationships with our society and environment. But if sustainable progress of this kind is not to be limited to the developed world, then there is one initial hurdle still to clear.

The Third World still lacks adequate investment in telecommunications. Telecom in the developing world needs about $30 billion a year, of which only $3 billion is presently available. The World Bank devotes only 2% of all its funding to telecommunications. Corporations are attracted by the prospect of immense long-term profit but frightened by political risk and the certainty of social and economic experimentation.

Along with a number of fellow telecom engineers and executives, I am now working to organize a special funding agency, similar to the World Bank, to support Third-World telecommunications. Without proper telecom institutions and infrastructure, sustainable development with freedom will be difficult to achieve. Without telecom development, we will never deliver 75% of the world's people to the civilization of the information age.

*In 1995, the 186 member nations of the International Telecommunication Union in Geneva voted to establish the global telecommunications development bank **Sam Pitroda** mentions at the end of his article, and they named him its first chairman. WorldTel, headquartered in London, is dedicated to narrowing the global communications gap by offering technical assistance and equity investment to commercial ventures in developing countries. Its sponsors include AT&T, Nokia, Sprint, Ameritech, Cable & Wireless, Teleglobe, and many more. WorldTel has made tentative agreements with China, Brazil, Kenya, Malawi, Tanzania, Ethiopia, Zaire, and Uganda for the creation of telecommunications infrastructure.*

In India, Sam Pitroda still serves as advisor to the prime minister on technology missions. The telephone program described in this article continues. India now has 12.4 million telephones (versus 5 million when he wrote this article), 420,000 digital exchanges, 250,000 public telephones, and 200,000 villages with telephone service.

5

The Purpose at the Heart of Management

KYE ANDERSON

I AM THE CHAIRMAN, CEO and president of a profitable, rapidly growing medical technology company that I founded on my dining room table. Single-mindedly, I invented a technology, sold my ideas to doctors and investors, and built a corporation with 130 employees and $15 million in sales. The drive to invent, found, sell, and build came from inside, from one of those legendary entrepreneurial wellsprings of zeal and inspiration. But where entrepreneurs are well equipped with passion, we are also notoriously bad managers. I hated delegating authority, for example, and I was not a good planner—or even a good communicator when it came to my employees. The ability and willingness to delegate, communicate, plan, and preach the vision—most of the skills it took to lead the company past the magic $10 million mark in sales—were capacities I had to acquire.

Companies as well as people have to grow up. In business, the name for this maturity is management. And yet that's only a half truth. To succeed, startup enterprises need both passion *and* good management. If youthful fire and intensity are not enough to build a successful company, technique alone is no better. Pushing a new enterprise past all the barriers to success takes learnable skills to be sure, but it also takes a tenacious inner passion bordering on monomania. This combination is what I call leadership.

When I was 13 years old, my father had a massive heart attack. He was 47 years old, an active man, a former athlete, but he was sometimes so short of breath that he would rush out of the house in a panic, thinking he'd be able to breathe better in the open air. He even went to the hospital, but the doctors could find nothing wrong with him; his electrocardiogram was normal. All they could say was, "Well, it's not your heart."

But it was his heart. Two weeks after his ECG, he had what was probably a myocardial infarction. When I heard, I left school and ran all the way to the hospital—a mile or so in the little town where we lived. Because I was so young, they wouldn't let me in, so I ran around the building looking in windows until I spotted my mother. I got her to come to the front desk and take me to Dad's room.

He wasn't dead, but he was in an oxygen tent with needles in his arms, and his face was blue. I stayed at the hospital all day, while my mother sat beside the bed and held Dad's hand. Every now and then a nurse would come in and check the tubes, and once a doctor came in and studied the ECG made earlier that day.

I sat up on top of the radiator cover and kept thinking two thoughts over and over again. The first was a prayer: "He's so sick, dear God, please help him."

The second had to do with the electrocardiograph. It was pretty high tech for Crosby, Minnesota in 1959, but I was so scared for my father, I simply wasn't impressed. I just kept staring at the tape that came out of it and thinking, "Is that all they know? He's so sick, and all they know is that squiggly line?"

I remember asking my mother what was wrong with him and her saying, "They don't know."

I understand now that they couldn't have known. There was almost no way for them to tell. Diagnostics was more an art than a science in those days because doctors had so little objective information to work with.

Worse yet for Dad and thousands of others, they had no way of detecting heart disease early enough to prevent a heart attack. The electrocardiograph was virtually their only diagnostic weapon, and what an ECG reveals is damage to the heart muscle. It can't detect a developing problem in time to head it off, it can only show anatomical changes as and after they occur. Probably, Dad's heart had been dying slowly for weeks. That was why he'd been so short of breath—his heart wasn't pumping enough blood to supply his body with oxygen. But 1950s diagnostics couldn't pinpoint the problem until after the harm was done. In the end, his heart was so diseased it couldn't pump at all, and it failed.

He died several days later in the middle of the night. None of us had believed he would die. It put us all in a state of shock. At the funeral home, I tried to wake him up. At the church and the reception afterward, I was numb. In most ways, I stayed numb about his death for years, even though it shaped the whole rest of my life. I finished high school, I went on to the university, I grew up, I became a medical technologist and an entrepreneur, but I was nearly middle-aged before I realized how his illness and death had given me the energy, determination, and inspiration to do almost everything I've done.

There were nine kids in my family—I was in the middle—and most of us had to go to work. I didn't even try to find something at a soda fountain or a drive-in or one of the summer resorts. I went straight to the hospital to get a job in the laboratory, and I worked there all through high school. Summers, my brothers and sisters would be tanned and healthy looking, and I'd be white as a ghost. I wasn't a brain. I was a fun-loving kid with a lot of friends, sort of a hellion in many ways, but every day after school my friends would drive me to the hospital, and even though I hated to leave them, I was always serious and excited about getting back to the lab, washing test tubes, doing blood counts and urinalyses.

My first mentor was Sister Mary Grace, who ran the lab and instilled in me the basic principle of working with patients. She had taught me to draw blood as well as test it, and one day when I had finished a test she asked me for the result. "Oh, 20 or 21," I said.

"Which was it?" she asked.

"What difference does it make?" I said. "Normal is 18 to 25."

"You have to know exactly," she said. "Put down what you're doing, go out there, redraw the blood, and come back here and do it again."

So I had to go out and restick the patient and redo the test. The result I got was 20.

"It's 20!" I told her. I was furious. I didn't really enjoy sticking needles into people.

"The doctor could be basing his medication on that number," she said, "so whether it's higher or lower than last time could be critically important." Then she looked at me hard. "Whenever you do a test, I want you to pretend you're doing it on your father."

At the time, I thought it was a cruel thing for her to say; she knew how close I'd been to him. But it's something I still say to Medical Graphics employees.

"Suppose you bring a parent or a child to an emergency room," I say. "Suppose it's your daughter, and she's having trouble breathing. Suppose the nurse wheels up a piece of Medical Graphics equipment to test her with and find out why. What is it you want to feel at that moment? A sense of relief—because you helped build the best equipment in the world, because you know it gives meaningful, accurate results, because it can save your child's life."

I WENT TO THE College of St. Scholastica in Duluth because it has a good program in medical technology. On top of all the math and chemistry and anatomy, I worked my way through school in hospital labs. I never thought of it as work, I liked it. I took it for granted. My motivation was so strong that nothing discouraged me.

I *knew* where I was going. I was going to prevent heart and lung disease. I didn't talk about it. I didn't even consciously connect it with my father's death, but that was my goal. I was going to make a difference. No one should die at 47.

After college, I landed a job in the cardiopulmonary lab at the University of Minnesota Hospital in Minneapolis, and I stayed there for eight years, working, studying, and doing research. I taught myself computer programming. I couldn't afford my own computer, but my husband, Stephen, was a salesman for Tektronix, and I worked on his demo. I figured out how to turn pages of diagnostic numbers—vital capacity, total lung capacity, minute ventilation, lung diffusion, oxygen consumption, carbon dioxide production, esophageal pressure, heart rate, blood pressure, plus a dozen other parameters—into computer graphics that incorporated all of it at once. I wrote software to produce such graphics from manually entered data, and I got the best doctors I could find to help me interpret the results so I could teach others to do the same. I went to medical conventions to show doctors my software. I had no strategic sales plan. I was just excited about what I could do. Nevertheless, several doctors hired me to automate and improve their laboratories, and one day Stephen suggested I build a business on the technology I was developing.

Stephen talked to his boss at Tektronix and got him to lend me $180,000 worth of equipment to demonstrate my software at medical conventions—and then I wouldn't give it back to him. I kept it for another month and then another, on the grounds that eventually I would start selling enough Tektronix computers along with my software that it would pay off for his company as well as for me. Eventually it did.

Finally, I began working with transducers and electronic analyzers, figuring out how to translate analog data directly into digital information and computer graphics. In theory, this would allow a doctor to read and interpret dozens of pieces of intricately related information as a graphic whole—and to do it in real time, or very nearly. It would allow people with shortness of breath to go to a doctor or a hospital, breathe into an apparatus that I was going to invent, and find out immediately whether they had a heart problem or a lung problem and, in many cases, what the problem was. Much of this information could be extracted simply by knowing at what rate a person was using oxygen. But I believed I could build equipment that would measure enough parameters to determine from an analysis of the breath alone—that is to say, completely *noninvasively*—whether a person had emphysema, asthma, bronchitis, a valve problem, coronary artery disease, congestive heart failure, or one of a dozen other circulatory system diseases.

I had a mission to help save lives. I was driven to do everything I could do to realize my mission—and to do all of it myself. I was a crusader, an inventor, a salesperson, an organizer, a hustler. I had been a kind of monomaniac, unconsciously, ever since my father died. Now I was beginning to be an entrepreneur.

One day in 1979, I got a call from Dr. Stephen Boros at St. Paul Children's Hospital, who told me a baby boy had been born with a rare disorder that caused him to stop breathing whenever he fell asleep. Boros and his staff had him on a respirator, but the long-term outlook was poor. In normal people, it is the level of carbon dioxide, or CO_2, in the blood that controls the depth and frequency of breathing. Here, they had to control breathing externally, and they had to get it right. Too much CO_2 could put the baby into a coma, too little would upset his internal chemistry. Their only recourse was to check CO_2 by taking repeated blood samples, a process that was awkward, painful, slow, and invasive.

Since life on a respirator is a kind of hell in any case, some felt the baby should be allowed to die. But Boros wanted to put a pacemaker on the nerve controlling the diaphragm, which might allow him to live a reasonably normal life. To get the breathing rate just right, he needed some way of measuring the baby's oxygen and CO_2 levels noninvasively, one breath at a time, and he knew I had done similar breath-by-breath testing on cats.

"But you're talking about a baby," I objected.

"You've got to help me," he said. It was the kind of system I wanted to build eventually, and now a baby's life was at stake; Boros was just forcing the issue. I told him I might be able to put one together in as little as a month. He asked me to do it in two weeks.

I put down the phone, picked it up again, and started putting in calls to suppliers, one in the Netherlands, others in Kansas City and Seattle. I asked them to ship me—overnight express—transducers, analyzers, computers, calibrators, pumps, a pneumotachograph for measuring the rate of respiration. I put them all together Rube Goldberg-style on my dining-room table. What this collection of equipment had to do was measure oxygen and carbon dioxide accurately in each small mass of expired air, translate the results into digital information, feed these data into a computer, and render the combined results precisely, sequentially, instantly, and in a graphic form that a doctor, nurse, or technician could quickly read and understand. That may *sound* easy, but no one had ever done it before. The software alone kept me up until four in the morning ten nights in a row.

Two weeks later I called Dr. Boros and told him I was ready. He met me at the hospital. We wheeled my apparatus in on a cart, adjusted a tiny mask on Colin's face—he now had a name—and started taking measurements. Everything worked. The video screen drew graphs showing the contents of Colin's expired air, breath by breath, exactly the way it should, and we could see that his CO_2 was dangerously high. Boros cautiously turned up the pacemaker, Colin began breathing a tiny bit faster, and his CO_2 began slowly dropping into the normal range. Within two or three days, Boros and his staff were able to stabilize the baby's unconscious breathing at an adequate, sustainable level. Colin lived.

Medical Graphics was born.

AN ENTREPRENEURIAL BUSINESS has an infancy, an adolescence, and a maturity. Entrepreneurs go through a similar kind of evolution, though the business and the person seldom develop at the same pace and in harmony from newly hatched all the way to adult. At the beginning, the entrepreneur and the business are identical. The idea, the vision, and the passion are all inside the entrepreneur, overflowing in every direction. An entrepreneur operates on the basis of abundance: grand opportunities, ambitious dreams, big plans, wide-open doors just waiting for someone to walk through them.

In my case, I saw a huge gap in the ability to diagnose heart and lung disease, and I set out to fill it. I built integrated, more compact versions of the equipment I had used on Colin. I lobbied the finest cardiologists and pulmonologists I could find and asked them to join my scientific advisory board. I wasn't shy. I'd go to medical meetings, pick out the leading doctor, insist on talking to him, tell him what Medical Graphics was, drag him back to our booth, and make him watch while I demonstrated the equipment. As soon as he got excited—and they always did—I'd say, "You can have this very equipment in your office next week for $20,000. But what I really want is for you to tell us how to make it better, tell us what you need. I want you to work with us and help us develop it further." They couldn't say no. They never did.

I traveled constantly. I stayed alone in hotels and drove lonely back roads by myself to get to hospitals and doctors in remote locations. I'd leave my two young children at home and fly off to a meeting in California and cry all the way to the coast, thinking, "I should be home taking care of my kids." But I did it. I did everything. I developed the products, wrote software, consulted with the doctors, did marketing and sales, wrote brochures, built a company, found a board of directors, issued stock, and delegated nothing. I was a typical infant entrepreneur and then a typical adolescent.

The company moved into the go-go stage. Sales climbed over $1 million. We had profits one year and no profits the next, but our R&D efforts were continuous. We introduced new systems or new software about every six months. We built devices that could measure 144 parameters of lung and heart activity. We developed a body plethysmograph to measure total lung capacity, airways resistance, and lung elasticity, and an inexpensive spirometer to screen people quickly for lung disease at the workplace or in a doctor's office. We made equipment that helped measure and control breathing and nutrition in intensive-care units. All of these systems were noninvasive, and all were unique. For years, Medical Graphics was the only player in the field. Sales climbed over $3 million.

We broadened our focus and got into sports medicine. NASA bought our equipment to test astronauts in space. General Motors used our systems to study the effects of explosive air-bag deployment. We went after markets in Europe, the Middle East, and the Soviet Union. We continued to introduce new products. Sales climbed over $7 million. I had my finger in every pie, I was everywhere and did everything—R&D, sales, marketing, planning, finances, and outreach. I was Medical Graphics, and Medical Graphics was Kye Anderson.

Then, under pressure from my board and the stress of my own frustration, I quit as CEO.

THERE IS AN OLD business axiom that says that no entrepreneur can take her own company beyond $10 million in sales. According to this view, entrepreneurs are fixed in the infant or adolescent stages of personal and company development and can never progress to adulthood. As Medical Graphics began to approach that $10 million threshold, I could see a lot of good reasons to believe the axiom was true.

In the first place, my talent was entrepreneurial, not managerial. I still burned with a kind of childish passion to save lives, to help cure heart and lung disease, to make a difference in the world.

I knew the technology, but I knew nothing about manufacturing. I knew the doctors and what they needed, but I was a marketing amateur.

Growth was too slow, and I had no idea how to plan. In fact, I never planned for anything but success. If someone said, "What do we do if we lose this order?" I'd figure he had to be mentally ill to be so negative.

I couldn't seem to get the company moving upward on an even keel. One year we'd make a profit, the next year we'd lose money. I didn't even care that much about profits. I wanted profits to keep the doors open, but I wasn't worried about bringing everything to the bottom line. What I really wanted was to get the products right for the market, so I kept putting more money into R&D. I figured if we got the products right, sales would take care of themselves.

Like so many entrepreneurs, I thought if I built a better

mousetrap, the world would beat a path to my door. I didn't see the need to advertise the mousetrap and pave the path, and I certainly didn't know how. Every doctor that bought one of our systems would wonder why he'd never heard of us before. One of them had said to me, "This stuff is the best-kept secret in the medical world."

I was working myself nearly to death, but I was frustrated and losing my confidence. The company's financial health became my bugbear. Quarterly earnings and the price of our stock kept me awake nights. A couple of my board members thought we should be making 10% profits after taxes, and though our earnings fluctuated wildly, they never swung as high as 10%. The board urged me to step aside and make way for professional management. I was ready. I knew it was the right thing to do.

I was wrong.

I ONCE HEARD an after-dinner speaker define entrepreneur as "a person who doesn't know any better." We all recognized ourselves and laughed. Entrepreneurs seldom do know what they're getting into when they start. They are people so fired up with a vision that they go blind to everyday realities—which is a good thing, since otherwise they would never even attempt to do the impossible things they so often succeed in doing. Moreover, entrepreneurs often lack a basic grasp of business skills. I certainly did.

But the definition is also true in another, more literal sense: entrepreneurs know nothing better than their own enterprises. They have the noblest missions and the finest products in the world. It doesn't matter if they make duct tape or artificial hearts; they believe they have what it takes to alter history. And they are right, at least for themselves and their own companies—and sometimes for history too.

In my own case, I was on a crusade to save lives by inventing and perfecting a technology that would aid the early detection and diagnosis of heart and lung disease. Maybe it's true, as some friends claim, that deep down I was still trying to save my father's life. On the surface, I was, in any case, building a company on the technology doctors needed to save the lives of patients *like* my father. The point is that it was a crusade and that I was its driving force.

I tried hard to stay away, and for more than a year I succeeded. I spent a lot of time on the phone with salespeople, working out strategies for particular customers, and I attended board meetings. I was still chairman. But despite a sense that people were losing their enthusiasm and despite the fact that we hadn't introduced a single new product or software refinement for a year, I stayed away and let the new professional managers run the show.

But then salespeople began quitting. And one day when I went to R&D to talk about our new cardiopulmonary exercise system, hardly anyone was there, and no one knew where they were. Working at home, maybe. Taking an early lunch. Out. Yet these were the people who used to chain themselves to their desks, so to speak, and work nights and weekends with enthusiasm.

I had to face the fact that the company was losing its way. We had developed a new focus on the bottom line, sales were up, a new distribution system was in place— but people didn't seem to care. And I could see why. The new distribution system focused on logistics, not on doctors and patients. The new management systems built walls between departments and emphasized hierarchy. The new improved bottom line pleased stockholders, I'm sure, but it had put out the fire in people's guts. I wanted to come back.

WHEN I LEFT Medical Graphics, I left behind a company with a lot of talented, motivated people, but I took away with me an intense excitement that some of my board seemed to feel the company had outgrown, or should outgrow. The board was right about one thing, the company did need to grow and mature. But maturity isn't simply a question of scrapping visions and adopting targets. People and companies that abandon all ardor and passion lose their purpose in life. Maybe I *had* been a little crazy, but I'd been crazy like a fox, crazy with determination, crazy about an idea and a vision. That kind of madness is a thing all companies desperately need and that entrepreneurs are uniquely qualified to offer.

As for the kinds of maturity I find more relevant— appreciating complexity, learning to plan, learning to learn—I'd changed in my year and a half at home. By delegating my entire business, I had discovered that I didn't need to do every single thing myself. By reading and studying a whole library of business books, I had taught myself a great deal about marketing, finance, strategy, and vision. I'd also had time to think about my own strengths and weaknesses as a manager and leader, and I had begun to come to terms with my own history as an entrepreneur and a person. In fact, I had reached some conclusions that convinced me I could run my own company not only better than I had before but better than any professional manager could hope to do.

This time I was right.

I talked to my board members one by one and persuaded the two who were least supportive to resign. I reassumed the role of CEO. I went out looking for a mentor who had built a successful company from nothing and found him in Earl Bakken, who developed the first wearable, external, battery-powered, transistorized pacemaker in 1957, founded Medtronic Inc. to produce it, and then took the company from a garage startup to $1 billion in sales in less than 35 years. By sheer persistence and good luck, I got him to join my board.

I regained my confidence. I realized that my earlier focus on R&D had been the right focus for Medical

Graphics at that stage in its development. The world was not going to beat a path to our door unassisted—marketing was necessary—but without the right products for our customers' needs, a superhighway to our door wouldn't have been much help. Now that we had the products, financial success was essential for everyone: me, my board, my managers, the employees with their stock options, even our patient stockholders. Profit is a wonderful and necessary thing. But my failure to achieve 10% after-tax profits in the mid 1980s had not been a failure at all. I had been right in my willingness to postpone profits for the sake of greater investments in research and development.

I had also come to see that our insistence on the patient as our ultimate customer was the right idea. We weren't supposed to be in business to please everyone. In my opinion, we were in business to please the patient and to give doctors the tools to prevent, diagnose, and treat heart and lung disease cost effectively and noninvasively. We were patient-driven—not sales-driven, not profit-driven, not even doctor-driven—and that fact helped give us our special sense of mission and purpose.

Earl Bakken taught me that a leader's greatest obligation is to preach. Before I took my year and a half off, I had my own private sense of purpose. It drove *me*, but I communicated it to no one else. I didn't see how I could go around telling people my goal was to do away with heart and lung disease. I'd sound like a megalomaniac. My problem was that I was so passionate about the product and getting it out to doctors and hospitals that I overlooked the most important piece of the whole operation—the people in my own organization who made it all happen. When I came back to the company, I started preaching the vision to them instead of running out to sell to the doctors.

With Earl's help, I put together a statement of higher purpose, along with statements articulating a mission,

eight values, and three strategies. This sounds complicated, and it is, but I didn't want to reduce everything to
a single slogan or phrase. Quality, service, innovation—
how do any of those words help people in a crisis? But
when mission and value statements talk about filling
unmet diagnostic needs, about improving the quality of
patients' lives, about maintaining competitive advantage
through quality and innovation, about profit, human dignity, ethics, cost-consciousness, cost-effective medicine,
about listening to customers, patients, and employees—
and when these values are spelled out under a banner
proclaiming, as a higher purpose, "To prevent heart and
lung disease, the leading causes of death and rising
healthcare costs," the result is a guide to behavior, to
planning, and to problem solving. I've been able to trace
back every difficulty I've ever encountered at Medical
Graphics, trivial as well as serious, to a violation of one
of these principles.

I had been violating them myself. Our involvement in
sports medicine and air bags, for example, had nothing
much to do with preventing heart and lung disease and
led us away from our higher purpose. I jettisoned both,
along with everything else that tempted us to wander off.
After all, Medical Graphics had invented everything new
in cardiorespiratory diagnostic equipment since 1977—
the graphic presentation of data, the breath-by-breath
technique for immediate results, diffusion measurement
by gas chromatography, the first fully computerized
plethysmograph, the first FDA-approved expert system
for the diagnosis of lung disease. Why did we want to
endanger that core competence by stretching ourselves
too thin?

If we were going to take our higher purpose seriously—and it had stood me in pretty good stead ever
since my father died—then it seemed clear to me and the
board that our future lay in prevention. We had always
worked closely with doctors, feeding on their needs,

ideas, and energies. They know the patients better than we do, and we know the technology. We were already doing our best to reach cardiologists, pulmonologists, asthmatologists, respiratory therapists, intensivists, and half a dozen other cardiorespiratory specialists. The next step was primary-care physicians. They see heart and lung disease before the specialists because they see the patients earlier.

The very first sign of heart and lung disease is often either shortness of breath or simple tiredness. But when people have those symptoms, they don't go to their personal cardiologist. In fact, they generally do nothing. They wait until they've got chest pains or grow so short of breath that they can't breathe normally. Then they see a physician, have some tests, and go on to a specialist, who discovers a serious problem. They wind up getting angioplasty for $10,000, or coronary bypass surgery for, say, $20,000, or a heart-lung transplant for maybe $200,000.

Our present strategic goal is to put inexpensive equipment in every general practitioner's office that can detect heart and lung disease while it can still be cured with drugs, exercise, nutrition, and other noninvasive therapies. Every time people have a physical—certainly if they're feeling short of breath or unusually tired—they'll breathe into our apparatus while performing simple exercise, and if their oxygen consumption fails to rise, then something is wrong with their circulatory systems. If such early detection prevented one single heart-lung transplant, the savings on the surgery alone would pay for thousands of doctor's-office physicals on our equipment, even at the present price of $30,000, and we're working hard to get the price down to $15,000 or $10,000 or even $5,000. With early detection, we believe we could eliminate more than 40% of surgeries and catheterizations. Our conservative estimate of this primary-care market is $1.2 billion.

WHEN I CAME BACK as active CEO after my year and a half at home, I began for the first time telling people the story of my father's death. To my surprise, nearly everyone I worked with had a similar story—a favorite aunt who was always short of breath until she died of undiagnosed heart disease, a father who passed a physical with flying colors and collapsed and died the next day, a mother dying horribly of emphysema, a spouse or a child getting the wrong treatment in intensive care. It turned out that all of us were in it for something more than money, and for ten years I had let that sense of higher purpose go unexpressed and unfulfilled.

It may be difficult, even painful, for an entrepreneur to expose the private emotions that drive her, but it is an indispensable piece of good entrepreneurial leadership. For Medical Graphics, it is a way of bringing all our technical and business skills to bear on the medical problems closest to our hearts.

Kye Anderson is the CEO and president of Medical Graphics Corporation of St. Paul, Minnesota, the company she founded in 1977. Since this article was written, the company has further reduced the cost of its cardiopulmonary exercise testing system and made it faster and easier to use. The newest version of the instrument, called the CPX Express, was launched in the fall of 1995. Its price tag—$18,000 (down from $30,000 when this article was written)—makes it afford-able diagnostic equipment for most of the healthcare facilities and med-ical practices that would like to use it in the routine prevention of heart-and-lung disease. (The CPX Express can also be used to find the aerobic rate at which a person most effectively improves cardiovascular performance—and burns fat—which creates a strong potential market at sports facilities and health clubs. The Spanish government bought 25 of a slightly earlier model for use at the Barcelona Olympics.)

Medical Graphics has also introduced new software that greatly enhances the capacity of its full-body plethysmograph to detect and diagnose asthma, which is today one of the five most expensive health problems (along with congestive heart failure, lower back pain, dia-betes, and accidents) in the U.S. healthcare system. Yet another new product is a CPX nutrition software package that measures calorie con-

sumption by analyzing aspirated air. It was designed to help hospitals avoid giving their patients too much food—especially in intensive care units, where overfeeding can be a problem—but it can also be used to monitor calo-rie expenditure in people who need to lose weight.

Since this article was written, annual sales revenues have risen from $15 million to $24 million.

The Harvard Business Review Book Series

Command Performance: The Art of Delivering Quality Service, With a Preface by John E. Martin
Manufacturing Renaissance, Edited with an Introduction by Gary P. Pisano and Robert H. Hayes
The Product Development Challenge: Competing through Speed, Quality, and Creativity, Edited with an Introduction by Kim B. Clark and Steven C. Wheelwright
The Evolving Global Economy: Making Sense of the New World Order, Edited with a Preface by Kenichi Ohmae
Managerial Excellence: McKinsey Award Winners from the *Harvard Business Review*, 1980–1994, Foreword by Rajat Gupta, Preface by Nan Stone
Fast Forward: The Best Ideas on Managing Business Change, Edited with an Introduction and Epilogue by James Champy and Nitin Nohria
First Person: Tales of Management Courage and Tenacity, Edited with an Introduction by Thomas Teal